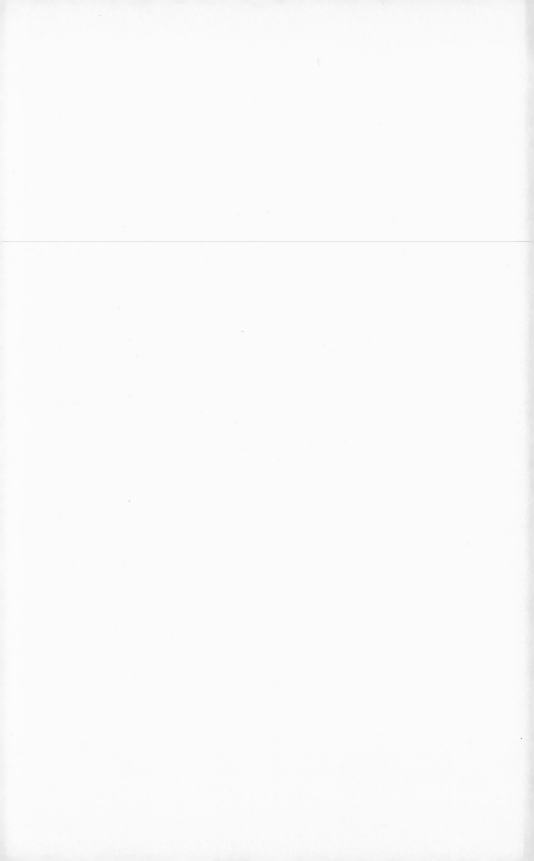

FROM APOSTLES TO BISHOPS

The Development of the Episcopacy
in the Early Church

THE NEWMAN PRESS
SIGNIFICANT SCHOLARLY STUDIES

The Newman Press imprint offers scholarly studies in historical theology. It provides a forum for professional academics to address significant issues in the areas of biblical interpretation, patristics, and medieval and modern theology. This imprint also includes commentaries on major classical works in these fields, such as the acclaimed Ancient Christian Writers series, in order to contribute to a better understanding of critical questions raised in writings of enduring importance.

FROM APOSTLES TO BISHOPS

The Development of the Episcopacy
in the Early Church

By Francis A. Sullivan, S.J.

THE NEWMAN PRESS
NEW YORK/MAHWAH, N.J.

The Publisher gratefully acknowledges use of the following: Excerpts from *Teaching Authority in the Early Church* (Message of the Fathers of the Church, vol. 14) by Robert Eno, S.S. Copyright 1984. Used by permission of Liturgical Press. Excerpts from *Tertullian: Treatises on Penance* (Ancient Christian Writers, no. 28) translated by William P. LeSaint, S.J. Copyright 1959. Used by permission of Paulist Press. Excerpts from *The Letters of Cyprian of Carthage* (Ancient Christian Writers, nos. 43, 44, 46, 47) translated by G. W. Clarke. Copyright 1984–89. Used by permission of Paulist Press. Excerpts from *Eusebius Pamphili: Ecclesiastical History* (Fathers of the Church, vol. 19) translated by Roy J. Deferrari. Copyright 1953. Used by permission of The Catholic University of America Press. Excerpts from *The Treatise on the Apostolic Tradition of St. Hippolytus of Rome* edited by Gregory Dix and Henry Chadwick. Copyright 1992. Used by permission of Curzon Press. Excerpts from *Early Christian Fathers* (Library of Christian Classics) edited by Cyril C. Richardson. Used by permission of Westminster John Knox Press. Excerpts from *Ecclesiastical Authority and Spiritual Power in the Churches of the First Three Centuries* by Hans von Campenhausen. Used by permission of Continuum Publishing.

The Newman Press is a trademark of Paulist Press, Inc.

Library of Congress Cataloging-in-Publication Data

Sullivan, Francis Aloysius.
    From apostles to bishops : the development of the episcopacy in the early church / by Francis A. Sullivan.
        p.   cm.
    Includes bibliographical references and index.
    ISBN 0-8091-0534-9
    1. Episcopacy—History of doctrines—Early church, ca. 30–600. I. Title.

BX1905 .S85 2001
262'.1213—dc21

                                                                        2001032736

Jacket design by Cheryl Finbow.

Case stamping design by Lynn Else.

Production editor and book designer was Joseph E. Petta.

Published by
THE NEWMAN PRESS
An imprint of Paulist Press
997 Macarthur Boulevard
Mahwah, New Jersey 07430

www.paulistpress.com

Printed and bound in the
United States of America

CONTENTS

PREFACE

On October 31, 1999, Edward Cardinal Cassidy, president of the Pontifical Council for Promoting Christian Unity, and Bishop Christian Krause, president of the Lutheran World Federation, signed a Joint Declaration on the Doctrine of Justification. The signing of this Joint Declaration meant that, after years of patient dialogue, the Catholic Church and the churches belonging to the Lutheran World Federation agreed that they no longer considered the doctrine of justification by God's grace through faith in Christ to be a church-dividing issue.

In the light of the agreement achieved on this question, which had for so long seemed a great barrier separating Catholics not only from Lutherans but from most Protestants as well, many Christians might think that now no formidable barriers stand in the way of restoring full communion between the churches.

In fact, however, some truly church-dividing issues remain. One such issue concerns the significance of episcopal ordination in the apostolic succession. The Catholic Church, the Orthodox and other Eastern churches, and most churches of the Anglican Communion teach that episcopal ordination in the apostolic succession is necessary for valid orders and ministry. While many Protestant churches do have bishops, none of them agrees that the validity of their orders and ministry depends on episcopal ordination in the apostolic succession. Few of them actually claim to have maintained the historic succession, and none admits that the lack of it renders their ministry or Eucharist invalid. Furthermore, Catholics hold that episcopal ordination confers on bishops a teaching role that is authoritative, and in some cases, infallible. No Protestants agree with this belief. These differences follow from the different answers given to an even more basic question: Is the episcopate the result of a purely human, historical development or is it of divine institution? While Protestants, who see the episcopate as the result of a purely human development, consider it a possibly useful, but not obligatory way to organize ministry, Catholics believe it to be an indispensable element of the divinely ordered structure of the Church.

The question whether the episcopate is of divine institution continues to divide the churches, even though Christian scholars from both sides agree that one does not find the threefold structure of ministry, with a bishop in each local church assisted by presbyters and deacons, in the New Testament. They agree, rather, that the historic episcopate was the result of a development in the post–New Testament period, from the local leadership of a college of presbyters, who were sometimes also called bishops *(episkopoi)*, to the leadership of a single bishop. They also agree that this development took place earlier in the churches of Syria and western Asia Minor, than it did in those of Philippi, Corinth and Rome. Scholars differ on details, such as how soon the church of Rome was led by a single bishop, but hardly any doubt that the church of Rome was still led by a group of presbyters for at least a part of the second century.

The question that divides Catholics and Protestants is not whether, or how rapidly, the development from the local leadership of a college of presbyters to that of a single bishop took place, but whether the result of that development is rightly judged an element of the divinely willed structure of the church. This question asks about the theological significance of a post–New Testament development, which history alone cannot answer. On the other hand, accurate knowledge of the history proves essential to arriving at the answer, for the question is whether the historical development took place in such a way that the resulting episcopate can rightly be deemed an essential element of the structure God willed for the church. An accurate knowledge of the history is also necessary in avoiding assertions about the link between the apostles and the bishops that cannot stand the test of historical investigation or critical exegesis.

In this book I present the historical development of the ministry of leadership in the early Church, beginning with the New Testament and ending with Saint Cyprian, the bishop of Carthage during the middle years of the third century. For the first part of this history, the reader will have the texts available in the New Testament. Early Christian writings after the New Testament are not so easily available, and for that reason I include passages of the works of that period that throw light on the development of the episcopate. As I have said, history alone cannot give the answer to the question whether bishops are the successors of the apostles by divine institution, and therefore, in my final chapter, I offer what seem to me the best reasons to support that belief. While I write as a Roman Catholic, I hope Protestants who may read this book will find my presentation of the history objective, and that they will at least find reasonable the grounds I offer for believing that the episcopate is an element of the divinely willed structure of the church.

I express my thanks to Joseph T. Lienhard, S.J., for his careful reading of this book in manuscript, as well as for the use I have made of his own book, *Ministry*, in the series Message of the Fathers of the Church (Wilmington: Michael Glazier, 1984).

I dedicate this book to the memory of Edward R. Callahan, S.J., and to the Jesuit community at Boston College.

Francis A. Sullivan, S.J.
Feast of the Ascension of the Lord, 2000

ABBREVIATIONS

BLE	*Bulletin de Littérature Ecclésiastique*
CA	*Confessio Augustana*
CCL	*Corpus Christianorum series latina*
CSEL	*Corpus Scriptorum Ecclesiasticorum Latinorum*
DV	*Dei Verbum*
GCS	*Griechische christliche Schriftsteller*
HE	Eusebius Pamphilus, *Ecclesiastical History*
JEH	*Journal of Ecclesiastical History*
JTS	*Journal of Theological Studies*
LG	*Lumen gentium*
RechSR	*Recherches de science religieuse*
RSPT	*Revue des sciences philosophiques et théologiques*
TS	*Theological Studies*
UR	*Unitatis redintegratio*

1
APOSTOLIC SUCCESSION IN THE EPISCOPATE: A CHURCH-DIVIDING ISSUE

The Catholic Refusal to Practice Open Communion

In October, 1998, the Catholic bishops of England, Wales, Scotland and Ireland issued a teaching document entitled *One Bread One Body*. In it they set forth the Catholic doctrine regarding the sacrament of the Eucharist, explained the present discipline of the Catholic Church with regard to the sharing of the Eucharist between Catholics and other Christians, and presented the theological basis for this discipline. The reactions this document received confirmed the observation of the editor of *The Tablet*, who began his comment on it by saying: "There is no area where more offence is caused to other Christians from other churches than in the Catholic refusal—on good theological grounds—to exercise a practice of open communion."[1]

A "practice of open communion" would mean welcoming all baptized Christians to receive the Eucharist when they attend Catholic Mass; if it were reciprocal, it would mean allowing Catholics to receive the Eucharist in other Christian churches. The "refusal of open communion" to which the editorial refers does not mean that other Christians are never allowed to receive the Catholic Eucharist. In fact, members of the Orthodox and other Eastern churches may receive the Catholic Eucharist if they spontaneously ask for it, and Catholics may also receive the Eucharist in those churches when it is impossible for them to receive it from a Catholic priest.

On the other hand, the discipline of the Catholic Church is quite restrictive with regard to sharing the Eucharist with members of "faith

1

communities rooted in the Reformation" (the description used in *One Bread One Body*). A Catholic priest may give the Eucharist to members of those churches only when they experience a grave and pressing need of the grace of the sacrament, cannot approach a minister of their own community, spontaneously ask for the sacrament, demonstrate catholic faith in regard to it, and are properly disposed. Catholics, however, are not allowed to receive the Eucharist from ministers of churches "rooted in the Reformation," among which the bishops included churches of the Anglican communion.[2]

"Based on Good Theological Grounds"

The *Tablet* editorial noted that the Catholic refusal to practice open communion was "based on good theological grounds." Indeed, a good part of *One Bread One Body* was devoted to explaining the theological reasons, both for the refusal of open communion and for the difference between the rules regarding the Orthodox and other Eastern Christians, on the one hand, and Christians of the Reformation churches on the other.

Briefly, the refusal to practice open communion is based on the intrinsic connection between eucharistic communion and ecclesial communion. The one signifies and calls for the other. There is a basic incongruity involved in regularly sharing the Eucharist in a church with which one is not in full communion, and in receiving it from a minister whom one does not recognize as one's pastor.

On the other hand, the limited sharing of the Eucharist the Catholic discipline does allow is based on the fact that despite the absence of full ecclesial communion, varying degrees of communion linking churches and their members with one another can still exist. The difference between the rules for eucharistic sharing between Catholics and Orthodox and other Eastern Christians, on the one hand, and between Catholics and members of the "communities rooted in the Reformation" on the other, is based on the differing degrees of communion linking these churches.

Differing Degrees of Ecclesial Communion

Ecclesial communion is measured by what churches have in common. What justifies the sharing of Eucharist between Catholics and the Orthodox and other Eastern Christians is that they not only share the same faith with regard to the sacraments of Holy Orders and Eucharist, but also recognize one another's Eucharist as fully valid, for those who celebrate it are ordained by bishops who stand in the historic apostolic succession. Because of this degree of communion the Second Vatican Council consistently used the term "churches" in referring to those Eastern communities. On the other hand, in its Decree on Ecumenism, it used the term "ecclesial communities" rather than "churches" in referring to those in which the Catholic Church does not recognize the presence of valid Holy Orders and hence a fully valid Eucharist. The Council's use of the term "ecclesial communities" as the subject of the following sentence in its Decree on Ecumenism highlights this fact:

> The ecclesial communities separated from us lack that fullness of unity with us which should flow from baptism, and we believe that especially because of the lack of the sacrament of orders they have not preserved the genuine and total reality of the Eucharistic mystery.[3]

The Council never explicitly named any individual Christian church as "lacking the sacrament of orders." Pope Leo XIII, however, in his bull *Apostolicae curae* of 1896, did declare Anglican orders null and void on the grounds that for the first hundred years after the Reformation Anglican ordinations used a defective formula, which in turn involved a defective intention on the part of the ordainers who used it. Recently, officials of the Congregation for the Doctrine of the Faith have described *Apostolicae curae* as an infallible papal declaration.[4]

Catholic Judgment on Protestant Orders

Although it has denied the validity of Anglican orders, the Catholic Church has never officially expressed its judgment about the validity of the orders in any particular Protestant church or about Protestant orders in general. However, the bishops who issued *One Bread One Body* explained why they are not considered valid when they said:

> It is essential that the one who presides at the Eucharist be known to be established in a sure sacramental relationship with Christ, the High Priest, through the sacrament of Holy Orders conferred by a bishop in the recognised apostolic succession. The Catholic Church is unable to affirm this of those Christian communities rooted in the Reformation. Nor can we affirm that they have retained the "authentic and full reality of the eucharistic mystery."[5]

This makes it obvious that the bishops have understood the term "ecclesial communities," as used in the above quotation from the Decree on Ecumenism, to designate "the Christian communities rooted in the Reformation."

The judgment that "the sacrament of Holy Orders conferred by a bishop in the recognised apostolic succession" cannot be affirmed of these communities rests on the fact that, at the time of the Reformation, the Calvinist communities renounced both the theory and practice of episcopal ordination of their clergy, and, in continental Europe, no Catholic bishop who might have handed on valid orders in Lutheran communities accepted the Lutheran reform. Evidence suggests that Luther and his early followers would have preferred to maintain the historic episcopate if Catholic bishops had joined them, but as none did, they resorted to the ordination of pastors by pastors, some of whom had been validly ordained as Catholic priests. It was one such Lutheran pastor who ordained the first Lutheran bishops for Norway and Denmark. In Sweden and Finland, however, the first Lutheran bishops were ordained by a man who had been a validly ordained Catholic bishop. To my knowledge, the Catholic Church has never officially expressed its judgment on the validity of orders as they have been handed down by episcopal succession in these two national Lutheran churches.

In any case, while the Lutheran Churches of Sweden and Finland have maintained the practice of ordination by bishops, they agree with the main body of Lutherans that the validity of orders does not depend on episcopal ordination in the historic apostolic succession. And on this point, they agree not only with other Lutherans, but with the whole Protestant world. If there is one doctrine on which all Protestants agree, it is that the validity of their orders and ministry does not depend on episcopal ordination in the historic apostolic succession. And they agree on this, whether their churches actually have bishops or not. A fundamental difference among the Catholic, Orthodox and Anglican churches, on the one hand, and the Protestant churches on the other, is not based on the presence or absence of bishops; in fact, many Protestant churches, including the Evangelical Lutheran Church in America, do have bishops. It is based rather on the doctrinal question whether the validity of orders and sacraments depends on episcopal ordination in the historic apostolic succession. This stands as a truly church-dividing issue, to which no solution has emerged from the many dialogues held between Catholics and representatives of the various Protestant churches.

The Issue of Episcopal Ordination in Agreements Between Anglicans and Lutherans

The same issue has loomed large in recent negotiations between some churches of the Anglican communion and some Lutheran churches that explored the possibility of establishing full communion. Anglicans have traditionally insisted, with Catholics and the Orthodox, that validity of ministry and sacraments depends on episcopal ordination in the historic apostolic succession. (They remain convinced that they have retained this, despite the negative judgment of Pope Leo XIII.) Consequently, until recently, Anglicans have always insisted that they could enter into full communion with a Lutheran church and accept its sacraments as valid, only if its pastors had been ordained by bishops who themselves were ordained in the apostolic succession. For Lutheran churches other than those of Sweden and Finland, this would mean "regaining" the apostolic succession by having their bishops co-ordained by an Anglican bishop. Not surprisingly, Lutheran churches have not accepted this, as it would mean accepting the view that such ordination proves necessary for valid ministry—which would imply that their previous ministry and sacraments had not been valid.

Recently, however, the British and Irish Anglican churches have formulated an agreement with the Scandinavian and Baltic Lutheran churches (in the "Porvoo Common Statement"), according to which these Anglican churches will immediately recognize as valid the ministry and sacraments in the Lutheran churches of Norway and Denmark, while in the future the bishops in those churches will be co-consecrated by bishops who stand in the historic succession.[6] The fact that the Church of Denmark declared itself unable to accept the Porvoo agreement reflects the reluctance of many Lutherans to accept the second of these conditions.

Similar negotiations have also taken place in the United States between the Episcopal Church and the Evangelical Lutheran Church, which have formulated a "Concordat of Agreement" with a view toward establishing full communion between them.[7] Here also the Episcopalians would recognize the present sacramental ministry of the Lutheran pastors as fully valid, while in the future Anglican bishops would take part in the consecration of Lutheran bishops. It was agreed that this concordat would require ratification by a two-thirds majority of the national convention of each church. The Episcopalians approved it by an even greater majority, but the measure failed, by a few votes, to achieve the required two-thirds at the 1997 Churchwide Assembly of the Evangelical Lutheran Church. The Assembly of 1999 approved it

by slightly more than two-thirds. At both Assemblies it was evident
that the opposition had focused on the requirement that, in the future,
Anglican bishops would take part in the ordination of Lutheran bishops. Many saw this as admitting the necessity of the historic episcopate.
Thus, as results of these efforts to achieve communion between
Anglican and Lutheran churches suggest, apostolic succession in the
episcopate remains a neuralgic issue.

Highlighting the complexities of the issue, Edward Yarnold, a
Catholic participant in the international Anglican-Catholic dialogue,
has raised the question whether, in recognizing the validity of the ministry of Lutheran pastors who have not been ordained by bishops in the
apostolic succession, the British, Irish and American Anglicans are being
consistent with principles with which Anglicans had expressed their
agreement in the international dialogue with Roman Catholics. He
observed that "both the *Final Report* of the first Anglican-Roman
Catholic International Commission (ARCIC I) and the *Clarifications*
to that report affirm the need for ordination to take place within an
unbroken episcopal succession." He went on to say: "I am glad to
acknowledge that the drafters of Porvoo made an effort not to contradict ARCIC, but although I have looked again and again, I cannot see
that they were successful."[8]

In another article on the Porvoo agreement, after analyzing the arguments by which the Anglicans had justified their acceptance of the validity
of Lutheran ministry without ordination by bishops in the apostolic succession, Father Yarnold concluded:

> The declaration has important implications for Roman
> Catholic–Anglican relations. If Roman Catholics could
> accept the Porvoo principle, many of the objections to
> Anglican orders would be nullified. If on the other hand, as
> seems more probable, they are bound to reject it, a new and
> important disagreement on the doctrine of ministry will have
> emerged.[9]

Yarnold could speak of this as a "new disagreement" between Roman
Catholics and Anglicans on the doctrine of ministry because the dialogues in which they engaged had manifested no substantial difference
on the necessity of ordination by bishops in the apostolic succession. In
fact, when one distinguished between a "catholic" and a "protestant"
view of ministry, one would have included the Anglicans as exemplifying
the "catholic" view. Now, however, Father Yarnold sees the "new disagreement on the doctrine of ministry" as exemplifying "a fundamental

difference between Anglican and Roman Catholic understandings of the Church."[10] That would seem to mean that he sees the Anglicans as having moved from a more "catholic" to a more "protestant" understanding of the Church.

Differing Understandings of Apostolicity

One of the fundamental differences between a "catholic" and a "protestant" understanding of the Church concerns elements necessary for the fullness of apostolicity. The most commonly used Christian creed professes the Church to be "one, holy, catholic and apostolic," and hardly any Christian church does not claim to be apostolic both in its faith and in its ministry. When churches explain what they hold as the necessary components of apostolicity in faith and ministry, however, fundamental differences appear between them.

While the typically "protestant" understanding of apostolicity in faith will insist on Scripture alone as the source and criterion of apostolic faith, a "catholic" understanding, while also looking to Scripture as source and criterion of faith, will regard the Church's tradition as providing an authentic interpretation of Christian revelation. Similarly, the typically "protestant" view will find divinely established apostolic ministry in the New Testament alone, judging the developments of ministry in the post–New Testament period as of merely human and historical value. The "catholic" view, on the contrary, will see some developments in the early Church as so evidently guided by the Holy Spirit that they can rightly be recognized as of divine institution.

Certainly, a number of ecumenical dialogues had made considerable progress on lessening the gap between the "catholic" and the "protestant" understandings of the Church's apostolicity.[11] In the past the "protestant" tradition had tended to identify apostolicity almost exclusively with fidelity to apostolic doctrine, while the "catholic" tradition had tended to identify it with apostolic succession in ministry. The concept of apostolicity expressed today in ecumenical agreements generally includes both of these major components. All agree that the church must be apostolic both in its faith and in its ministry. However, a basic difference remains concerning the nature of the link between apostolicity of ministry, on the one hand, and ordination by bishops who stand in the historic apostolic succession, on the other.

Progress Noted in the Lima Report

One of the clearest indications of the progress made on this issue, and of the difference that remains, is found in the document *Baptism, Eucharist and Ministry,* also known as the *Lima Report,* which was the fruit of lengthy discussion by the Faith and Order Commission of the World Council of Churches. The commission that prepared this document included representatives from virtually all the Christian traditions, including the Roman Catholic. It does not claim to have reached consensus, but rather to represent "significant theological convergence" and a "large measure of agreement."[12] The following statements from its section IV, "Succession in the Apostolic Tradition," indicate the degree of agreement that has been reached, and the important difference that remains.

> 35. The primary manifestation of apostolic succession is to be found in the apostolic tradition of the Church as a whole. The succession is an expression of the permanence and, therefore, of the continuity of Christ's own mission in which the Church participates. Within the Church the ordained ministry has a particular task of preserving and actualizing the apostolic faith. The orderly transmission of the ordained ministry is therefore a powerful expression of the continuity of the Church throughout history; it also underlines the calling of the ordained minister as guardian of the faith....
>
> 36. Under the particular historical circumstances of the growing Church in the early centuries, the succession of bishops became one of the ways, together with the transmission of the Gospel and the life of the community, in which the apostolic tradition of the Church was expressed. This succession was understood as serving, symbolizing and guarding the continuity of the apostolic faith and communion.
>
> 37. In churches which practice the succession through the episcopate, it is increasingly recognized that a continuity in apostolic faith, worship and mission has been preserved in churches which have not retained the form of historic succession. This recognition finds additional support in the fact that the reality and function of the episcopal ministry have been preserved in many of these churches, with or without the title "bishop." Ordination, for example, is always done in them by

persons in whom the Church recognizes the authority to transmit the ministerial commission.

38. These considerations do not diminish the importance of the episcopal ministry. On the contrary, they enable churches which have not retained the episcopate to appreciate the episcopal succession as a sign, though not a guarantee, of the continuity and unity of the Church. Today churches, including those engaged in union negotiations, are expressing willingness to accept episcopal succession as a sign of the apostolicity of the life of the whole Church. Yet, at the same time, they cannot accept any suggestion that the ministry exercised in their own tradition should be invalid until the moment that it enters into an existing line of episcopal succession. Their acceptance of the episcopal succession will best further the unity of the whole Church if it is a part of a wider process by which the episcopal churches themselves also regain their lost unity.

The above section of the *Lima Report* manifests a significant convergence in that churches that, since the Reformation, have not maintained the episcopate are "expressing willingness to accept episcopal succession as a sign of the apostolicity of the life of the whole Church." The remaining difference, however, is also evident, in that Protestants cannot recognize episcopal succession as a necessary element of the apostolicity of the Church, as this could suggest that the ministry in their churches would be invalid until it entered into the historic episcopal succession. On the other hand, the Catholic position, as expressed recently in *One Bread One Body,* holds that ordination by bishops in the apostolic succession is so necessary for valid orders and ministry that the Catholic Church cannot affirm that the churches rooted in the Reformation have retained the authentic and full reality of the eucharistic mystery. The contrast between these two positions makes it evident that, despite the progress that has been made, apostolic succession in the episcopate remains a church-dividing issue.

To this point, I have considered this issue as it affects the different understandings churches have concerning the requirements for valid ministry, with the consequences that follow for the possibility of reciprocal sharing of ministry and sacraments. Another important dimension of the problem, however, also requires attention. It concerns the role of bishops in the transmission and interpretation of the Christian faith.

Bishops as Authoritative Teachers in Matters of Faith

The doctrine of the Catholic Church maintains that bishops, as successors to the apostles, have an essential role to play in the faithful transmission of the apostolic faith. Statements made by the Second Vatican Council in its Dogmatic Constitutions on the Church and on Divine Revelation authoritatively express this belief.

> Among the various ministries which have been exercised in the church from the earliest times the chief one, according to tradition, is that performed by those who, having been appointed to the episcopate through an unbroken succession going back to the beginning, are transmitters of the apostolic seed. Thus, according to the testimony of St. Irenaeus, the apostolic tradition is manifested and preserved throughout the world by those whom the apostles made bishops and by their successors down to our own time.[13]

> The sacred synod teaches that the bishops have by divine institution taken the place of the apostles as pastors of the church in such wise that whoever hears them hears Christ and whoever rejects them rejects Christ and him who sent Christ.[14]

> Episcopal consecration confers, together with the office of sanctifying, the offices of teaching and ruling, which, however, of their very nature can be exercised only in hierarchical communion with the head and members of the college.[15]

> Although the individual bishops do not enjoy the prerogative of infallibility, they do, however, proclaim infallibly the doctrine of Christ when, even though dispersed throughout the world but maintaining among themselves and with Peter's successor the bond of communion, in authoritatively teaching matters to do with faith and morals, they are in agreement that a particular teaching is to be held definitively. This is still more clearly the case when, assembled in an ecumenical council, they are, for the universal church, teachers of and judges in matters of faith and morals, whose definitions must be adhered to with the obedience of faith.[16]

> In order that the full and living Gospel might always be preserved in the church the apostles left bishops as their successors. They gave them "their own position of teaching authority."

...Thus the apostolic preaching, which is expressed in a special way in the inspired books, was to be preserved in a continuous line of succession until the end of time.[17]

The task of giving an authentic interpretation of the word of God, whether in its written form or in the form of tradition, has been entrusted to the living teaching office of the church alone. Its authority in this matter is exercised in the name of Jesus Christ. This authority is not superior to the word of God, but is rather its servant. It teaches only what has been handed on to it.[18]

As noted above, if there is one doctrine on which all Protestants agree, it is that the validity of their orders and ministry does not depend on episcopal ordination in the historic apostolic succession. All Protestants also stand united in rejecting the Catholic doctrine that ordination in the apostolic succession confers on bishops an authoritative and eventually infallible teaching role in the Church. The question of the teaching office of bishops is undoubtedly among the most intractable issues dividing Catholics and Protestants today.

Teaching Authority in Churches "Rooted in the Reformation"

It is true that the most authoritative of the Lutheran confessional documents, the *Confession of Augsburg* of 1530, does say: "According to divine right, it is the office of the bishop to preach the Gospel, forgive sins, judge doctrine and condemn doctrine that is contrary to the Gospel."[19] However, because Catholic bishops refused to accept the Lutheran reform, pastors who were not bishops, as well as the university faculties of theology, carried on the teaching role in most Lutheran churches.

In the past century, especially since the end of the First World War, many Lutheran churches that previously did not have bishops conferred that title on those exercising episcopal oversight over regions of their church. However, the teaching role of such bishops is commonly exercised in synods or general conventions in which pastors and laity also have an influential voice. Thus, as we have seen, it was the Churchwide Assemblies of the Evangelical Lutheran Church in America that voted on the acceptance of the Concordat of Agreement with the Episcopalians.

It is the understanding of Lutherans that a doctrinal statement made by a synod would have its authority not from the bishops taking part in it, but from the conformity of its doctrine with the truth of the Gospel. An outstanding example of such a declaration in modern times was made by the first synod of the "Confessing Church" in Barmen, Germany, in May, 1934. The "Barmen Declaration," drawn up by a group of pastors led by Martin Niemöller and by theologians inspired by Karl Barth, was directed against the Nazi-dominated "German Christians." It proposed six "evangelical truths," calling Christians to place their trust in God's grace rather than in earthly realities and to find God's word in Jesus Christ, the one valid source of revelation. Evangelical Christians rightly look upon the "Barmen Declaration" as having great authority, but its authority comes from what was said, enhanced by the heroism of the pastors who dared to say it in defiance of the Nazi regime. It presents a far different example of teaching authority from that, for example, exercised by the Catholic bishops at Vatican II.

While bishops now lead a good many churches "rooted in the Reformation," none attributes to its bishops a divinely instituted teaching office, received through ordination in the apostolic succession. The Anglicans do not recognize the bishops who gather every tenth year for the "Lambeth Conference," and are believed to be ordained in the apostolic succession, as possessing such teaching authority on that account. In Western Christianity, only the Catholic Church believes that episcopal ordination confers a teaching office by which bishops can teach with authority in the name of Jesus Christ, and, as a college united with its head, can proclaim the doctrine of Christ with infallibility.

Successors of the Apostles "by Divine Institution"?

Thus far, we have seen that the Protestant churches reject two of the principal doctrines affirmed by Vatican II concerning episcopal ordination in the apostolic succession—namely, that valid ministry depends on it and that it confers an authoritative teaching office. These are truly church-dividing issues. But, the passage quoted from Vatican II includes another affirmation that goes more deeply to the root of the problem: "The sacred synod teaches that the bishops have by divine institution taken the place of the apostles as pastors of the church in such wise that whoever hears them hears Christ and whoever rejects them rejects Christ and him who sent Christ."[20]

The distinctive Catholic doctrines concerning the role of bishops in the Church ultimately depend on the truth of the claim that "by divine institution" the mandate and authority Christ gave to the college of apostles as "teachers of doctrine, priests for sacred worship and ministers of government"[21] have been perpetuated in the college of bishops. This provides the foundation of the Catholic belief that through episcopal ordination "the grace of the Holy Spirit is given, and a sacred character is impressed, in such a way that bishops, eminently and visibly, take the place of Christ himself, teacher, shepherd and priest, and act in his person."[22]

Belief that bishops are the successors of the apostles by divine institution grounds the Catholic insistence that episcopal succession comprises an essential element of the permanent structure of the Church, on which the validity of its sacramental ministry and the authority of its official teachers depend.

Obviously, then, those who do not share Catholic belief on these latter points deny the more basic claim that the episcopate is of divine institution. Their denial is usually based on the fact that the divine institution of the episcopate cannot be proven from the New Testament. As I have pointed out above, Protestants will find divinely established apostolic ministry in the New Testament alone, judging the developments of ministry in the post–New Testament period as of merely human and historical value.

A Simplistic Presentation of the Catholic Position

Admittedly the Catholic position, that bishops are the successors of the apostles by divine institution, remains far from easy to establish. It is unfortunate, I believe, that some presentations of Catholic belief in this matter have given a very different impression. One finds a recent example of this in the Vatican Response to the *Final Report* of the First Anglican–Roman Catholic International Commission (ARCIC I).[23] The Response called for "further clarification" of what ARCIC I said on the question of apostolic succession. Presumably to insist on a point that had not been asserted clearly enough in the *Final Report,* the Vatican Response said: "The Catholic Church recognizes in the apostolic succession...an unbroken line of episcopal ordination from Christ through the apostles down through the centuries to the bishops of today."[24]

This statement of the Vatican Response itself needs further clarification. To speak of "an unbroken line of episcopal ordination from Christ through the apostles" suggests that Christ ordained the apostles as bishops, and that the apostles in turn ordained a bishop for each of the churches they founded, so that by the time the apostles died, each Christian church was being led by a bishop as successor to an apostle. There are serious problems with such a theory of the link between apostles and bishops.

Problems with a Simplistic Notion
of Apostolic Succession

The first problem has to do with the notion that Christ ordained the apostles as bishops. On the one hand, it is no doubt true that the mandate Christ gave to the apostles included the threefold office of teaching, ruling and sanctifying, which Vatican II described as conferred by episcopal consecration (*LG* 21). However, the correctness of describing the apostles themselves as "bishops" is another question. A "bishop" is a residential pastor who presides in a stable manner over the church in a city and its environs. The apostles were missionaries and founders of churches; there is no evidence, nor is it at all likely, that any one of them ever took up permanent residence in a particular church as its bishop.

A second question also arises: Did the apostles ordain a bishop for each of the churches they founded? The New Testament contains good evidence that the churches founded by St. Paul had local leaders, to whom the apostle urged the community to be submissive. In the salutation of his letter to the Philippians Paul made special mention of the *episkopoi* and *diakonoi:* terms that literally mean "overseers and servants" but in Christian usage came to mean "bishops and deacons." During his final journey to Jerusalem, Paul gave a farewell address to the leaders of the church of Ephesus, whom Luke calls "presbyters," but whom he has Paul describe as having been appointed *episkopoi* by the Holy Spirit (Acts 20:17–35). So there is good evidence that during the period of the New Testament, Christian churches had local leaders, some of whom, at least, were called "bishops."

However, it remains unclear whether these "bishops" of whom Paul speaks were actually appointed or ordained by him. Secondly, there is no evidence that St. Paul or any other apostle ever appointed one of these local leaders as the chief pastor of the whole church in a particular city. Rather, the evidence suggests that up to the end of the New Testament period, leadership and other ministry were provided in each local church by a group of "elders" or "overseers," with no one person in charge except when the apostle or one of his coworkers was actually present. The New Testament offers no support for a theory of apostolic succession that supposes the apostles appointed or ordained a bishop for each of the churches they founded.

Nor do we find support for such a theory in the earliest Christian writings that we have from the post–New Testament period. According to the *Didache,* a Christian community that lacked the leadership of a prophet should choose worthy men and appoint them as bishops and deacons. It contains no suggestion that they would derive their authority in any way from a founding apostle. The letter of the Romans to the Corinthians, known as *I Clement,* which dates to about the year 96, provides good evidence that about thirty years after the death of St. Paul the church of Corinth was being led by a group of presbyters, with no indication of the presence of a bishop with authority over the whole local church. However, *I Clement* does affirm that the founding apostles had appointed the first generation of local church leaders and had laid down the rule that when those men died, others should be appointed to succeed them. This letter, then, does attest to the principle of apostolic succession in ministry, but it gives no support to the idea that the apostles had appointed a bishop for each church they founded. For *I Clement,* the principle of apostolic succession was realized in the college of duly appointed presbyters. Most scholars are of the opinion that the church of Rome would most probably have also been led at that time by a group of presbyters. A Roman document of the early second century known as *The Shepherd of Hermas* supports this opinion.

The letters of Ignatius of Antioch, generally dated to about 115, are the first Christian documents that witness to the presence of a bishop who is clearly distinct from the presbyterate and is pastor of the whole church of a city. However, this testimony is certain only for the church of Antioch and for several churches of western Asia Minor in the vicinity of Ephesus. A letter that Polycarp, Bishop of Smyrna, wrote to the Philippians a few years later indicates that the church of Philippi at that time was still being led by a group of presbyters. More importantly, nothing in the letters of Ignatius suggests that he saw his episcopal authority as derived from the mandate Christ gave to the apostles. While the role and authority of the bishop comprised a major theme in his letters, he never invoked the principle of apostolic succession to explain or justify it

There exists a broad consensus among scholars, including most Catholic ones, that such churches as those of Alexandria, Philippi, Corinth and Rome most probably continued to be led for some time by a college of presbyters, and that only during the course of the second century did the threefold structure become generally the rule, with a bishop, assisted by presbyters, presiding over each local church.

Need for an Objective Examination of the Evidence

One conclusion seems obvious: Neither the New Testament nor early Christian history offers support for a notion of apostolic succession as "an unbroken line of episcopal ordination from Christ through the apostles down through the centuries to the bishops of today." Clearly, such a simplistic approach to the problem will not do. On the other hand, many reputable Catholic scholars, who share the consensus regarding the gradual development of the episcopate in the early church, remain convinced that we do have solid grounds for holding that bishops are the successors of the apostles. Such scholars agree that along with the evidence from the New Testament and early Christian documents, one must invoke a theological argument based on Christian faith to arrive at the conclusion that bishops are the successors of the apostles "by divine institution." At the same time, they insist that the evidence from the New Testament and early Christian literature is crucial, and must be treated with scholarly integrity. It is counterproductive to put forth arguments that will not stand the test of critical exegesis or historical investigation.

The rest of this book examines the evidence in the New Testament and in Christian writings up to the middle of the third century, which throws light on the development of the ministry of leadership in the early Church. I have found this a fascinating chapter in the history of the Church, and it is my hope that this book will allow many others to share my fascination with it. But I hope also to show that while it is not easy to establish a link between apostles and bishops, those who believe that bishops derive their ministry from Christ as successors to the apostles do have sound reasons for their belief.

2
THE APOSTLES

THE TWELVE

A lthough the term "the twelve apostles" is very familiar to us, in fact it appears only twice in the New Testament: once in a Gospel (Matt 10:2) and once in the Book of Revelation (Rev 21:14). On the other hand, the term "the Twelve" appears in the four Gospels more than twenty-five times in all and is the term St. Paul used to designate the first group of disciples to whom Christ appeared after his resurrection (1 Cor 15:5). The fact that here St. Paul is "hand[ing] on...as of first importance" the profession of faith he had "received" (15:3) shows that "the Twelve" had an essential place in the earliest Christian tradition. The fact that Judas, who betrayed Christ, is described in all four Gospels as "one of the Twelve" provides the most cogent evidence for the historicity of the choice of the Twelve by Jesus during his ministry (see Matt 26:47; Mark 14:10,43; Luke 22:3,47; John 6:71.)

All four Gospels witness to the fact that Jesus formed a special group of twelve disciples during his public ministry (see Matt 10:1–4; Mark 3:13–19; Luke 6:12–16; John 6:70). According to Luke's account, Jesus selected the Twelve out of a larger number of disciples: "He called his disciples to himself, and from them he chose Twelve..." (Luke 6:13). Matthew, on the contrary, tends to identify "the disciples" with "the Twelve," as in the phrase "his twelve disciples" (Matt 10:1; 11:1). In any case, the evangelists agree that Jesus chose these twelve; it was he who chose them, not they who chose him (cf. John 15:16). Mark's expression of this is particularly vigorous: "He went up the mountain and summoned those whom he wanted and they came to him. He appointed [literally: "he made"] twelve..." (Mark 3:13–14). Mark also indicates the purpose for which he chose them: "...that they might be with him and he might send them forth to preach and to have authority to drive out demons" (Mark 3:14–15). Here we can distinguish their two roles: first, as disciples ("with him") and second as apostles ("sent out to preach"). Significantly, Mark only speaks of the Twelve as "apostles" when they returned from the mission on which Jesus sent them during his public ministry (Mark 6:30). Matthew likewise calls them "apostles" only once, when giving the names of "the twelve apostles" (Matt 10:2). Luke, on the other hand, speaks of the Twelve as "apostles" six times in his Gospel and far more frequently in Acts. The way Mark and Matthew use the term suggests their understanding that only when they had been "sent out" were they properly called by the name that means "men sent out." In his Gospel, Luke anticipates the use of the term by which they will be known in his second book.

The Names of the Twelve and Significance of the Number

Each synoptic Gospel lists the names of the Twelve (Mark 3:16–19; Matt 10:2–4; Luke 6:14–16). Each list has the names arranged in three groups of four. The first name in each group is the same in all lists (Peter heads the first group, Philip the second and James of Alphaeus the third). The same names appear in each group, although not always in the same order. However, in the third group, Mark and Matthew have Thaddaeus while Luke has Judas of James. Judas Iscariot is always in the last place. This structure would seem a mnemonic device, suggesting the intention of the Christian community to retain the names of the Twelve when they were no longer on the scene. The variation between Thaddaeus and Judas of James suggests that the names of the less prominent among the Twelve were not so well remembered by the time the Gospels were written. This also suggests that the Twelve as a group were more significant than the names of some of the individuals among them.

The "Q" source used by Matthew and Luke provided a saying of Jesus that indicates the symbolic meaning of the number twelve: "Amen, I say to you that you who have followed me, in the new age, when the Son of Man is seated on his throne of glory, will yourselves sit on twelve thrones, judging the twelve tribes of Israel" (Matt 19:28; cf. Luke 22:29–30). On the significance of the number twelve, I quote the New Testament scholar, Gerhard Lohfink:

> Reference to the twelve tribes evoked a central point of Israel's eschatological hope. Although the system of twelve tribes had long since ceased to exist...the complete restoration of the twelve-tribe people was expected for the eschatological time of salvation....Against the background of this very lively hope Jesus' constitution of twelve disciples could only be grasped as a *symbolic action*. The Twelve exemplified the awakening of Israel and its gathering in the eschatological salvific community, something beginning then through Jesus. They exemplified this gathering simply through the fact that they were created as *Twelve,* but they also exemplified it through being sent out to all of Israel. Institution and mission were two aspects of one and same symbolic action.[1]

Lohfink also offers the following comment on the text quoted above from the "Q" source: This saying of Jesus "shows conclusively that the Twelve can only be understood as a sign *for the people of God.* But it also shows that they are not only a sign *promising salvation,* but also a sign of judgment. At the last judgment they will testify against Israel if Israel does not repent."[2]

The Mission of the Twelve during Jesus' Ministry

The three synoptic Gospels record the fact that at least on one occasion Jesus sent his twelve disciples out on a mission to do what he himself was doing: to preach repentance in view of the coming kingdom of God and to heal the sick (Matt 10:1–21; Mark 6:7–13; Luke 9:1–6). Each of these passages brings out the idea that their mission was an extension of Jesus' own ministry. They shared his message and his power over illness and evil spirits, and the consequences for those who refused to listen were as serious as for those who refused to listen to Jesus himself (cf. Matt 10:14–15: "Whoever will not receive you or listen to your words—go outside that house or town and shake the dust from your feet. Amen, I say to you, it will be more tolerable for the land of Sodom and Gomorrah on the day of judgment than for that town.") Jesus expresses this positively when he says: "Whoever receives you receives me, and whoever receives me receives the one who sent me" (Matt 10:40; cf. John 13:20).

While the Gospels record such sayings of Jesus as being said to the disciples on the occasion of their temporary mission, the early Church certainly understood them as also applying to the apostles when they were fully commissioned by the risen Christ. In fact, it is evident that in the "missionary discourse" attributed to Jesus in Matthew 10:5–42, one has to distinguish between what applied to their temporary mission in Galilee and what applied to the eventual preaching of the Gospel to the pagan world. Thus, the saying: "Do not go into pagan territory or enter a Samaritan town. Go rather to the lost sheep of the house of Israel" (Matt 10:5–6) clearly applied to the mission in Galilee. At the same time, as G. Lohfink points out, the Twelve

> were sent by Jesus to proclaim the message of the reign of God to *the whole house of Israel*. They exemplified Jesus' claim on Israel as a whole. The lost sheep of Matt 10:6 are not a reference to only a part of the people—such as sinners or apostates—but to the *entire* people, which is compared to a scattered flock that has been led astray.[3]

On the other hand, the prediction that "you will be led before governors and kings for my sake as a witness before them and the pagans" (Matt 10:18) reflects the experience of persecution after the Gospel had begun to be preached to the Gentile world. While this can well be understood as an instance of the evangelist's attributing to Jesus something reflective of the experience of the church of his own time, the command not to go into pagan territory or to the Samaritans could hardly have been other than an authentic word of Jesus during the public ministry.

A number of passages in the Gospels indicate that one of the reasons why Jesus chose the Twelve was that he might teach them privately and instruct them more fully than he did the rest of his followers (cf. Matt 11:1; 13:10–18; Mark 4:10ff.; 8:31; 9:30–37; 10:32; Luke 18:31). This suggests that Jesus was preparing them for a future ministry of teaching, when they would be like "scribe[s] who [have] been instructed in the kingdom of heaven" (Matt 13:52).

Other passages of the Gospels, especially that of Matthew, suggest that Jesus prepared the Twelve for a future role of leadership, with authority over a community. One example of this appears in Matthew 18, a chapter that begins with the question put to Jesus by his disciples: "Who is greatest in the kingdom of heaven?" In the light of Matthew's identification of "the disciples" with "the Twelve" and the fact that such a question is elsewhere attributed to the Twelve (Mark 9:34–35), there is good reason to take this discourse as reflecting instructions Jesus gave to the Twelve in view of a role of leadership that he intended them to have. He warns the disciples against giving scandal to the "little ones" or despising them. They are to be like the shepherd who goes after the straying sheep (Matt 18:6–14). This discourse also includes the saying: "Amen, I say to you, whatever you bind on earth shall be bound in heaven, and whatever you loose on earth shall be loosed in heaven" (Matt 18:18).

In contemporary rabbinic literature, the image of "binding and loosing" expressed the idea of making authoritative decisions, declaring something forbidden or permitted by the Law. It was also used of imposing or lifting a ban of excommunication, to which it refers in the immediate context. In that context, it seems to be directed to the local community ("the church" of v. 17), rather than to the Twelve, but the fact that Jesus gave the authority to "loose and bind" to Peter, the leader among the Twelve (cf. Matt 16:19), suggests the likelihood that in another context he may have directed this saying to the Twelve. Anton Vögtle has suggested that it comprises one of the "church-founding" sayings addressed to the Twelve by the risen Christ.[4]

The Mission of the Eleven by the Risen Christ

The profession of Christian faith that Paul had received and "handed on as of first importance" included the belief that Christ appeared after his resurrection first to "Cephas and then to the Twelve" (1 Cor 15:5). The use of the term "the Twelve," despite the fact that the group had been reduced to eleven by the desertion of Judas, indicates how embedded in the tradition the term had become. All four Gospels and Acts bear witness to the belief of the early Church that these men, who had been Jesus' special disciples during his public ministry, were sent out by the risen Christ to "make disciples," "baptize" and "teach" (Matt 28:19–20); to "proclaim the gospel" (Mark 16:15); to be his "witnesses" (Luke 24:48; Acts 1:8); and to "forgive" sins (John 20:21–23).

It is no doubt true that the actual wording of the commission as found in these texts reflects further developments that had taken place by the time the Gospels were written. Only later did Jewish Christians come to know that they should "make disciples of all nations" (Matt 28:19) and "proclaim the gospel to every creature" (Mark 16:15). Likewise, the command to "baptize in the name of the Father, and of the Son, and of the holy Spirit" is generally recognized as a subsequent development of the rite of baptism. Such influence of later Christian experience on the formulation of sayings attributed to Jesus, however, is understandable in the light of the purpose for which the Gospels were written, and is not a reason to reject the fact that the men who had been Jesus' special disciples during his ministry were sent out by the risen Christ to preach his Gospel. Otherwise, one could hardly explain the origin of the Christian Church or the authority that the early Church recognized these men as having.

Luke's Twelve Apostles

As noted above, the term "the twelve apostles" appears only twice in the New Testament. However, clearly Luke, in both his Gospel and in Acts, believed "the Twelve" and "the apostles" to be identical groups of men. They are "apostles" because they are "men sent on a mission." Luke's identification of the apostles with the Twelve would seem to follow from his understanding of what they were sent out to do. In both the Gospel (Luke 24:48) and in Acts (1:8) the risen Christ gives to the eleven the mission to be his "witnesses." "Thus it is written that the Messiah would suffer and rise from the dead on the third day,...you are witnesses of these things" (Luke 24:46–48).

Luke's account of the choice of Matthias to take the place of Judas makes it clear that, for Luke, being an apostle meant being able to witness not only to the resurrection of Christ, but to all that Jesus had said and done, from his baptism by John until his ascension into heaven (Acts 1:21–22). Because for Luke the apostles were sent to witness to "these things," their number was restricted to the twelve men capable of such witnessing and chosen for this task. The original twelve had been chosen by Jesus; the choice of Matthias was made by casting lots, which meant that he was chosen by the Lord (Acts 1:24). That only male disciples were eligible to be chosen (Luke has Peter use the term *andrôn*) is understandable for two reasons: because the Twelve symbolized the twelve patriarchs of Israel and because that culture did not consider women reliable witnesses.

For Luke, "the Twelve" were "the apostles," for they were uniquely qualified to be Christ's witnesses and were sent out by him to fulfill that task. While Luke has Christ say that they were to be his witnesses "in Jerusalem, throughout Judea and Samaria, and to the ends of the earth" (Acts 1:8), this was more his description of how the Gospel would spread than of the part that the Twelve would actually play in it. It was Philip, not one of the Twelve, who brought the Gospel to Samaria, and it was Paul who would carry the message to "the ends of the earth."

The mention of Paul raises the question whether Luke recognized him as an apostle. Obviously Paul could not meet the requirement laid down by Luke of being a witness to all that Jesus had said and done from his baptism to his ascension into heaven. However, Acts does refer to Paul and Barnabas as apostles in the context of the missionary journey on which they were sent out by the church at Antioch (Acts 14:4,14). One explanation of this might be that in this passage Luke was following a source that applied the term to any missionary sent out to preach the Gospel. If this were the case, it suggests that Luke did not altogether reject such a broader use of the term, although he did not prefer that meaning.

The Ministry of the Twelve

Of the individual members of the Twelve, Luke tells us only about the ministry of Peter, who is sometimes accompanied by John as a kind of shadow-figure. However, in several places Luke does speak of the role of "the apostles" as a group. Thus, he describes how Peter "stood up with the Eleven" to deliver his Pentecost address (Acts 2:14). Those "cut to the heart" by Peter's sermon asked him and the other apostles, "What are we to do, my brothers?" (2:37). Those baptized that day "devoted themselves to the teaching of the apostles" (2:42). Luke tells us that "many wonders and signs were done through the apostles" (2:43), and that "with great power the apostles bore witness to the resurrection of the Lord Jesus, and great favor was accorded them all" (4:33). The fact that the people who sold their possessions "put [the proceeds] at the feet of the apostles" who saw to their distribution (4:35) suggests the pastoral role of the apostles in the Jerusalem community. When the Hellenists complained that their widows were being neglected, Luke tells us that the Twelve called together the community and that the apostles prayed and laid hands on the men chosen to take care of this need (6:1–6). The same passage attributes to the Twelve a special role of "prayer" and the "ministry of the word" (6:4). When "the apostles in Jerusalem" heard that Samaria had accepted the word of God, they sent Peter and John to them (8:14). When the dispute over the circumcision of Gentile converts broke out in Antioch, "it was decided that Paul, Barnabas, and some of the others should go up to Jerusalem to the apostles and presbyters about this question" (15:2). When the decision in favor of freedom of the Gentiles from the law of circumcision had been taken, Luke says that it was "the apostles and presbyters, in agreement with the whole church," who addressed a letter to the Gentile Christians of Antioch, Syria and Cilicia, and sent their representatives to carry the message to them (15:15–23).

In summing up what we know from the New Testament about the role of "the twelve apostles" in the early church, we have to admit that, apart from what we know about Peter, our information comes mostly from what we find in Acts about their ministry as a group in the primitive church of Jerusalem. The first half of Acts witnesses to the Church's memory of the founding role the Twelve played during the first years of the mother church of Jerusalem. Having been the specially chosen disciples of Jesus during his lifetime on earth, they provided the primary link between Jesus and the postresurrection Church. Their witness to Jesus' teaching, his miracles and, above all, to his death and resurrection was foundational for the Church. The earliest Christian community was the fruit of their witness and grew under their leadership. Their confirmation of the authenticity of the missionary work done by others—by Philip in Samaria, by the men of Cyprus and Cyrene in Antioch, and eventually by Paul of Tarsus—testifies to their openness to unexpected initiatives and their role of oversight over churches beyond the limits of Judea.

The role of the Twelve as symbolizing the twelve patriarchs of Israel meant that they had a unique role to play, precisely as a group of twelve, in the very origin of the Church. This called for the choice of a twelfth man to take the place of Judas, prior to Pentecost, so that on that day Peter "stood up with the Eleven" (Acts 2:14) when he gave his first witness to the risen Christ. On the other hand, some years later, when James, the son of Zebedee and brother of John, was put to death by Herod (Acts 12:2), there was no question of again completing the number of the Twelve. By then the initial "foundation time" was completed.

The silence of Acts about the ministry of James, even though it must have been notorious enough to move Herod to kill him, suggests that one should be cautious about drawing conclusions from the silence of Acts about missionary journeys by members of the Twelve other than Peter. It seems clear that they were no longer in Jerusalem at the time of Paul's last visit there, when James and the presbyters received him (21:18). Of course one cannot rely on the legendary accounts of their dispersal to various regions of the world, and of their martyrdom in the places where they are said to have founded churches. There is good reason to doubt that they understood themselves as sent to preach the Gospel to Gentiles. If, in fact, they never undertook missionary activity to the Gentile world, were they apostles in the sense in which St. Paul used this term? We can look to St. Paul for some light on this question.

Did St. Paul Recognize the Twelve as "Apostles"?

It is obvious that Paul's notion of what being an apostle required differs from Luke's, for Paul insisted that he himself was an apostle of Jesus Christ, even though he had never been one of Jesus' disciples. We shall later go into detail about Paul's concept of an apostle, but for now suffice it to say that it certainly included being sent to preach the Gospel to those who had not heard it. He knew that he himself had been sent to preach the Gospel to Gentiles. Can one conclude that, if the Twelve were not active as missionaries to the Gentile world, Paul would not have considered them apostles? There are good reasons against drawing such a conclusion.[5]

First of all, speaking of the time immediately after his conversion, Paul says: "...nor did I go up to Jerusalem to those who were apostles before me" (Gal 1:17). This clearly shows that he knew of apostles before him, and that they were in Jerusalem. Given the role the Twelve played in the early years of the Jerusalem community, it seems likely that the Twelve were among those to whom Paul referred as "apostles before me."

Secondly, Paul certainly recognized the leader of the Twelve as an apostle. In fact, Paul saw his own apostleship confirmed by its equality with that of Peter.

> [W]hen they saw that I had been entrusted with the gospel to the uncircumcised, just as Peter to the circumcised, for the one who worked in Peter for an apostolate to the circumcised worked also in me for the Gentiles, and when they recognized the grace bestowed on me, James and Cephas and John, who were reputed to be pillars, gave me and Barnabas their right hands in partnership, that we should go to the Gentiles and they to the circumcised. (Gal 2:7–9)

Several points are noteworthy in this passage. First, while Paul knew himself to be sent as an apostle to the Gentiles, he also recognized that an apostolate to the Jews had been given to Peter. Secondly, Paul's conclusion, that "*we* should go to the Gentiles and *they* to the circumcised" (emphasis added) indicates that it was not Peter alone who had received the mission to the Jews; at least one other member of the Twelve, John, is named. It would seem arbitrary to think that Paul recognized two members of the Twelve, but not the others, as "apostles to the circumcised."[6]

The plentiful evidence about Paul's missionary activity, and the little we know about Peter's makes it clear that the division of the apostolate Paul describes here was not understood as a rigid separation. Paul consistently began his work in a new city by going to the synagogue and preaching about Christ to the Jews. He tells us that in Antioch Peter had been sharing meals with the Gentile Christians, which suggests that he saw his mission as directed to them as well as to Jews. On the other hand, the passage noting that "when they [some people from James] came, he...separated himself" (Gal 2:12) can well be understood as indicating that Peter's primary mission was to the Jews, and that he felt obliged to avoid the breach with the church in Jerusalem that could have followed had he continued to eat with the Gentiles rather than with the emissaries from Jerusalem while they visited the community in Antioch.[7]

Evidence from archaeology and early Christian writing suggests that Peter's missionary activity took him as far as Rome, and there is some evidence that John, the other "pillar" among the Twelve, worked in Ephesus. We have no reliable evidence about any missionary journeys undertaken by other members of the Twelve. Significantly, however, Paul tells us that the "brothers of the Lord" engaged in missionary journeys, and we can presume that they preached to Jews. One can only guess the identity of the "rest of the apostles" to whom, along with Kephas, Paul also refers in this context (1 Cor 9:5).

The "apostolate to the circumcised" was certainly not restricted to Judea and Galilee; at that period communities of Jews existed in every major city of the Roman Empire. It is important to note that the author of Acts has given us a selective history of the spread of the Gospel. Luke was primarily interested in the propagation of the Gospel in the Gentile world and in its progress northward and westward from Jerusalem to Rome. He tells us nothing about its spread to the south or east, except that it had reached Damascus even before Paul's conversion. That Luke knew of communities of Jews in those regions seems clear from his description of Pentecost, where he notes that some of the Jews who witnessed the events were "Parthians, Medes and Elamites, inhabitants of Mesopotamia... Egypt and the districts of Lybia near Cyrene" (Acts 2:9–10). Acts tells us nothing about how the Gospel reached those regions.

There is good reason to believe that not only Peter and John, but the rest of the Twelve as well, understood themselves as "apostles to the circumcised." Given the evidence that, at the time of Paul's last visit to Jerusalem, they no longer resided there, it seems likely that they had left to preach the Gospel to predominantly Jewish communities. The fact that Acts says nothing about this is not a sufficient reason to conclude that they did not engage in missionary activity. On the other hand, it remains true that they made their major contribution to the life of the Church in their role as the primary witnesses to the ministry, death and resurrection of Christ and as the founders of the mother church of Jerusalem. The author of the Book of Revelation had good reason to describe the foundation of the heavenly Jerusalem as inscribed with the names of the twelve apostles of the Lamb (Rev 21:14).

PAUL, AN APOSTLE OF JESUS CHRIST

In his letters, St. Paul speaks of two kinds of apostles: the "apostles of Jesus Christ" and the "apostles of the churches." The latter are envoys or messengers sent out by a local church to perform some function on behalf of that church, such as those mentioned at 2 Corinthians 8:23 and Philippians 2:25. Their role resembled that of the *sheluhim* who are mentioned in rabbinic writings of the second century. These were envoys sent out by the Jewish authorities with the power to represent them and act in their name. *Sheluhim* were not missionaries; neither were the "apostles of the churches."

For Paul, however, "apostles of Christ" were sent out by the risen Christ to preach his Gospel. The fact that his adversaries challenged his right to be recognized as an apostle forced him to defend his claim and thus to name the criteria by which he would have recognized others as apostles as well. The following passages of Paul's letters spell out the grounds on which he based his claim to be an apostle of Jesus Christ.

In 1 Corinthians 9:1–2, Paul asks: "Am I not free? Am I not an apostle? Have I not seen Jesus our Lord? Are you not my work in the Lord? Although I may not be an apostle for others, certainly I am for you, for you are the seal of my apostleship in the Lord." Here we can identify two criteria: to have seen the risen Lord and to have founded a church by the preaching of the Gospel.

In 1 Corinthians 15:8–10, after listing those to whom Christ appeared after his resurrection, Paul adds: "Last of all, as to one born abnormally, he appeared to me. For I am the least of the apostles, not fit to be called an apostle, because I persecuted the church of God. But by the grace of God I am what I am, and his grace to me has not been ineffective." Here we see the same two criteria: his having seen the risen Lord and the effectiveness of his ministry.

In 2 Corinthians 11:22–29 Paul compares himself with the men whom he calls "false apostles, deceitful workers, who masquerade as apostles of Christ" (11:13). Here he bases his claim to be even more a "minister of Christ" than they are, on the far greater sufferings he has undergone in his missionary work. The detail with which he lists his sufferings for the Gospel suggests how important a criterion of his apostleship he considered them. In the following chapter (12:12) Paul speaks of "the signs of an apostle," which the Corinthians had witnessed in his ministry to them: "signs and wonders and mighty deeds" that were performed among them "with all endurance."

When presenting himself to the Romans as "a slave of Christ Jesus, called to be an apostle and set apart for the gospel of God," Paul declares that "through him [Jesus Christ our Lord] we have received the grace of apostleship, to bring about the obedience of faith, for the sake of his name, among all the Gentiles" (Rom 1:1,5). Here we see that Paul's credentials include both the source and the goal of his apostleship.

In the letter to the Galatians we find a more lengthy exposition of the grounds on which Paul based his claim of apostleship. He begins by describing himself as "an apostle not from human beings nor through a human being but through Jesus Christ and God the Father who raised him from the dead" (Gal 1:1). Verses 15 and 16 again highlight the divine source of Paul's call: "But when [God], who from my mother's womb had set me apart and called me through his grace, was pleased to reveal his Son to me, so that I might proclaim him to the Gentiles...." Here we can distinguish three points: (1) the call is from God; (2) it involves receiving divine revelation; (3) it is a call and mission to preach Christ to the Gentiles.

In chapter 2 of Galatians, Paul mentions the criteria by which "the pillars" recognized him as an apostle:

> [W]hen they saw that I had been entrusted with the gospel to the uncircumcised, just as Peter to the circumcised, for the one who worked in Peter for an apostolate to the circumcised worked also in me for the Gentiles, and when they recognized the grace bestowed upon me, James and Cephas and John, who were reputed to be pillars, gave me and Barnabas their right hands in partnership, that we should go to the Gentiles and they to the circumcised. (2:7–9)

From these texts of St. Paul we can draw out his criteria for an apostle of Jesus Christ: (1) to have seen the risen Christ; (2) to have received from him a mission to preach the Gospel; (3) to have one's ministry confirmed by its fruitfulness, by signs and wonders and by one's sufferings for the sake of the Gospel.

Evidently Paul's opponents also claimed to meet the criteria of apostleship. Paul responded that whatever criteria one could claim, he himself had them to a higher degree and, in addition, could claim his many sufferings for the Gospel—a criterion that perhaps he alone employed.

Rudolf Schnackenburg has raised the question whether Paul also used the term "apostle" in a more generic sense, of Christian missionaries who had not seen the risen Lord or been sent directly by him.[8] As an example of such use he refers to 1 Thessalonians 2:7, where Paul seems to refer not only to himself but also to Silvanus and Timothy as "apostles of Christ." Likewise, in 1 Corinthians 9:5–6, Schnackenburg suggests that "the rest of the apostles" could include missionaries who had not been sent directly by the risen Christ. In the same context, Paul names Barnabas as an apostle who has the same rights as himself. Barnabas belonged to the Jerusalem community, but it is not certain that he was among "all the apostles" to whom the Lord appeared (1 Cor 15:7). The same uncertainty applies to the case of Andronicus and Junia (Rom 16:7). Schnackenburg describes them as Hellenist Jews, who are not likely to have been members of the Jerusalem Christian community during the early period of the appearances of the risen Christ. In 1 Corinthians 12:28 Paul names apostles as the first among those gifted with charisms, whom God has designated for service in the Church. Schnackenburg takes Paul to be speaking of apostles here in the commonly accepted sense in the Hellenist communities: that is, missionaries designated for this work by the charism God had given them for it. Schnackenburg concludes that in his earlier period, Paul used the term "apostles" in the broader sense of "missionary founders of churches," and later, when his own credentials were challenged, he insisted on the more demanding qualifications that made him an "apostle of Jesus Christ," namely, that he had seen the risen Christ and had been sent by him.

Our knowledge of the ministry carried on by individual apostles is limited to what the New Testament tells us about the ministry of Peter and Paul. Acts and the letters of Paul provide information about both of them.

APOSTOLIC MINISTRY OF PETER

According to Paul, Peter had received the apostolate to the circumcised (Gal 2:7–8). However, Peter also spent some time in Antioch, where he "used to eat with the Gentiles" (Gal 2:12), a fact that suggests that he did not direct his ministry exclusively to Jews. Paul also speaks of Peter as engaging in what were no doubt missionary journeys, on which he took along his wife (1 Cor 9:5). The fact that some of the community at Corinth declared themselves to "belong to Cephas" (1 Cor 1:12) suggests that Peter may have visited Corinth and spent some time in ministry there. Peter was evidently not in Rome when St. Paul wrote his Letter to the Romans, but it is generally recognized as certain, based on evidence from archaeology and early Christian writings, that he died there a martyr in the persecution of Nero. Hence there is good reason to believe that Peter engaged in apostolic activity in several major cities of the Roman Empire.

Luke's account in Acts, however, makes no mention of this. Apart from Jerusalem, where most of Peter's apostolic activity takes place, Luke mentions only his ministry in Samaria (8:14 ff.), Lydda (9:32–35), Joppa (9:36–43) and Caesarea (ch. 10). In the first three places, he describes Peter as visiting Christian communities founded by others; in Caesarea, on the contrary, Peter takes the initiative, under the guidance of the Spirit, to preach the Gospel for the first time to Gentiles. With regard to other missionary journeys undertaken by Peter, Acts includes only the laconic statement that after his release from prison in Jerusalem, "he left and went to another place" (12:17).

Peter's apostolic ministry in Jerusalem, as described in Acts, embraces both his preaching to those who had not yet accepted the Gospel and his leadership of the Christian community. He founded the community by preaching the Gospel to receptive Jewish listeners, first at Pentecost (2:14 ff.) and then in Solomon's Portico (3:12 ff.). Subsequently, he defended his message before a hostile audience in his addresses to the Sanhedrin (4:8 ff.; 5:29 ff.). His ministry was confirmed by miracles of healing (3:1–10; 5:15) and by his joyfully accepting suffering for the sake of the Gospel (5:41).

Peter's leadership of the Jerusalem community first manifested itself when he took the initiative with regard to choosing another to take the place of Judas among the Twelve (1:15–22). Later it meant invoking the judgment of God upon Ananias and Sapphira for deceiving the church (5:1–11). When Peter was questioned about his having entered the house of Cornelius, he took pains to explain what he had done "step by step" to the Jerusalem community, with the result that "they stopped objecting and glorified God" (11:1–18). Finally, the prominence of Peter's ministry in Jerusalem is attested by Herod's having him arrested and kept in prison (12:1–5).

The ecumenical study *Peter in the New Testament* has called attention to the trajectory of images associated with Peter in the New Testament.[9] The dominant image in the chronologically earlier books is the fisherman: (Mark 1:17; Matt 4:19; 17:17), obviously suggesting his work as a missionary; the image in the last chapter of the Fourth Gospel, on the contrary, is the shepherd who has the care of both lambs and sheep (John 21:15–17). The First Letter of Peter likewise attributes a pastoral role to him. There he counsels presbyters as a "fellow presbyter," urging them to be examples to the flock assigned to them, so that when the chief Shepherd appears they will receive the unfading crown of glory (1 Pet 5:1).

The eminent New Testament scholar, James D. G. Dunn, has recognized another aspect of the pastoral ministry of Peter, describing him as *"probably in fact and effect the bridge-man who did more than any other to hold together the diversity of first-century Christianity."* He justifies this description of Peter in the following way:

> James and Paul, the two other most prominent leading figures in first-century Christianity were too much identified with their respective "brands" of Christianity, at least in the eyes of Christians at the opposite end of this particular spectrum. But Peter, as shown particularly by the Antioch episode in Gal. 2, had both a care to hold firm to his Jewish heritage which Paul lacked, and an openness to the demands of developing Christianity which James lacked....So it is Peter who becomes the focal point of unity for the whole Church.[10]

In the light of Dunn's appreciation of Peter's role as "bridge-man," one could add that in his pastoral concern to hold together the Jewish and Gentile elements of early Christianity, Peter resembled St. Paul in his "anxiety for all the churches" (2 Cor 11:28).

APOSTOLIC MINISTRY OF PAUL

As the first half of Acts focuses on Peter among the Twelve, so the second half focuses on Paul, the apostle to the Gentiles. Here I distinguish between his work as a missionary and founder of churches and as a pastor caring for the churches he had founded.

Preaching and Founding Churches

Toward the end of his Letter to the Romans, Paul describes his own work as missionary to the Gentiles in the following way (Rom 15:15–21):

> But I have written to you rather boldly in some respects to remind you, because of the grace given me by God to be a minister of Christ Jesus to the Gentiles in performing the priestly service of the gospel of God, so that the offering up of the Gentiles may be acceptable, sanctified by the holy Spirit. In Christ Jesus, then, I have reason to boast in what pertains to God. For I will not dare to speak of anything except what Christ has accomplished through me to lead the Gentiles to obedience by word and deed, by the power of signs and wonders, by the power of the Spirit [of God], so that from Jerusalem all the way around to Illyricum I have finished preaching the gospel of Christ. Thus I aspire to proclaim the gospel not where Christ has already been named, so that I do not build on another's foundation, but as it is written:/ "Those who have never been told of him shall see,/and those who have never heard of him shall understand."

In keeping with his intention to proclaim the Gospel where Christ had not already been named, when Paul told the Romans that he intended to visit their church, he made it clear that it would be only in passing, as he intended to continue on to Spain (Rom 15:28).

In the First Letter to the Thessalonians we have Paul's own description of how he founded that church:

> For you yourselves know, brothers, that our reception among
> you was not without effect. Rather, after we had suffered and
> been insolently treated, as you know, in Philippi, we drew
> courage through our God to speak to you the gospel of God
> with much struggle. Our exhortation was not from delusion
> or impure motives, nor did it work through deception. But as
> we were judged worthy by God to be entrusted with the
> gospel, that is how we speak, not as trying to please human
> beings, but rather God, who judges our hearts. Nor, indeed,
> did we ever appear with flattering speech, as you know, or with
> a pretext for greed—God is witness—nor did we seek praise
> from human beings, either from you or from others, although
> we were able to impose our weight as apostles of Christ.
> Rather, we were gentle among you, as a nursing mother cares
> for her children. With such affection for you, we were deter-
> mined to share with you not only the gospel of God, but our
> very selves as well, so dearly beloved had you become to us.
> You recall, brothers, our toil and drudgery. Working night and
> day in order not to burden any of you, we proclaimed to you
> the gospel of God. (1 Thess 2:1–9)

The second half of Acts describes Paul's work of founding churches by
proclaiming the Gospel in places where Christ had not yet been named. In
each place, Paul first preached his message to the Jews, and when most of
them rejected it, he turned to the Gentiles who proved more receptive to
it. This pattern is repeated in his founding of churches in Antioch of
Pisidia (Acts 13:14–52), in Iconium (14: 1–7), in Philippi (16:11–15), in
Thessalonika (17:1–9), in Beroea (17:10–13), in Corinth (18:4–7) and in
Ephesus (19:8–9).

Pastoral Care of Churches

We can distinguish between the pastoral care Paul exercised while actually present in a church and that which he carried on while absent,
through his letters and by sending one of his coworkers.

PASTORAL MINISTRY WHILE PRESENT

While Paul stayed only briefly in some of the churches he founded,
Luke tells us that after the initial preaching of the Gospel in Corinth, Paul
"settled there for a year and a half and taught the word of God among

them" (Acts 18:11). Presumably, he directed much of this teaching to those whom he had already converted to Christ. Similarly, at Ephesus, after three months of debating with Jews in the synagogue, Paul "withdrew and took his disciples with him and began to hold daily discussions in the lecture hall of Tyrannus. This continued for two years with the result that all the inhabitants of the province of Asia heard the word of the Lord, Jews and Greeks alike" (Acts 19:9–10).

Elsewhere, Acts describes Paul as engaged in a ministry of teaching, whether directed to the whole Christian community, as in Antioch (11:26; 15:35), or especially to the presbyters, as in Ephesus (20:20). Consistent with these accounts, Paul speaks of his own ministry in the churches he founded as teaching (cf. 1 Cor 4:17: "He [Timothy] will remind you of my ways in Christ [Jesus], just as I teach them everywhere in every church."). In his First Letter to the Thessalonians, Paul reminds them of the "instructions" he had given them during his time with them.

> Finally, brothers, we earnestly ask and exhort you in the Lord Jesus that, as you received from us how you should conduct yourselves to please God—and as you are conducting yourselves—you do so even more. For you know what instructions we gave you through the Lord Jesus....[w]e urge you, brothers, to progress even more, and to aspire to live a tranquil life, to mind your own affairs, and to work with your [own] hands, as we instructed you, that you may conduct yourselves properly toward outsiders and not depend on anyone. (1 Thess 4:1–12)

PAUL'S PASTORAL MINISTRY WHILE ABSENT

Paul spoke of "the daily pressure" put upon him by his "anxiety for all the churches" (2 Cor 11:28). His letters give eloquent testimony to this "anxiety" and to the kind of pastoral care he lavished on his beloved communities. Chapters 4 and 5 of 1 Thessalonians provide an example. Along with exhortations to holiness and mutual charity, he also offered consolation to those who mourned their deceased by his teaching about the resurrection. The pastor's care for his flock is especially evident in the following exhortation given them toward the end of his letter:

> Therefore, encourage one another and build one another up, as indeed you do. We ask you, brothers, to respect those who are laboring among you and who are over you in the Lord and who admonish you, and to show esteem for them with special love on account of their work. Be at peace among yourselves.

> We urge you, brothers, admonish the idle, cheer the faint-
> hearted, support the weak, be patient with all. See that no one
> returns evil for evil; rather, always seek what is good [both] for
> each other and for all. Rejoice always. Pray without ceasing. In
> all circumstances give thanks, for this is the will of God for you
> in Christ Jesus. Do not quench the Spirit. Do not despise
> prophetic utterances. Test everything; retain what is good.
> Refrain from every kind of evil. (1 Thess 5:11–22)

1 Corinthians deals mainly with the problems afflicting that church: factions, a case of incest, lawsuits, sexual immorality, scandal caused by eating
meat sacrificed to idols, the lack of charity at the Eucharist, rivalry about
charisms and disorder in the use of these gifts. In his letter, Paul addresses
these problems one by one, offering pastoral advice for their solution. He
calls the Corinthians his "beloved children," reminding them that he
"became [their] father in Christ Jesus through the gospel" (1 Cor
4:14–15). His fatherhood gave him the right to exercise paternal authority
over those "inflated with pride" (1 Cor 4:18). Paul warned them: "I will
come to you soon, if the Lord is willing, and I shall ascertain not the talk of
these inflated people but their power. For the kingdom of God is not a
matter of talk but of power. Which do you prefer? Shall I come with a rod,
or with love and a gentle spirit?" (1 Cor 4:19–21).

The Second Letter to the Corinthians provides the most powerful
example of the kind of "anxiety" Paul felt for his churches. It also shows
how Paul exercised the authority that he felt confident his role as founding
apostle had given him. He spoke of this authority in the following way:

> [E]ven if I should boast a little too much of our authority, which
> the Lord gave me for building you up and not for tearing you
> down, I shall not be put to shame. May I not seem as one fright-
> ening you through letters. For someone will say: "His letters are
> severe and forceful, but his bodily presence is weak, and his
> speech contemptible." Such a person must understand that
> what we are in word through letters when absent, that we are
> also in action when present. (2 Cor 10:8– 11)

If need be, Paul could be severe in the use of his authority (cf. 2 Cor
13:10), but when he had to write a strong admonition, it was "out of
much affliction and anguish of heart" and "with many tears" (2 Cor 2:4).
His anguish was like that of a woman in labor, such was his affection for
those whom he had brought to birth in Christ (cf. Gal 4:19).

DID THE APOSTLES HAVE "SACRAMENTAL" MINISTRY?

The New Testament shows the apostles engaged in two kinds of ministry: founding new churches by preaching the Gospel to those who had not yet heard it and providing pastoral care to the churches already established. The latter, as already seen, included the ministry of teaching and of authoritative leadership.

A Catholic might ask whether the apostles also engaged in what we would call sacramental ministry. One must reply that the New Testament provides very scanty evidence of this.

Baptism

As we have seen, the "great commission" in Matthew 28:19–20 included the command to "make disciples of all nations, baptizing them in the name of the Father, and of the Son, and of the holy Spirit." Scholars generally agree that the trinitarian formula reflects a later development of baptismal liturgy. On the other hand, it would be difficult to explain the importance the New Testament attributes to baptism and its role as a distinctive sign of Christian initiation if it were not based on a command given by the risen Christ. However, it remains unclear whether the apostles felt called to be the actual ministers of baptism for their converts. In addressing the divided community at Corinth, Paul says:

> I give thanks [to God] that I baptized none of you except Crispus and Gaius, so that no one can say you were baptized in my name. (I baptized the household of Stephanas also; beyond that I do not know whether I baptized anyone else.) For Christ did not send me to baptize but to preach the gospel.... (1 Cor 1:14–17)

The account in Acts of Paul's dealing with the twelve disciples who had received the baptism of John seems to reflect Paul's view that he was not sent to baptize but to preach the Gospel. It tells us that when these men had heard Paul's explanation of the difference between John's baptism and that of Jesus, "they were baptized in the name of the Lord Jesus. And when Paul laid [his] hands on them, the holy Spirit came upon them..." (Acts 19:5–6). The account of the conversion of Cornelius and his household also uses the passive voice in connection with baptism; "Peter responded: 'Can anyone withhold the water for baptizing these people, who have received the holy Spirit even as we have?' He ordered them to be baptized in the name of Jesus Christ" (Acts 10:46–48). In neither case are we told who actually did the baptizing, but it does not seem to have been the apostle himself. In Acts the only person described as actually baptizing someone is Philip "the evangelist" (Acts 8:38; cf. 21:8). However, when the jailer and his household in Philippi were converted, "he and all his family were baptized at once," (Acts 16:33) and the only ones who could have baptized them, according to this account, were Paul and Silas.

Eucharist

The three synoptic Gospels specify the Twelve as the companions of Jesus at supper on the night on which he was betrayed (Matt 26:20; Mark 14:17; and Luke 22:14 has "the apostles," whom Luke identifies with the Twelve). The same three Gospels and 1 Corinthians have an account of the institution of the Eucharist during this supper (Matt 26:26–29; Mark 14:22–25; Luke 22:17–20; and 1 Cor 11:23–25). Yet only the version handed on by Paul and Luke contains the words of Jesus: "Do this in remembrance of me" (1 Cor 11:24; Luke 22:19). Catholic tradition understands these words as establishing a eucharistic ministry that, in view of the recognition of the Eucharist as a liturgical sacrifice, came to be understood as Christian priesthood. The first to receive this ministry were the Twelve. However, the New Testament says nothing about their exercise of such a ministry.

Luke tells us that the first Christians in Jerusalem "devoted themselves to the teaching of the apostles and to the communal life, to the breaking of the bread and to the prayers" (Acts 2:42). He also says that "every day they devoted themselves to meeting together in the temple area and to breaking bread in their homes" (2:46). It seems certain that Luke is referring to the Eucharist by the term "breaking of the bread," but he gives no information as to who presided at the table and actually "broke the bread" and distributed it to the rest. The fact that they broke the bread in their homes suggests a multiplicity of such gatherings, which would call for a multiplicity of presiders.

The one account of a gathering in which an apostle is said to have "broken the bread" is found in Acts 20:7–12. The occasion was Paul's one-week stay in Troas during his final journey to Jerusalem. Luke begins the account by saying: "On the first day of the week when we gathered to break bread, Paul spoke to them because he was going to leave on the next day." After interrupting Paul's discourse with the account of how he restored the young man who fell from the window to life, Luke continues: "Then he returned upstairs, broke the bread and ate; after a long conversation that lasted until daybreak, he departed" (20:11). Given the way Luke begins this account, one can hardly doubt that he means that this vigil ended with Paul's presiding at the Eucharist. It would seem reasonable to presume that whenever an apostle was present, he would preside at the Eucharist. However, apostles can hardly have been the only ones who did this.

Luke's account of the sending of Barnabas and Saul on their first missionary journey begins with his naming five "prophets and teachers" of the church of Antioch who were "worshiping the Lord and fasting" (Acts 13:1–2). From the liturgical role attributed to these men we can surmise that in the early Church, people recognized as prophets and teachers would have presided at the Eucharist. One recalls that Paul named apostles, prophets and teachers as first, second and third among those whom "God has designated" for ministry in the Church (1 Cor 12:28). We look in vain to the New Testament for a certain answer to the question of whether persons other than members of these three groups presided at the Eucharist.

The Laying On of Hands

The laying on of hands is an important component of the sacraments of confirmation and ordination. I conclude this study of the ministry of the apostles by recalling the passages of the New Testament where the apostles make use of this sign.

Acts contains two references to the laying on of hands by apostles for the reception of the gift of the Holy Spirit. In the first instance, Peter and John laid hands on the Samaritan converts.

> [W]hen the apostles in Jerusalem heard that Samaria had accepted the word of God, they sent them Peter and John, who went down and prayed for them, that they might receive the holy Spirit, for it had not yet fallen upon any of them; they had only been baptized in the name of the Lord Jesus. Then they laid hands on them and they received the holy Spirit. (Acts 8:14–17)

In the second case Paul laid hands on the men at Ephesus who had previously received John's baptism. "When they heard this, they were baptized in the name of the Lord Jesus. And when Paul laid [his] hands on them, the holy Spirit came upon them, they spoke in tongues and prophesied" (Acts 19:5–6).

The New Testament also includes two references to the laying on of hands by apostles in commissioning persons for ministry in the Church. When the Hellenists in the Jerusalem community complained that their widows were being neglected in the daily distribution, the Twelve called upon the community to select seven men to take care of this matter. Having chosen them, "[t]hey presented these men to the apostles who prayed and laid hands on them" (Acts 6:6). In the Second Letter to Timothy, Paul is quoted as saying to him: "I remind you to stir into flame the gift of God that you have through the imposition of my hands" (2 Tim 1:6).

CONCLUSION

The "great commission" in the Gospel of Matthew concludes with the promise: "And behold I am with you always, until the end of the age" (Matt 28:20). Such a promise evidently looks to the future, when Jesus' immediate disciples will no longer be on the scene. If Jesus is going to continue to be with his apostles until the end of the age, it will be through his presence with those who will carry on the ministry he entrusts to them. In our next chapter we shall seek to identify those whom the apostles looked to as their successors.

3

SHARERS IN THE
APOSTLES' MINISTRY

Because God chose the economy of incarnation to redeem humanity, the Good News of salvation was announced to the world in human speech addressed to human hearers. No doubt, God could have illuminated the mind of every person on earth with infused knowledge of his plan of salvation, but he chose to do it in a different way. Jesus announced the coming of the reign of God to his fellow men and women in the same way men and women speak to one another. An inevitable consequence of this choice is that he could not reach everyone with his message; he would need others to share this task. The following passage of the Gospel of Matthew illustrates this point.

> Jesus went around to all the towns and villages, teaching in their synagogues, proclaiming the gospel of the kingdom, and curing every disease and illness. At the sight of the crowds, his heart was moved with pity for them because they were troubled and abandoned, like sheep without a shepherd. Then he said to his disciples, "The harvest is abundant but the laborers are few; so ask the master of the harvest to send out laborers for his harvest." Then he summoned his twelve disciples and gave them authority over unclean spirits to drive them out and to cure every disease and every illness....Jesus sent out these twelve after instructing them thus, "Do not go into pagan territory or enter a Samaritan town. Go rather to the lost sheep of the house of Israel. As you go, make this proclamation: 'The kingdom of heaven is at hand.' Cure the sick, raise the dead, cleanse lepers, drive out demons. Without cost you have received; without cost you are to give." (Matt 9:35–10:8)

Obviously much about Jesus' ministry was uniquely his and could not be shared with his disciples; after all, he alone was the Savior of the world. At the same time, as indicated in the above gospel passage, he needed other laborers to bring in the harvest. A comparison between Matthew's description of Jesus' Galilean ministry and the instruction Jesus gave to the disciples shows that he sent them out to do exactly what he himself was doing. Likewise, the command to go not to pagans or Samaritans, but rather to the lost sheep of the house of Israel corresponds to Jesus saying of himself: "I was sent only to the lost sheep of the house of Israel" (Matt 15:24). Jesus could not share with the disciples his unique role as the lamb of God who would take away the sins of the world, but he could and did share with them the ministry of teaching and healing he undertook during the brief years of his public life.

As noted in the previous chapter, all four Gospels and Acts testify that the risen Christ sent out these same disciples (minus Judas) with a mandate to carry his message of reconciliation to the world. Subsequently, two leaders among them, Peter and John, recognized that Christ had appeared to Paul, the former persecutor of the Church, and had sent him as an apostle to the Gentiles. These men, and perhaps some others, were uniquely "apostles of Jesus Christ." The risen Christ had appeared to them and had personally commissioned them to preach the Good News of the salvation he had accomplished by his death and resurrection. He sent them to make disciples and to teach them to observe all that Jesus had commanded them.

"Making disciples" meant founding communities of believers who would form the *ekklesia tou theou,* the "assembly of God" of the New Covenant. In the building of this Church, the "apostles of Jesus Christ" had a unique foundational role. No one of the next generation could give the eyewitness testimony to the life, death and resurrection of Jesus the Twelve could give; no one of the next generation could claim to have received his commission directly from the risen Lord as they and Paul had received it. They could share with no one else their mission as "apostles of Jesus Christ," for that mission had to be given by the risen Lord himself.

As we have seen, Jesus' own mission was unique, but he could and did share his ministry with his disciples, both during his public life and by sending them out after his resurrection. Analogously, while in many respects the apostles had a unique mission that could not be handed on, their ministry of preaching the Gospel, making disciples and teaching them to observe all Jesus had taught them could be shared with others. Indeed it had to be shared with others, as they obviously could not do it all by themselves. The following passages of the New Testament illustrate how the apostles shared their ministry with others.

THE SEVEN

In the first four chapters of Acts, Luke twice describes the early Jerusalem community as one in which "[a]ll who believed were together and had all things in common; they would sell their property and possessions and divide them among all according to each one's need" (Acts 2:44–45; cf. 4:34–35). However, this idyllic picture is marred in chapter 5 by the story of Ananias and Sapphira and in chapter 6 by the complaint of the Hellenists that their widows were being neglected by the Hebrews in the daily distribution.[1] Luke, who probably relied on an early tradition in his account of the affair,[2] attributes the solution of this problem to the Twelve, who

> called together the community of the disciples and said: "It is not right for us to neglect the word of God to serve at table. Brothers, select from among you seven reputable men, filled with the Spirit and wisdom, whom we shall appoint to this task, whereas we shall devote ourselves to prayer and the ministry of the word." (Acts 6:2–4)

When the community had chosen seven men, all with Greek names and therefore most likely from among the Hellenists, "[t]hey presented these men to the apostles who prayed and laid hands on them" (6:6).

On this detail, Joseph Fitzmyer comments:

> "Laying on of hands" is known in the OT, where it usually expresses a solidarity between persons, a self-identification of one with the other in some blessing, spiritual gift, or office or rank. Thus Moses is told by God to commission Joshua, son of Nun, as his successor (Num 27:18–23); the Levites are so commissioned in Num 8:10.[3]

Given this background, it is not surprising that the apostles would adopt this gesture in commissioning the Seven for their ministry.

As Luke tells the story, the Seven were commissioned to serve at tables, and he may have intended his readers to see the origin of the diaconate in this episode. However, the fact that the community was told to select men "filled with the Spirit and wisdom" and that subsequently two of them, Stephen and Philip, engaged in activities that required a greater fullness of Spirit and wisdom than serving at tables suggests that the Seven were really chosen for a leadership role among the Hellenists. Raymond Brown refers to them as "the Hellenist leaders," and "administrators for the Hellenist believers." He adds:

> The choice of administrators in 6:6 is done in the context of praying and the laying on of hands. Although the develop-ment of church structure reflects sociological necessity, in the Christian self-understanding the Holy Spirit given by the risen Christ guides the church in a way that allows basic structural development to be seen as embodying Jesus Christ's will for his church.[4]

The "sociological necessity" brought out by this episode reflects the fact that as the community grew in numbers and complexity, the apostles simply could not do everything that needed to be done; they had to share their ministry. In meeting this need, they had the example of Jesus to guide them. In his commentary on this passage, Joseph Fitzmyer points to the analogy between what Jesus did and what the apostles did: "As Jesus chose the Twelve (Luke 6:13), so the community and the Twelve now choose the Seven."[5] Actually, while the community chose the Seven, the Twelve laid down the criteria for making the choice and appointed these men to their task, with prayer and laying on of hands. One can hardly doubt that in thus commissioning the Seven, the apostles con-ferred on them a share in the mission and mandate that they themselves had received from the Lord.

As Raymond Brown has remarked, Acts tells us relatively little about the Twelve.[6] Thus, it is not surprising that in Acts we read of no other instance where Peter or any other member of the Twelve shared his apostolic ministry. However, the references to Silvanus and Mark in the conclusion of the First Letter of Peter (1 Pet 5:12–13) do suggest that Peter had coworkers. Here Silvanus is described as a "faithful brother," through whom Peter writes his letter, and Mark, his "son," sends his greetings along with those of the Roman church. These two compan-ions of Peter should probably be identified with men who had also been coworkers of Paul. Paul associates Silvanus with himself in 1 Thessalonians 1:1; 2 Thessalonians 1:1; and 2 Corinthians 1:19, and he describes Mark as one of his coworkers in the conclusion of his letter to Philemon (Phlm 24). While it remains uncertain whether 1 Peter was written by the apostle himself, the references to Silvanus and Mark in the conclusion of the letter tend to confirm the antecedent probability that he had companions with whom he shared his ministry, as Paul did. We stand on surer ground when we look to Paul's letters for evidence of his own practice in this regard.

PAUL'S COWORKERS

In describing Paul's apostolic ministry in the previous chapter, I distinguished between his missionary work of founding churches by preaching the Gospel to those who had not heard it and his pastoral care of the churches he had founded. As we shall now see, coworkers assisted him in both these tasks. We know little more than the names of most of them, but we have a fair amount of information, both from Acts and from Paul, about several of them. Since this information complements our understanding of ministry in the apostolic period, it is worth considering in some detail.

Barnabas

Luke introduced Barnabas into his story as a Levite, a Cypriot by birth, who received his name, which means "son of encouragement," from the apostles and who sold a piece of property he owned and "brought the money and put it at the feet of the apostles" (Acts 4:36–37). When Saul came to Jerusalem after his conversion, Barnabas brought him to the apostles and assured them of his sincerity (9:27). When the church in Jerusalem heard that Gentiles in Antioch had accepted the Gospel, they sent Barnabas to look into it. When he "saw the grace of God" at work there, he went to Tarsus to find Saul and bring him to Antioch; the two of them then worked together for a year, teaching and building up the community (Acts 11:22–26).

The beginning of Acts 13 lists Barnabas and Saul among five prophets and teachers in the church at Antioch. They are then sent out as missionaries, designated for this task by the Holy Spirit (13:1–4). As they had worked together in pastoral ministry at Antioch, they now cooperated in preaching the Gospel, first on the island of Cyprus and then on the mainland of Asia Minor. They had their greatest success with Gentiles, and agreed that these converts should not be obliged to accept circumcision. When a dispute about this arose at Antioch, Paul and Barnabas went to Jerusalem to present their case to the apostles and presbyters (Acts 15:2).

At this point Luke's account is confirmed by Paul, who says that he went up to Jerusalem with Barnabas and that "when they recognized the grace bestowed on me, James and Cephas and John, who were reputed to be pillars, gave me and Barnabas their right hands in partnership, that we should go to the Gentiles and they to the circumcised" (Gal 2:9). Before undertaking their next missionary journey, Paul and Barnabas had a falling out and did not travel together after that.[7] However, some years later Paul commended Barnabas for the fact that, like Paul, he worked to support himself, rather than receiving support from the communities to which he preached (1 Cor 9:6).

As seen above, Barnabas and Paul were designated as partners in missionary work by the Holy Spirit. After his separation from Barnabas, however, it seems Paul chose his own coworkers. This is clearly the case with regard to Silvanus and Timothy.

Silvanus (Silas)

Luke, using the name Silas, describes him as a prophet, sent by the church at Jerusalem to convey to Antioch the decision concerning the freedom of the Gentile converts from the law of circumcision (Acts 15:27,32). Paul evidently came to know him during his stay at Antioch and chose him as his companion for his second missionary journey (Acts 15:40). In Philippi Paul and Silas were stripped, beaten and thrown in jail, freed by the earthquake and then asked by the magistrates to leave their city (Acts 16:19–40). The two of them then preached the Gospel in Thessalonika (Acts 17:1–9), a fact confirmed by Paul, who associates Silvanus with himself in the salutation of both his letters to the Thessalonians. Silvanus also helped Paul evangelize the Corinthians, as we know both from Acts 18:5 and from Paul, who reminds the Corinthians that the Son of God was proclaimed to them by Silvanus, Timothy and himself (2 Cor 1:19).

Timothy

Luke's account of Paul enlisting Timothy as a coworker (Acts 16:1–3) stresses the fact that Paul chose Timothy to accompany him and Silas on their mission. Luke uses the same word here that Mark used in describing the choice of the Twelve by Jesus; as Jesus "summoned those whom he wanted" (Mark 3:13), so Paul "wanted him [Timothy] to come along with him" (Acts 16:3). We hear that "[t]he brothers in Lystra and Iconium spoke highly of him" (Acts 16:2), and according to 1 Timothy 4:14, Timothy was also recommended to Paul by a prophetic word. But Paul clearly made the choice. Luke also tells us that "[o]n account of the Jews of that region, Paul had him circumcised, for they all knew that his father was a Greek" (Acts 16:3). This would seem to reflect Paul's practice of first preaching the Gospel to Jews, who might have been put off by his having an uncircumcised coworker whose mother was known to be of Jewish origin.

The number of references to Timothy in Paul's letters make it clear that Timothy assisted Paul both in founding churches and in the pastoral care of churches they had founded. Timothy's role in the founding of the church of the Thessalonians is evident from the salutations of the two letters Paul wrote to that community. Paul may also have referred to him and Silvanus as "apostles of Christ" (1 Thess 2:7), depending on the meaning of the pronoun "we" Paul used in the first two chapters of 1 Thessalonians. In 2 Corinthians 1:19, Paul names Timothy, along with himself and Silvanus, as those who had proclaimed the Son of God, Jesus Christ, to the Corinthians.

Paul speaks at greater length about Timothy's role in the pastoral care of the churches they had founded. In his First Letter to the Thessalonians, Paul complains of being thwarted in his desire to see them in person, and continues:

> That is why, when we could bear it no longer, we decided to remain alone in Athens and sent Timothy, our brother and co-worker for God in the gospel of Christ, to strengthen and encourage you in your faith, so that no one be disturbed in these afflictions....But just now Timothy has returned to us from you, bringing us the good news of your faith and love, and that you always think kindly of us and long to see us as we long to see you. (1 Thess 3:1–6)

Two references to Timothy appear in the First Letter to the Corinthians: "For this reason I am sending you Timothy, who is my beloved and faithful son in the Lord; he will remind you of my ways in Christ [Jesus], just as I teach them everywhere in every church" (1 Cor 4:17); and "If Timothy comes, see that he is without fear in your company, for he is doing the work of the Lord just as I am" (1 Cor 16:10). In his Letter to the Philippians Paul says:

> I hope, in the Lord Jesus, to send Timothy to you soon, so that I too may be heartened by hearing news of you. For I have no one comparable to him for genuine interest in whatever concerns you. For they all seek their own interests, not those of Jesus Christ. But you know his worth, how as a child with a father he served along with me in the cause of the gospel. (Phil 2:19–22)

Several elements in these texts justify the conclusion that Paul shared with Timothy the mandate for apostolic ministry he himself had received from Christ. The description of Timothy as his "beloved and faithful son" who served along with Paul "as a child," suggests that Paul was the source from whom Timothy received his ministry. The repeated reference to Paul's "sending" Timothy on missions confirms this. Significantly, while Paul speaks of Apollos and himself as "God's co-workers" (1 Cor 3:9), he never speaks of "sending" Apollos on a mission. He does say, rather: "I urged him strongly to go to you with the brothers, but it was not at all his will that he go now. He will go when he has an opportunity" (1 Cor 16:12). The difference between "urging" Apollos and "sending" Timothy brings out the fact that Timothy received his task and mandate from Paul.

Titus

Titus is not mentioned in Acts, and we do not know how Paul chose him as his coworker. That he was a Gentile is clear from the fact that when Paul went up to Jerusalem to settle the question about the freedom of his Gentile converts from the law of circumcision, he made the point that "not even Titus, who was with me, although he was a Greek, was compelled to be circumcised" (Gal 2:3). From a number of references to him in the Second Letter to the Corinthians, we know that Paul shared with him the pastoral care of the Corinthian church at a time of great tension between Paul and that community.

In his first reference to him Paul describes Titus as his "brother," whom he had hoped in vain to find in Troas with a report about affairs in Corinth (2 Cor 2:13). Paul next describes his own encouragement at the arrival of Titus in Macedonia, as well as "the encouragement with which he was encouraged in regard to you, as he told us of your yearning, your lament, your zeal for me, so that I rejoiced even more" (2 Cor 7:7). Paul goes on to say: "And besides our encouragement, we rejoice even more because of the joy of Titus, since his spirit has been refreshed by all of you....And his heart goes out to you all the more, as he remembers the obedience of all of you, when you received him with fear and trembling" (2 Cor 7:13,15). Addressing the Corinthians, Paul described Titus as "my partner and co-worker for you" (2 Cor 8:23), to whom he entrusted an important role in the collection for the church in Jerusalem (8:6), a matter of great concern both for Paul and for Titus (8:16–17). Paul insists that neither he nor Titus took advantage of the Corinthians, asking: "Did Titus take advantage of you? Did we not walk in the same spirit? And in the same steps?" (12:18). One can surely feel justified in concluding that in making Titus his "partner and co-worker," Paul transmitted to him a share in the mission he himself had received from the risen Christ.

Thus far the chapter has focused on the four coworkers of Paul about whom we have the best information; however, Paul mentions a considerable number of others in his letters, generally with terms that express their association with his work. The following list details the terms Paul used, along with the information the New Testament provides about the persons he designated by them.

Coworkers (Sunergoi)

PRISCA (PRISCILLA) AND AQUILA

In the final chapter of his Letter to the Romans, Paul says: "Greet Prisca and Aquila, my co-workers in Christ Jesus, who risked their necks for my life, to whom not only I am grateful but also all the churches of the Gentiles; greet also the church in their house" (Rom 16:3–5). 1 Corinthians 16:19 clearly indicates that they also had a house-church in Ephesus: "Aquila and Prisca together with the church at their house send you many greetings in the Lord." From Acts we learn that Paul lodged and worked with them during his initial stay in Corinth (Acts 18:2–3) and that when he left there he traveled with them as far as Ephesus (18:18–19). When Apollos came to Ephesus and began to speak about Jesus in the synagogue, Luke tells us that Priscilla and Aquila "took him aside and explained to him the Way [of God] more accurately" (18:26).

EPAPHRODITUS

Paul multiplies his terms in describing this man: "my brother and co-worker and fellow soldier, your messenger and minister in my need" (Phil 2:25). He sends him back to the Philippians, urging them to "[w]elcome him then in the Lord with all joy and hold such people in esteem, because for the sake of the work of Christ he came close to death, risking his life to make up for those services to me that you could not perform" (2:29–30).

EUODIA, SYNTYCHE, CLEMENT

In the same letter to the Philippians, Paul says: "I urge Euodia and I urge Syntyche to come to a mutual understanding in the Lord. Yes, and I ask you also, my true yokemate, to help them, for they have struggled at my side in promoting the gospel, along with Clement and my other coworkers, whose names are in the book of life" (Phil 4:2–3).

PHILEMON, MARK, ARISTARCHUS, DEMAS AND LUKE

Paul's Letter to Philemon names all five of these men as coworkers, and Paul also describes Philemon as "beloved" by whom "the hearts of the holy ones have been refreshed" (1,7,23).

Fellow Slaves (Sundouloi)

EPAPHRAS, TYCHICUS

In the Letter to the Colossians, Paul reminds them that they heard the word of truth, the Gospel, "from Epaphras our beloved fellow slave, who is a trustworthy minister of Christ on your behalf and who also told us of your love in the Spirit" (Col 1:7– 8). Later on in the same letter, Paul says: "Tychicus, my beloved brother, trustworthy minister, and fellow slave in the Lord, will tell you all the news of me. I am sending him to you for this very purpose, so that you may know about us and that he may encourage your hearts" (Col 4:7–8).

Fellow Soldiers

EPAPHRODITUS, ARCHIPPUS

As seen above, this was one of the terms Paul applied to Epaphroditus. In the letter to Philemon he also used it of Archippus (Phlm 2).

Fellow Prisoners

ANDRONICUS, JUNIA, EPAPHRAS

In the last chapter of the Letter to the Romans, among the many persons Paul asks the Romans to greet are Andronicus and Junia. Paul describes them as "my relatives and my fellow prisoners; they are prominent among the apostles and they were in Christ before me" (Rom 16:7). For a long time the Greek name *Iounian* was taken to be masculine, but now it is more commonly taken as feminine. It is also now generally accepted that Paul numbers this pair among the apostles: However, as indicated in the previous chapter, that does not necessarily mean that they had seen the risen Lord and been missioned by him.[8] We do not know on what occasion they shared imprisonment with Paul, but this fact, along with his naming them "apostles," suggests that at some time they shared his work as a missionary.

In his Letter to Philemon, Paul also mentions Epaphras as his "fellow prisoner in Christ Jesus" (Phlm 23). Apparently, Epaphras was in prison with Paul when he wrote this letter. It remains unclear which of Paul's several imprisonments this one was.

Women among Paul's Coworkers

Included among those just mentioned are several women: Prisca (Priscilla), Euodia and Syntyche. In the last chapter of his Letter to the Romans, Paul sends his greetings to several other women: Mary, who, he says, "has worked hard for you" (Rom 16:6); Tryphaena and Tryphosa, who are "workers in the Lord" (16:12); and the "beloved Persis," who also "has worked hard in the Lord" (16:12). In Paul's vocabulary, "working hard in the Lord" can only mean taking part in the kind of work Paul himself did. Hence we have good reason to believe that Paul shared his ministry with women as well as with men. On the other hand, there is no indication that any of those women accompanied Paul on his missionary journeys, although Prisca and Aquila did accompany him from Corinth to Ephesus (Acts 18:18–19). It seems more likely that these women "workers in the Lord" helped to spread the Good News of the Gospel in the places where they lived.

LOCAL LEADERS IN PAUL'S CHURCHES

After Paul had founded a new church by his preaching of the Gospel, he continued to exercise his pastoral care of that community by personal visits, by letters and by sending one of his coworkers. To use modern terminology, one could say that while it doesn't appear that Paul ever appointed any one person as "resident bishop" of any of his churches, he himself clearly exercised *episkopê*, episcopal oversight, over all the churches he founded. At the same time, it seems that each of Paul's churches had local leadership, in the form of a group of persons responsible for the welfare of the community.

In his very first letter to a church he had founded, Paul exhorts the Thessalonians: "We ask you, brothers, to respect those who are laboring among you and who are over you in the Lord and who admonish you, and to show esteem for them with special love on account of their work"

(1 Thess 5:12–13). Toward the close of his First Letter to the Corinthians, Paul urges the faithful there to be subordinate to Stephanas and his household, and "to everyone who works and toils with them," as "they have devoted themselves to the service of the holy ones" (1 Cor 16:15–16). In his Letter to the Galatians he reminds them that those who instruct others in the faith should receive recompense for their work (Gal 6:6). In the salutation of his Letter to the Philippians, Paul gives special greetings to the *episkopoi* and *diakonoi* in that community (Phil 1:1). The terms used by Paul mean "overseers" and "ministers," indicating that some persons had a role of oversight in that church, while others performed some kind of service on its behalf.

Paul also speaks of a *diakonos* of the church at Cenchreae, whom Paul commends to the Romans in the warmest of terms: "I commend to you Phoebe our sister, who is [also] a minister *[diakonos]* of the church at Cenchreae, that you may receive her in the Lord in a manner worthy of the holy ones, and help her in whatever she may need from you, for she has been a benefactor *[prostatis]* to many and to me as well" (Rom 16:1–2). The term *diakonos* indicates that Phoebe had a recognized ministry in that local church. Joseph Fitzmyer translates *prostatis* as "patroness," and says:

> Although many commentators have understood this title *pro-statis* figuratively, as "helper, support," it actually denoted a person of prominence in the ancient Greco-Roman world.... In giving Phoebe this title, Paul acknowledges the public service that this prominent woman has given to many Christians at Cenchreae. *Prostatis* may be related to *proistamenos* (Rom 12:8; cf. 1 Thess 5:12) so Phoebe was perhaps a superior or at least a leader of the Christian community at Cenchreae, as some commentators suggest....[9] She probably owned a house there and, as a wealthy, influential person involved in commerce, was in a position to assist missionaries and other Christians who traveled to and from Corinth.[10]

The fact that Cenchreae was the port city of Corinth, where one would wait for a ship to take one across the Aegean (cf. Acts 18:18), would make such assistance particularly welcome.

Looking back over these texts from undoubtedly authentic Pauline letters, we find that in four of the principal churches founded by Paul (Thessalonika, Corinth, Galatia and Philippi) a recognized group of persons exercised a role of leadership. They were "over" the others "in the Lord"; they "admonished" others; the others were to be "subordinate" to them; some of them "instructed" others and were to be compensated for their work; some, called *episkopoi*, had a role of oversight.

In these texts, Paul also exhorted the communities to "respect" those over them, to "esteem them with special love," to be "subordinate to them" and to give them "recompense" for their work. It is also important to recall the motives that Paul gives for this: it is "on account of their work" and because "they have devoted themselves to the service of the holy ones."

Significantly, in none of these texts do we find Paul mentioning the charisms these persons have received as qualifying them for leadership or as reasons for esteeming them or being subordinate to them. However, in the light of Paul's teaching about the charisms (1 Cor 12–14; Rom 12:6–8), it seems unlikely that Paul did not know, or at least presume, that these persons had received the charisms necessary for the ministry they performed. Among the spiritual gifts Paul mentioned were *kuberneseis* ("administration" [NAB], or "forms of leadership" [NRSV] [1 Cor 12:28]) and the role of the *proistamenos* ("one [who] is over others" [NAB], or "the leader" [NRSV]) [Rom 12:8]).

DID PAUL APPOINT THE LEADERS IN HIS CHURCHES?

Scholars have disputed the question of whether the local church leaders whom Paul mentions in his authentic letters can be said to have received their mandate for ministry from Paul, so that they would have shared in his oversight over their respective churches. On this question, Pierre Grelot has criticized Hans Küng and Edward Schillebeeckx on the grounds that they so minimized the role of Paul in the selection and appointment of those leaders as to make it doubtful that their authority had the apostle as its source.[11] Grelot, on the contrary, insists that after founding a church and spending a year or two in building it up, Paul would not have left it without providing for its leadership. Hence, he finds it highly improbable that only after Paul's departure did "spontaneous leaders" emerge to take over the leadership of a church he had founded.[12] Grelot remains convinced that Paul himself must have had a direct role in the selection and appointment of leaders for his churches.

I think one has to admit the probability of Grelot's conjecture—but it is still a conjecture. While Paul personally chose his missionary coworkers, he says nothing about selecting and appointing leaders in his churches. At the same time, he expected that members of those churches would engage in various kinds of ministry on the basis of the charisms they received from the Spirit. This raises the question whether the oversight exercised by the local leaders in the Pauline churches can be described as a participation in the apostolic mandate Paul received from Christ.

In answer to this question, I would suggest that while Paul's authentic letters do not tell us what role he himself had in the appointment of those leaders, they do tell us that Paul confirmed their authority, supporting their leadership role with his own authority as founding apostle. This is obviously what Paul was doing when he exhorted the Thessalonians to "respect" those who are "over you in the Lord and who admonish you" (1 Thess 5:12) and when he urged the Corinthians to "be subordinate" to the household of Stephanas and to others who toiled with them (1 Cor 16:16). While the authority of those leaders would also have been based on the community's recognition of their charisms and their devoted service, still there can be no doubt that Paul put his own apostolic authority behind theirs, so that in obeying their local leaders, the community would be obeying Paul as well. In that sense, I believe one can say that their leadership role in Paul's communities was a participation in Paul's own leadership and that they shared in the mandate the apostle had received from Christ.

Having examined the evidence in the authentic letters of Paul of the presence of local leaders in the churches he founded, we also must, in order to give a balanced account of the matter, note the fact that these local leaders played only a minor role in solving the problems faced by Paul's churches. Undoubtedly, Paul himself, assisted by his coworkers, played the major role. Next in importance came the Spirit-filled communities, in whose guidance by the Spirit Paul put great confidence. Paul does not address his letters to the local leaders; he addresses them to the whole local church. Even when a church encounters serious problems, he does not give instructions to the local leaders as to how they should intervene. Paul himself gives directions to the whole community, and the whole community is to carry them out. (As an example, take the case of the man guilty of incest, 1 Cor 5:1–5.) It is true that while Paul was writing 1 Corinthians, he had Stephanas, accompanied by Fortunatus and Achaicus, with him in Ephesus (1 Cor 16:17), so that one might think that Paul then gave him orally the instructions they needed. On the other hand, in that letter Paul clearly expects the Corinthian community itself to undertake the measures he proposes for the correction of their failings, and he says nothing about the part the local leaders should play in bringing this about. Paul did not leave his churches without local leaders, but he attributed the major roles to himself, his coworkers and his Spirit-filled communities.

CONCLUSION

Just as Jesus shared with the Twelve his work of preaching and healing during his Galilean ministry, so also his apostles, during their lifetime, shared their work of founding churches and pastoring the churches they founded with a number of coworkers, both men and women.

We also know that before Jesus returned to his Father, he commissioned the same Twelve to carry on the work of preaching the Good News and making disciples, promising to be with them in this task "to the end of the age." A few years later, the risen Lord also sent Paul to carry his message to the Gentile world. One can expect that as the apostles followed Jesus' example in sharing their ministry with others during their lifetime, they would also have provided for the continuation of their ministry when they themselves had gone to rejoin the Lord.

In many respects the apostles had a unique role, one they could not hand on to others in its fullness. However, the ministry the apostles shared with others during their lifetime had to be handed on for the church to continue and grow to maturity.

The next chapter will explore the question: By whom was the ministry of the apostles carried on in the next generation? And in what sense can those who carried it on be termed "successors of the apostles"?

4
MINISTRY IN THE
SUBAPOSTOLIC PERIOD

I use the term "subapostolic period" the way Raymond Brown used it in his book *The Churches the Apostles Left Behind*.[1] He argues that the "apostolic period" closed by the year 67, when Peter, Paul and James the "brother of the Lord"—the only apostles about whose role in the early Church we have detailed knowledge—had disappeared from the scene. The "subapostolic period," then, would comprise the last third of the first century, during which most of the New Testament (with the exception of the undisputed letters of Paul) was written, although the New Testament authors wrote without using their own names, in some cases attributing their work to an apostle. Brown suggests that the "postapostolic period" began at the end of the first century, when early Christian writings, such as the letter to the Corinthians known as *I Clement* and the *Didache*, which are not part of the New Testament, appear.

In the previous chapter, I based the study of ministry during the apostolic period mostly on the authentic Pauline letters. In the present chapter, I shall consider the evidence concerning ministry in the subapostolic generation as found in the parts of the New Testament written during that period. Some of these writings, especially Acts, give information about ministry during the apostolic generation as well. This chapter, of course, shall take note of such information, although its main interest is the ministry as it continued during the generation that followed the death of the great apostles.

While it is reasonably certain that all the books of the New Testament considered in this chapter were written during the subapostolic era, establishing a certain chronology among them remains difficult. However, following the dates Raymond Brown, in his *Introduction to the New*

Testament, suggests as the most probable, I shall begin with the Letter to the Hebrews (ca. 80), and end with the Pastoral Letters (ca. 100) and 3 John (shortly after 100).

LETTER TO THE HEBREWS

While this letter was accepted into the canon of the New Testament largely because of its attribution to St. Paul, modern scholars agree that its author is unknown. Brown remarks: "We have to be satisfied with the irony that the most sophisticated rhetorician and elegant theologian of the New Testament is an unknown."[2] The argument of the letter suggests that the author wrote it for a Christian community that valued the religious wealth of Judaism, especially its cultic liturgy. The author thinks that some in this community put too much value on the Israelite cultic heritage, not appreciating the enormous changes brought about through Christ. Brown suggests that the letter may have been addressed to the Roman community; the mention of persecution suffered in the past (10:32–34) could well refer to the persecution by Nero (64–68). In any case, of particular interest here are the references to "leaders" found in the final chapter of the letter.

The author addresses this exhortation to his readers: "Remember your leaders who spoke the word of God to you. Consider the outcome of their way of life and imitate their faith. Jesus Christ is the same yesterday, today, and forever"(13:7–8). The author clearly refers here to the "leaders" of the previous generation: those who founded the community by their preaching and whose lives ended in a way worthy of admiration. Their faith, which should be imitated, is the abiding faith in Jesus Christ, who is the same forever. Significantly, the author describes "those who spoke the word of God to you" as "your leaders," where the Greek word is the participial form of the verb "to lead" *(hegoumenoi).* This form was used commonly to describe persons in authority; we find an example of this usage in Luke 22:26, where Jesus, in response to his disciples who were arguing about which of them was the greatest, says: "[L]et the greatest among you be as the youngest, and the leader *[ho hegoumenos]* as the servant." The use of this word in the Letter to the Hebrews, referring to "those who spoke the word of God to them," suggests that the persons who had evangelized the community also became its leaders, exercising pastoral ministry over those whom they had brought to faith.

Ten verses later in the same final chapter of Hebrews, we read: "Obey your leaders and defer to them, for they keep watch over you and will have to give an account, that they may fulfill their task with joy and not with sorrow, for that would be of no advantage to you"(13:17). Here the author clearly refers to those now exercising leadership in the community; the use of the same term *(hegoumenoi)* suggests the continuation of the ministry from the apostolic generation to the subapostolic. The exhortation: "Obey your leaders and defer ['submit': NRSV] to them" echoes that of Paul to the Thessalonians to "respect" those who are "over" them in the Lord (1 Thess 5:12) and to the Corinthians to "be subordinate" to Stephanas and his household (1 Cor 16:16). Also similar to Paul's exhortations is the motivation given for such obedience: "...for they keep watch over you and will have to give an account." Obviously, the leaders must give an account of their ministry to the Lord, which suggests that they have received it from him.

The third reference to "leaders" occurs toward the end of the letter, when the author sends his "greetings to all your leaders and to all the holy ones" (13:24). The term "all your leaders" highlights the fact that a number of persons shared leadership in the community; this also corresponds to what we have seen in our study of the Pauline communities.

These references to "leaders" in the Letter to the Hebrews lead to the following conclusions: (1) that the leadership exercised by the founders of the community was carried on in the following generation by other leaders; (2) that the "holy ones" were expected to obey those leaders, who in turn had to give an account of their ministry to the Lord; (3) that leadership in this second generation was still exercised collegially, with no indication of any one being over the rest; (4) that the generic term *hegoumenoi* was used of such leaders. This, of course, does not exclude the possibility that the leaders in the church to which Hebrews was written were also being called "presbyters," even though the author of Hebrews did not use that term. As we shall see, this would become the term most commonly used of local church leaders in the subapostolic period. However, we shall now look at another letter of that period in which this term does not appear.

LETTER TO THE EPHESIANS

According to Raymond Brown, four out of five scholars now consider this letter to be deutero-Pauline, that is, written not by St. Paul but by one of his disciples. Brown suggests that "we should think of Eph as the continuation of the Pauline heritage amid his disciples who came to see how the unified church of Jews and Gentiles (now existing in Asia Minor?) fitted into God's plan and brought to culmination the gospel proclaimed by Paul."[3]

Whereas the undisputed letters of Paul use the term *ekklesia* most often of the local Christian community, Ephesians always uses it to refer to the universal Church, which is seen as the body of Christ, uniting Jew and Gentile in "one new person" (Eph 2:15). The unity of the Church comprises a major theme of this letter, especially in chapter 4. In this context those called to exercise various ministries are described as "gifts" that the risen and glorious Christ has bestowed on his Church in order to perfect it in unity.

> The one who descended is also the one who ascended far above all the heavens, that he might fill all things. And he gave some as apostles, others as prophets, others as evangelists, others as pastors and teachers, to equip the holy ones for the work of ministry, for building up the body of Christ, until we all attain to the unity of faith and knowledge of the Son of God, to mature manhood, to the extent of the full stature of Christ....(Eph 4:10–13)

One has to compare this passage with what Paul says in 1 Corinthians 12:27–28:

> Now you are Christ's body, and individually parts of it. Some people God has designated in the church to be, first, apostles; second, prophets; third, teachers; then, mighty deeds; then gifts of healing, assistance, administration, and varieties of tongues.

Just as Paul saw apostles, prophets and teachers as placed in the Church by God, so the author of Ephesians described them as gifts of Christ for the building up of his body, the Church. Both letters describe the persons themselves, and not just the charisms with which they are equipped for their ministry, as divine gifts. This indicates the importance both authors attributed to the roles apostles, prophets and teachers played in the life of the Church.

Also significant is a previous passage in which the author of Ephesians refers to apostles and prophets. Addressing the Gentile members of the church community, he says: "So then you are no longer strangers and sojourners, but you are fellow citizens with the holy ones and members of the household of God, built upon the foundation of the apostles and prophets, with Christ Jesus himself as the capstone"(2:19–20). Here the foundational role of the apostles and prophets suggests that they belong to the first Christian generation. Are the apostles and prophets in Ephesians 4:11 also understood as among those who laid the foundation of the church? The mention of "evangelists" as distinct from apostles could point in that direction. Elsewhere the New Testament uses this term of men who continued the work begun by the apostles. Thus, Philip, one of the "Seven," is called "the evangelist" (Acts 21:8), and Timothy is exhorted to "perform the work of an evangelist" (2 Tim 4:5).

The Greek text of Ephesians 4:11 highlights the fact that apostles, prophets and evangelists are different persons by introducing each of these words with a new definite article. In contrast to this, the last two titles, "pastors [shepherds] and teachers" are linked by the same definite article. This suggests that, for the author of Ephesians, the same person would normally fulfill the functions of pastoring and teaching. One would also associate these tasks with the ongoing care of a local community, after the initial work of an apostle had been accomplished. It is therefore also the kind of ministry that would continue into the succeeding generation. We have reason, then, to think that the author of Ephesians looked back to the apostles and prophets as belonging to the foundational apostolic era, and saw evangelists, pastors and teachers as gifts that the risen Christ continued to provide to the Church during the period when the author was writing.

The author clearly tells us that the persons named in this list performed works of ministry. There is a dispute, however, regarding the punctuation, and hence, the translation, of the phrase: "to equip the holy ones for the work of ministry, for building up the body of Christ." The question concerns whether there should be a comma after "the holy ones." (The original Greek did not use commas). Putting a comma there would identify the apostles, prophets, evangelists, pastors and teachers as the "holy ones" whom Christ equips for the work of ministry. Omitting the comma (as do the NAB and NRSV) means interpreting the phrase the way the note in the NAB does: "The ministerial leaders in v. 11 are to equip the whole people of God for their work of ministry."

In his recent book, *Are All Christians Ministers?*, John N. Collins has argued strongly against this interpretation of the text.[4] He insists that in its genuine classical and biblical meaning, the word *diakonia* does not mean a kind of lowly service that practically anyone can perform, but rather a service one is authorized to perform on behalf of a higher authority.[5] He answers the question: "Are all Christians ministers?" with a blunt "no." In his view, it takes more than good will and a readiness to undertake some service to justify using the term "ministry," if one does not wish to empty it of the strong meaning it had in its classical and biblical usage.

Because this question is a very real one today, I have mentioned it; however, I do not attempt to answer it here. For our present purpose, it is sufficient to note that whether or not the author of Ephesians saw all Christians as called to ministry, he certainly recognized apostles, prophets, evangelists, pastors and teachers as special gifts of the risen Christ for the building up of his body the Church.

More to the point here, I offer some observations about two terms the author has used in describing these "gift-persons," namely, "evangelists" and "pastors" (literally: "shepherds"). Elsewhere in the New Testament, only Philip, one of the Seven, and Timothy, Paul's coworker, are called evangelists. Even more noteworthy, Ephesians 4:11 is the only place in the New Testament where leaders of Christian communities are called shepherds. Elsewhere the term is used only of Christ, who speaks of himself as the "good shepherd" (John 10:11) and is described as "the great shepherd of the sheep" (Heb 13:20) and "the shepherd and guardian of your souls" (1 Pet 2:25). The verb form, however, does appear, describing the task the risen Christ assigned to Peter (John 21:16) and which the author of 1 Peter attributed to presbyters (1 Pet 5:2). Strikingly, however, Ephesians 4:11 is the only place in the New Testament where church leaders are called pastors.

The reference to 1 Peter 5:2 reminds us that we find the term "presbyters" neither in Hebrews nor in Ephesians. As we shall now see, all the other New Testament books of the subapostolic period that speak of persons engaged in ministry will use this term.

ACTS OF THE APOSTLES

While Acts dates from the subapostolic period, it also provides us with most of the information we have about the mother church of Jerusalem during the apostolic era. The previous chapter discussed how the apostles shared a portion of their ministry with the Seven, whom they appointed as leaders of the Hellenist members of the Jerusalem community. In this study of Acts, I shall first consider some other information Luke has given about the development of ministry during the apostolic period and then see what we can learn from him about ministry during the 80s, when it seems most likely that he was writing.

Presbyters in the Jerusalem Church

Luke tells us that in the early period of the Jerusalem community, "those who owned property or houses would sell them, bring the proceeds of the sale, and put them at the feet of the apostles, and they were distributed to each according to need" (Acts 4:34–35). This, along with the following story about Ananias and Sapphira (Acts 5:1–11) indicates that at this early stage the apostles were directly involved in caring for the material needs of the poor in the community. However, the appointment of the Seven meant that others would take over this burden, so that the apostles could "devote [themselves] to prayer and to the ministry of the word" (6:4).

It seems likely that a comparable group of responsible persons cared for the needy among the Hebrew-speaking members of the church, but Luke does not mention them in this context. However, several chapters later, he says that when the Christians in Antioch heard about a coming famine and decided to send relief to the brothers who lived in Judea, they sent it "to the presbyters" (11:30). Since the Hellenists had been dispersed as a result of the persecution that broke out after the martyrdom of Stephen (8:1), the Jerusalem church was now composed only of Hebrew-speaking Christians. The fact that Luke does not explain how the church of Jerusalem came to have presbyters suggests that he presumed his readers would take it for granted that such a community would have "elders" to take care of its needy members.

While the term "elder" literally means "older men," it was more often used in the Old Testament to refer to authority figures among the Hebrew people; it was used in the same way in the New Testament, as in references to members of the Sanhedrin (e.g. Acts 4:5, 8, 23). Fitzmyer says: "There were 'elders' also in the Hellenistic world, and the Greek use of that term may also have influenced Christians in their adoption of the title for author- ity figures in their communities."[6] In any case, we have good reason to accept as historical Luke's information about the presence of presbyters in the Jerusalem church in the apostolic period and their role in caring for the poor. Luke gives no information about how they were chosen or appointed. However, in the light of his account of the choice and appointment of the Seven, it seems a reasonable conjecture that both the community and the apostles were similarly involved in choosing Jerusalem presbyters.

The next reference to presbyters in that church has them sharing a decision-making role with the apostles. Luke tells us that when dissen- sion arose in Antioch as to whether Gentile converts should accept cir- cumcision, "it was decided that Paul, Barnabas, and some of the others should go up to Jerusalem to the apostles and presbyters about this question" (15:2). Several times in his account of the "council" in Jerusalem, Luke indicates that presbyters helped arrive at the decision with the apostles (15:6, 22, 23). Actually, it is more likely that Luke combined two distinct events into his account of the "council": (1) the decision that Gentile converts were not obliged to accept circumcision; and (2) the decision calling on Gentile converts in Antioch, Syria and Cilicia to observe some provisions of the Jewish Law. Many commenta- tors believe that the "council" took only the first of these decisions and that the second was taken some time later by James, the "brother of the Lord" as leader of the Jerusalem church. If these were actually two different decisions, Luke indicates that the presbyters of the Jerusalem church took part in both of them.

These presbyters are again associated with James in Luke's account of Paul's last visit to Jerusalem, when he went up to deliver the money his Gentile communities had collected for the poor of Judea. It appears in one of Luke's "we" passages: "When we reached Jerusalem the brothers welcomed us warmly. The next day, Paul accompanied us on a visit to James, and all the presbyters were present" (Acts 21:17–18). Here James is presented as the leader of the Jerusalem church, and the presbyters as his council. The other apostles are obviously no longer on the scene. It would seem that Luke intends to show that the presbyters did not merely play a silent role, for in the following exchange with Paul, not only James speaks, but a collective "we." Naturally, the "we" had a spokesman, but in Luke's account it was not just James, but the combined leadership of the Jerusalem church.

Having seen the evidence in Acts concerning the role of presbyters in Jerusalem during the apostolic period, I must now say something about the role James played in the mother church during that same period.

James, "The Brother of the Lord"

Both Matthew 13:55 and Mark 6:3 mention James as one of four brothers of Jesus. All four Gospels indicate that neither James nor his brothers were followers of Jesus during his public ministry; John explicitly says that Jesus' brothers did not believe in him (7:5). However, after the resurrection, they are mentioned as praying with the followers of Jesus, along with Mary his mother (Acts 1:14). Paul, who lists James among those to whom the risen Lord appeared (1 Cor 15:7), gives an explanation for this change of heart, at least on the part of James. It would seem that in Paul's eyes, this appearance of the Lord established James as an apostle. At least this represents one possible interpretation of the account he gives of his first visit to Jerusalem after converting, when he "went up to Jerusalem to confer with Cephas." He says: "But I did not see any other of the apostles, only James the brother of the Lord" (Gal 1:19).

In any case, Paul recognized James as one of the men "of repute" to whom he presented the Gospel he preached to the Gentiles, so that he "might not be running, or have run, in vain" (Gal 2:2). He also named James among the "pillars" who gave him and Barnabas "their right hands in partnership"(Gal 2:9). In his account of the incident at Antioch in which he rebuked Peter, Paul speaks of "some people who came from James" as causing Peter to withdraw from eating with the Gentiles.

There is good evidence, then, both from Paul and from Acts, that at some point James became the leader of the Jerusalem church. It seems likely that his blood relationship with Jesus, and Jesus' special appearance to him after the resurrection, factored into his being granted such leadership. That Peter recognized his role is indicated by the fact that when Peter had been delivered from prison and was about to leave Jerusalem, he said to the disciples gathered in the house of Mary the mother of Mark: "Report this to James and the brothers" (Acts 12:17).

James's leadership role in the Jerusalem church eventually brought upon him the enmity of the high priest Ananus, who took advantage of the death of the procurator Festus in the year 61 to have James put to death, a fact reported by the Jewish historian Josephus.[7] Writing in the fourth century, the Christian historian Eusebius describes James as "the brother of the Lord, to whom the throne of the episcopacy in Jerusalem had been entrusted by the apostles."[8] We have good reason to think that Peter and the others recognized James's role as leader of the Jerusalem church, but it seems unlikely that the term "bishop" was used at Jerusalem during his lifetime. On the other hand, later church writers would understandably describe him as the first bishop of Jerusalem. He is, in fact, the only example in the New Testament of a single residential leader of a local church.

Prophets and Teachers as Leaders of the Church in Antioch

Antioch was the third-largest city of the Roman Empire. Its Christian community, including both Gentiles and Jews, was founded not by an apostle, but by Hellenist Jewish Christians, originally from Cyprus and Cyrene, who had fled from Jerusalem during the persecution that followed the martyrdom of Stephen (see Acts 11:19–20). When the Jerusalem church heard about the conversion of Gentiles at Antioch, they sent Barnabas to look into it; when he had "seen the grace of God" at work there, he brought Saul from Tarsus to help in building up the new community. At the beginning of Acts 13, Luke describes the leadership of the church at Antioch:

> Now there were in the church at Antioch prophets and teachers: Barnabas, Symeon who was called Niger, Lucius of Cyrene, Manaen who was a close friend of Herod the tetrarch, and Saul. While they were worshiping the Lord and fasting,

the holy Spirit said, "Set apart for me Barnabas and Saul for the work to which I have called them." Then, completing their fasting and prayer, they laid hands on them and sent them off. (Acts 13:1–3)

Most likely Luke intends to describe all five men as both prophets and teachers, and he clearly presents them as the leaders of the church at Antioch. According to Paul, God designated prophets and teachers in the Church (1 Cor 12:28), and according to the author of Ephesians, they are gifts of the risen Christ for building up his body (Eph 4:11–12). The men exercising leadership at Antioch at this early stage of the community's development were designated for their task by their charismatic gifts, which the community recognized and accepted. What "the holy Spirit said" no doubt was said through the mouth of one of these prophets. While three of them remain otherwise unknown, Luke had already told us about Barnabas being sent to Antioch by the Jerusalem church and how the risen Christ had appeared to Saul to make him his "chosen instrument" (Acts 9:15). As Fitzmyer puts it: "Now the Spirit takes over and inaugurates the joint missionary work of the two, especially of Saul, who becomes 'the apostle to the Gentiles.'"[9] Luke's description of their return to Antioch after completing their missionary journey highlights the significance of the laying of hands on Barnabas and Saul: "[T]hey sailed to Antioch, where they had been commended to the grace of God for the work they had now accomplished" (Acts 14:26). In other words, the laying on of hands implied the blessing of God upon their missionary work.

When the Jerusalem church had already begun to organize itself, with the appointment of the Seven to care for the Hellenists and with presbyters to care for the rest of the community, the church in Antioch was led by men designated for their task by their charismatic gifts. This reflects the kind of leadership one finds in the churches founded by Paul, as described in his undisputed letters.

The fact that those letters make no mention of presbyters has led most commentators to question the historicity of Luke's statement that as Barnabas and Paul retraced their steps after founding churches in several towns and cities of Asia Minor, "[t]hey appointed presbyters for them in each church" (Acts 14:23). Fitzmyer observes that presbyters were undoubtedly a fixture in local churches by the time Luke writes, so the notice may simply be a Lucan anachronism.[10] Others, however, have noted that Barnabas was the senior partner on this first missionary journey and he could have initiated the appointment of presbyters. That he had belonged to the Jerusalem community, which had presbyters, might explain why.[11] In any case, as the authentic letters of Paul show, when he had founded a church, he did not leave it without local leaders, even though he did not refer to them as presbyters. Neither did he say that he himself had appointed them.

Paul's Farewell Address to the Presbyters of the Church of Ephesus

Luke tells us that Paul made a first brief visit to Ephesus at the end of his second missionary journey, leaving Priscilla and Aquila there and promising to return (Acts 18:18–21). At the beginning of his third missionary journey, he returned and stayed for three years (Acts 19). After a brief visit to the churches in Greece and Macedonia, Paul was on his way to Jerusalem when he stopped at Miletus, a port city about forty miles from Ephesus. Luke tells us: "From Miletus he had the presbyters of the church at Ephesus summoned" (Acts 20:17), and then reports the farewell speech Paul addressed to them. Needless to say, this speech was composed by Luke, who in this respect followed the practice of ancient historians. In it, Paul warns his hearers about what will happen in the future, when he is no longer with them. Written some twenty-five years after Paul's death, this more likely reflects the situation of the writer's time than of Paul's. For this reason, scholars believe that it tells us more about local ministry in Pauline churches during the subapostolic period than about the church of Paul's own time.

The speech reveals that a group of presbyters were responsible for the pastoral care of the church at Ephesus. Paul's exhortation contains the following description of their role: "Keep watch over yourselves and over the whole flock of which the holy Spirit has appointed you overseers, in which you tend the church of God that he acquired with his own blood" (Acts 20:28). The word translated by "tend" is the Greek *poimainein,* which literally means "to shepherd"; correspondingly, the Christian community is described as a "flock" (Greek *poimnion*). Recall that "pastors" (literally "shepherds") were among the gifts of the risen Christ to the church in Ephesians 4:11.

In his narrative, Luke spoke of these men as "the presbyters of the church at Ephesus" (20:17). However, he has Paul say to them: "...the holy Spirit has appointed you overseers, in which you tend the church of God" (20:28). The word "overseers" translates the Greek *episkopous,* which will eventually come to mean "bishops." Here it is best rendered by the literal meaning of the word, for historically a bishop is the single leader of a local church who presides over the group of presbyters as well as over the whole community. We have seen in the previous chapter that at the beginning of his Letter to the Philippians, Paul addressed his salutation to "all the holy ones in Christ Jesus who are in Philippi, with the overseers and ministers" (Phil 1:1). From this undisputed letter, we know Paul did use the term *episkopoi* of local leaders in his churches. The fact that Luke puts this term on Paul's lips, although he himself had described these same men as presbyters, suggests that he may have known that Paul spoke of local leaders as *episkopoi* rather than as *presbuteroi*. It also suggests that in Luke's day, local church leaders could be called either elders or overseers, without a clear distinction between the terms. As we shall see, this was still the case when the Letter to Titus was written.

Another noteworthy point in Paul's discourse is the fact that the Holy Spirit appointed these men as overseers. In Ephesians also, pastors and teachers are seen as gifts of the risen Christ to his body the Church (Eph 4:11). Taking these texts as reflective of the understanding of the origin of ministry common in the 80s (when they were written), Anton Vögtle stresses the fact that neither the author of Ephesians nor Luke in Paul's farewell address suggests that second-generation local church leaders had received their pastoral authority through appointment by apostles. Rather, even in the subapostolic period such authority was seen as coming directly from the Holy Spirit or the risen Christ. Vögtle agrees that these men in fact carried on the pastoral ministry begun by the apostles in the churches they founded, but he insists that there is no indication here that their authority to do so had been transmitted to them by an apostle. He concludes that in these texts one finds the Pauline idea that ministry is conferred directly by charismatic gift, rather than the later idea that it is handed on from one generation to the next by apostolic succession.[12]

In his farewell address to the elders of Ephesus Luke has Paul say that the Holy Spirit made them overseers, and the text includes nothing about apostles or other human agents being involved in their appointment. However, this farewell address is a Lucan composition and thus should be interpreted in the light of what he says elsewhere in Acts. That the Holy Spirit is so deeply involved in every step of the church's progress that it can simply be described as the work of the Spirit is a recurring theme in Acts. But such attribution to the Spirit did not exclude the role human agents played in it. Thus, for instance, the Holy Spirit designated Barnabas and Saul for their mission from Antioch (Acts 13:2), but this did not exclude the role of the other prophets and teachers in sending them (13:3). The same Luke who has Paul say that the Holy Spirit appointed the overseers at Ephesus has Barnabas and Paul appoint presbyters in the churches they founded in Asia Minor (14:23). And Luke tells us that in the church of Jerusalem the apostles prayed and laid hands on the Seven for their ministry (6:6).

It would seem risky, therefore, to conclude from the fact that Luke has Paul say to the elders of Ephesus, "The holy Spirit has made you over-seers" that Luke himself, and the subapostolic church for which he wrote, did not think pastoral authority had been transmitted from the apostles to those actually carrying on the apostles' work. In any case, Paul's farewell address makes clear that while Paul had been with them he had prepared these men for their ministry and he expected them to carry it on after his departure. He had prepared them by his teaching, his admonitions, and his example: "I did not at all shrink from telling you what was for your benefit, or from teaching you in public or in your homes" (20:20); "I did not shrink from proclaiming to you the entire plan of God" (20:27); "[F]or three years, night and day, I unceasingly admonished each of you with tears" (20:31); "In every way I have shown you that by hard work of that sort we must help the weak" (20:35).

Paul expected them to carry on his pastoral care of the church:

> I know that after my departure savage wolves will come among you, and they will not spare the flock. And from your own group, men will come forward perverting the truth to draw the disciples away after them. So be vigilant....And now I commend you to God and to that gracious word of his that can build you up and give you the inheritance among all who are consecrated. (20:29–32)

Teaching the truth of the Gospel and defending it against all perversions had been paramount in Paul's ministry, and it continued to be a primary concern of those who carried on his ministry. They had received from Paul the Gospel they were to teach and defend; one surely has good reason to think that Luke understood, even if he did not have Paul say so, that they had also received from Paul the commission to carry on this ministry. Luke would have seen no contradiction in also saying that the Holy Spirit had made them overseers to tend the Church of God.

FIRST LETTER OF PETER

According to Raymond Brown, of all the Catholic epistles, 1 Peter has the best chance of being written by the figure to whom it is attributed, but, with many other scholars, he thinks it more probable that a disciple of Peter wrote it after his death.[13] It was written in Rome (disguised with the name "Babylon" [5:13]) and addressed to the Christian communities of northern Asia Minor, which, while largely composed of Gentiles, had most likely been evangelized from Jerusalem, as Rome had been. 1 Peter has many traits in common with the authentic letters of Paul; one of the most striking is its exhortation concerning the use of charismatic gifts.

> As each one has received a gift [Greek: *charisma*], use it to serve one another as good stewards of God's varied grace. Whoever preaches [literally: "speaks"], let it be with the words of God; whoever serves, let it be with the strength that God supplies, so that in all things God may be glorified. (1 Pet 4:10–11)

A comparison between this text and the teaching of Paul on the charisms in 1 Corinthians 12–14 and Romans 12:6–8 shows how much they have in common. Paul insists that the charisms are given by the Spirit, not for vain show but for a useful purpose (1 Cor 12:7)—to build up the Church (14:5). 1 Peter says the same: Charisms are to be used in service to one another; those who receive charisms should act not as proprietors of these gifts, but as stewards. Paul mentions a number of different charisms; 1 Peter names only two: speaking and serving. 1 Peter also includes the phrase "God's varied grace," which suggests the variety of ways people could use their charisms to serve one another. Those who use their charisms in serving should do this "with the strength that God supplies" (1 Pet 4:11), so also for Paul, "there are different workings but the same God who produces all of them in everyone" (1 Cor 12:6).

When Paul wrote his Letter to the Romans, he had not yet visited that church. His exhortation to them about using their charisms makes it evident that he presumed a variety of charismatic gifts in that community. 1 Peter 4:10–11 would indicate that when this letter was written, charisms still played an important role in the life of local churches, both that of Rome and those of Asia Minor to which it was addressed. If this text gave us the only information we had about ministry in those churches, we could conclude that little had changed since the time Paul's letters were written. However, 1 Peter 5:1–5 gives us further information, which makes it clear ministry had developed in ways we do not find in the authentic letters of Paul. 1 Peter 5 begins as follows:

> So I exhort the presbyters among you, as a fellow presbyter and witness to the sufferings of Christ and one who has a share in the glory to be revealed. Tend the flock of God in your midst, [overseeing] not by constraint but willingly, as God would have it, not for shameful profit but eagerly. Do not lord

> it over those assigned to you, but be examples to the flock.
> And when the chief Shepherd is revealed, you will receive the
> unfading crown of glory. Likewise, you younger members, be
> subject to the presbyters. (5:1–5)

This exhortation to the presbyters, and the author's description of himself as a "fellow-presbyter," indicates that at this time, in both the church of Rome and the churches of northern Asia Minor, there existed not only charismatic ministry, but also the more structured ministry of a group of presbyters. If, as Brown believes, these churches had been founded by Jewish Christians from Jerusalem, one might attribute their adoption of the presbyterate to a tendency to follow the example given by the mother church. In any case, one must observe that these communities evidently saw no incompatibility between charismatic ministry and that of presbyters. Indeed, it would seem likely that persons were chosen as presbyters because they manifested the gifts for such ministry.

1 Peter 5:1–5 gives valuable information about the ministry exercised by presbyters in these churches. Their role consisted of being pastors of the flock; the word translated "tend" is *poimainein,* literally "to shepherd." The NAB puts the word "overseeing" *(episkopountes)* in brackets, because it is not found in some of the most authoritative New Testament manuscripts. However, the term so clearly corresponds to the sense of the passage that one can easily see how it could have been introduced into the text.

The exhortation to perform their ministry "not by constraint but willingly, as God would have it" indicates that some of those chosen for this task may have been reluctant to undertake it; this also suggests the role of the community in choosing its presbyters. The warning: "not for shameful profit" points to the responsibility of presbyters for the material needs of the poor, which would involve handling money collected for this purpose. It could also indicate that presbyters received payment for their ministry. The exhortation: "Do not lord it over those assigned to you, but be examples to the flock" is the clearest indication that presbyters exercised authority in the community. In doing this they were to heed the warning Jesus had given to his disciples: "You know that the rulers of the Gentiles lord it over them...but it shall not be so among you" (Matt 20:25–26). 1 Peter 5:3 has the same Greek word as Matthew 20:25 for "lord it over." In both cases, the question concerns how authority is exercised. The next verse reminds the presbyters that the flock does not belong to them, but to the "chief Shepherd," from whom they will receive the reward for their labors. Exactly who are included among the "younger members" who are urged to be subject to the presbyters remains a matter of dispute among scholars; in any case, the phrase "be subject to" confirms the role of authority exercised by the presbyters.

We have good reason to believe that the presbyteral structure of Christian church leadership was first introduced in the mother church of Jerusalem. If, as Brown and others believe, the churches of Rome and of northern Asia Minor were evangelized by Christians from Jerusalem, it is not surprising that these churches also adopted the presbyteral system. At the same time they recognized that persons could have charismatic gifts for ministries of the word and of service (1 Pet 4:10–11). One should note also the presence of charismatic gifts in the church of Jerusalem: miracles of healing (Acts 3:1–10; 5:15–16); signs and wonders (Acts 5:12; 6:8); prophets (Acts 11:27; 15:32).

The fact that 1 Peter addressed communities mainly of Gentile composition (cf. 2:10: "Once you were 'no people,'/but now you are God's people") means that a structure more typical of Jewish communities was also adopted in those made up of Gentiles. However, it was even more likely to be found in Jewish-Christian circles. We shall now see the special role given to presbyters in a letter that, according to Brown, was addressed to Christians strongly identified by Jewish heritage.[14]

THE LETTER OF JAMES

The James named as the writer of this letter is the "brother of the Lord," whom we have seen described as the leader of the Jerusalem community. If he actually wrote the letter, he did so before 61, when the high priest Ananus put him to death. However, it is more probable that a disciple who admired the image of James as the Christian authority most loyal to Judaism wrote it in the 80s or 90s.

The Christian churches addressed in this letter evidently had a group of presbyters, but also had members they recognized as teachers. The reference to teachers comes as a warning: "Not many of you should become teachers, my brothers, for you realize that you will be judged more strictly, for we all fall short in many respects" (Jas 3:1–2). This suggests that persons could aspire to be teachers in the community, and then be appointed for this task. Such teachers would then become part of the structure of the community, and most likely receive payment for their work. In the early Pauline churches, teachers were so designated by God (1 Cor 12:28) and by their charism for teaching (Rom 12:7); now the role of teacher in the community appears more like an office one could undertake.

In the Pauline churches certain persons were also gifted with charisms for healing (1 Cor 12:9, 28, 30). In the Letter of James, what was previously a charismatic gift is now seen as a ministry performed by the official leaders in the community. James advises:

> Is anyone among you sick? He should summon the presbyters of the church, and they should pray over him and anoint [him] with oil in the name of the Lord, and the prayer of faith will save the sick person, and the Lord will raise him up. If he has committed any sins, he will be forgiven. (Jas 5:14–15)

Brown raises the question whether this role assigned to presbyters may be a continuation of the healing ministry Jesus had given to the apostles when he sent them on their mission in Galilee (Matt 10:1,8).[15] While Mark does not say that Jesus told them to anoint the sick with oil, he does say that on that mission "they anointed with oil many who were sick and cured them" (Mark 6:13). Brown notes that "throughout Jas there are echoes of the Jesus tradition," so it is not impossible that they based this practice on the belief that Jesus had told his disciples to do this. In that case, the presbyters would be seen as carrying on the ministry Jesus had given to the apostles.

Evident from this passage of James is the fact that the presbyters had an official role of prayer in the community and their prayer was expected to be efficacious both for healing and for the forgiveness of sins. While no other functions of the presbyters are mentioned, one can reasonably conclude that they would have had a leading role in other practices of community prayer, including eucharistic worship. The New Testament is remarkably silent on the question of who presided at the Eucharist, but the ministry of prayer that James gives to the presbyters does shed some light on it.

THE PASTORAL LETTERS

The two Letters to Timothy and the Letter to Titus have, from ancient times, been called "pastoral" because of their contents, which deal primarily with the pastoral care of the churches of Ephesus and Crete, entrusted to Timothy and Titus. They are presented as written by Paul, but most modern scholars believe they were written some years after Paul's death by one (or two) of his disciples. Hence they are thought to reflect church structure as it developed during the subapostolic period. Of the three letters, two provide more information about such development, Titus reflecting an earlier and 1 Timothy a later phase of it. Some scholars think 2 Timothy was written soon after Paul's death by a different author than the other two and that it is more closely related in thought and language to the authentic Pauline letters.[16] Most critics believe the other two were written toward the end of the first century. Given this book's focus on ministry, I shall first consider the roles these letters ascribe to Timothy and Titus.

Ministry of Timothy and Titus

The previous chapter explored how Paul shared his missionary and pastoral task with these principal coworkers, frequently sending them on delicate missions to the churches they had evangelized together. The Pastorals Letters present them as still working under Paul's direction, sent by him to churches he had founded with their help: Timothy to Ephesus, and Titus to Crete. Just as they work under Paul's direction, so also they have received from him the pastoral authority they exercise in those communities. Both letters to Timothy speak of a gift of grace *(charisma)* given to him through the imposition of hands. In 1 Timothy 4:14 these are the hands of the presbyterate, while in 2 Timothy 1:6 they are Paul's own hands.[17] 1 Timothy 1:18 and 4:14 also refer to words of prophecy that had been uttered about Timothy's calling to ministry. One recalls how Barnabas and Saul were designated for their missionary task by the Holy Spirit, no doubt speaking through one of the prophets at Antioch, who also imposed hands on them.

In our liturgical calendar Timothy and Titus are called "bishops," but Paul did not leave them as permanent residential leaders of those churches; they remained missionaries and were to rejoin Paul when they had completed their present task (Titus 3:12; 2 Tim 4:9, 11, 21). The task was not evangelization, but the pastoral care of established Christian communities. This principally involved the teaching of sound doctrine, the choice and appointment of local leaders and the instruction of the community in proper conduct.

A major concern of these letters is the danger of false doctrine, which Timothy and Titus were to counteract by their sound teaching. Thus, Paul says: "I repeat the request I made of you when I was on my way to Macedonia, that you stay in Ephesus to instruct certain people not to teach false doctrines..." (1 Tim 1:3). "Until I arrive, attend to the reading, exhortation and teaching" (1 Tim 4:13). "Whoever teaches something different and does not agree with the sound words of our Lord Jesus Christ and the religious teaching is conceited, understanding nothing..." (1 Tim 6:3–4). A key idea in these letters is that the true doctrine of Christ makes up a sacred "deposit" that must be kept safe and handed on incorrupt. Thus, 1 Timothy concludes: "O Timothy, guard what has been entrusted to you. Avoid profane babbling and the absurdities of so-called knowledge. By professing it, some people have deviated from the faith" (1 Tim 6:20–21). Similarly, 2 Timothy notes: "Take as your norm the sound words that you heard from me, in the faith and love that are in Christ Jesus. Guard this rich trust with the help of the holy Spirit that dwells within us" (2 Tim 1:13–14).

The choice and appointment of local church leaders comprise a major theme of Titus and 1 Timothy, with this difference: In Crete, Titus inaugurated a structure of leadership in the local churches of the island, whereas such a structure was already established in Ephesus. After the initial salutation, the Letter to Titus begins: "For this reason I left you in Crete so that you might set right what remains to be done and appoint presbyters in every town, as I directed you..." (Titus 1:5). One of Paul's instructions to Timothy deals with handling accusations against a presbyter (1 Tim 5:19); this suggests that presbyters were already well known in Ephesus. (One recalls that Acts 20 also attests to the role of presbyters in that church in the subapostolic period). However, 1 Timothy also contains explicit instructions to Timothy with regard to the qualifications of the persons he is to choose as *episkopoi* and *diakonoi* at Ephesus (1 Tim 3:1–13). Clearly a major responsibility of both Titus and Timothy consisted of providing the right kind of persons for the ongoing leadership of the churches to which Paul had sent them.

A third element of the pastoral care Paul enjoined on his coworkers was instruction of the whole community on the conduct expected of them. Timothy was to tell both men and women how to deport themselves when the community gathered for common prayer (1 Tim 2:1–15). He was to pass on Paul's detailed instruction concerning the conduct of widows (1 Tim 5:3–16) and another for Christian slaves (6:1–2). Similarly, Titus was to teach specific rules of behavior appropriate for older men, older women, younger women, younger men and slaves (Titus 2:1–10).

Ministry of Local Leaders

In both 1 Timothy and Titus, Paul gives detailed instructions regarding the qualifications of the persons whom his coworkers are to choose and appoint for ministry. As seen above, Paul says that he left Titus in Crete so that he "might set right what remains to be done and appoint presbyters in every town" (Titus 1:5). The first qualification for a man chosen as presbyter is that he be "blameless" (1:6); the next verse, however, continues: "For a bishop *[episkopos]* as God's steward must be blameless...." One can hardly avoid the conclusion that the author of this letter called the same persons "elders" or "overseers." One recalls that in Acts 20, Luke spoke of the "presbyters of Ephesus" (v. 17), but had Paul describe the same persons as *episkopoi* (v. 28). In 1 Timothy, Paul lays down the qualifications of a person appointed as *episkopos*, and then of those chosen as deacons (3:1–13). In this context he says nothing about presbyters, but later in the same letter it becomes evident that there is a group of presbyters at Ephesus whose role is to "preside" (5:17).

A possible reason why the letter lacks a list of qualifications for presbyters could be that in 1 Timothy, as in Acts 20 and Titus 1:5–7, the same men were called both "elders" and "overseers." Because the word *episkopos* occurs only in the singular in these letters, some commentators have concluded that the "monepiscopal" structure had already emerged when the Pastorals were written. However, the word occurs only twice, and in both texts the Greek expression is *dei ton episkopon,* which is an example of the generic singular. Most commentators agree that there is no real evidence that the Pastorals witness to the presence of a single bishop, distinct from the group of presbyters.

On the other hand, 1 Timothy does provide evidence of differentiations within the group of presbyters at Ephesus, according to the tasks they performed. "Presbyters who preside well deserve double honor, especially those who toil in preaching and teaching" (1 Tim 5:17). The word translated here as "honor" can also mean "pay," and the following verse indicates that this is the meaning here. In other words, while all the presbyters presided and were paid for their work, some were recognized as presiding especially well and were deserving of double pay. Among these, some also toiled in preaching and teaching; this would indicate that not all the presbyters engaged in these tasks.

John P. Meier has argued that at Ephesus only the presbyters who preached and taught were called *episkopoi,* whereas this differentiation had not yet taken place in the less developed churches of Crete.[18] In any case, both 1 Timothy and Titus witness to the importance of the teaching role entrusted to the men whom Timothy and Titus appointed as local leaders of these churches. One of the requirements of the man chosen as *episkopos* in 1 Timothy 3:2 is that he be *didaktikos:* an apt teacher. In Titus 1:9, the candidate must be a man "holding fast to the true message as taught so that he will be able both to exhort with sound doctrine and to refute opponents."

Another requirement that sheds light on the task of those chosen as elders/overseers concerns a man's marital and family status: He must be "married only once....He must manage his own household well, keeping his children under control with perfect dignity; for if a man does not know how to manage his own household, how can he take care of the church of God?" (1 Tim 3:2, 4). Similarly Titus 1:6 states that he may be "married only once, with believing children who are not accused of licentiousness or rebellious." From these qualifications, we can see that the pastoral role was clearly seen as analogous to that of the father of a family, with the corresponding duties of paternal care and the maintaining of appropriate discipline. The requirement that he be "married only once" indicates that the remarrying of widowers, while tolerated, was not regarded as the ideal.

The candidate was also expected to practice the virtues of the ideal father of a family and manifest none of the faults or vices that would disqualify him for such a role. In general, the qualifications listed in these letters can be described as "domestic" or "down-to-earth"; they differ widely from the charismatic gifts that qualified persons for ministry in the early Pauline communities.

Besides the qualifications for *episkopoi,* 1 Timothy also lists the qualifications for *diakonoi.* One recalls that Paul greeted persons with these two titles in the salutation of his Letter to the Philippians. The qualities required for deacons resemble those required for overseers, with the exception of the ability to teach. After three verses that list these qualities, the next verse continues: "Women, similarly, should be dignified, not slanderers, but temperate and faithful in everything" (3:11). Some have identified these women as the wives of deacons; however, the word "similarly" works against this interpretation. It seems strange to mention the qualities required in the wives of deacons when nothing is said about the wives of *episkopoi.* It is reasonably certain that women deacons are meant. One recalls that Paul described Phoebe as *diakonos* of the church in Cenchreae (Rom 16:1). Presumably the next verse refers to women as well as to men: "Deacons may be married only once and must manage their children and their households well" (3:12).

From the absence of any mention of teaching ability as a qualification for deacons, one can conclude that this was not part of their ministry. The author of 1 Timothy excluded women from this role in any case. He says: "I do not permit a woman to teach or to have authority over a man" (2:12). On the other hand, the Letter to Titus, probably written by the same author, does give a teaching role to older women. He describes them as "teaching what is good, so that they may train younger women to love their husbands and children, to be self-controlled, chaste, good homemakers..." (Titus 2:3–5). The teaching by women excluded in 1 Timothy 2:12 would seem to refer to the teaching in the assembly of the community, which was done by those among the presbyters who "toil in preaching and teaching" (5:17).

As mentioned above, one of the instructions given to Timothy concerns the handling of an accusation against a presbyter.

Do not accept an accusation against a presbyter unless it is supported by two or three witnesses. Reprimand publicly those who do sin, so that the rest also will be afraid. I charge you before God and Christ Jesus and the elect angels to keep these rules without prejudice, doing nothing out of favoritism. Do not lay hands too readily on anyone, and do not share in another's sins. Keep yourself pure. (1 Tim 5:19–22)

In this translation (NAB), the phrase "those who do sin" clearly refers to sinning presbyters; however, some have taken the Greek term to refer more generally to sinners in the community. Meier has given several cogent reasons for interpreting it in reference to presbyters.[19] Those who claim it refers to sinners in general also understand the advice "Do not lay hands too readily on anyone" to refer to using this gesture in the reconciliation of penitent sinners. However, as Meier points out, the New Testament contains no other instance of the imposition of hands being used in this way, and in fact neither does Christian literature prior to the third century. On the other hand, the other two instances of the laying on of hands in the Pastorals refer to Timothy's receiving a gift of grace for ministry (1 Tim 4:14 and 2 Tim 1:6). There are very good reasons, therefore, to take it, as Meier and many others do, as referring to the ordination of those chosen for the presbyterate. The NRSV simply translates the advice as: "Do not ordain anyone hastily."

A Succession of Teachers Handing on the Deposit of Truth

The Second Letter to Timothy does not mention the choice and appointment of local church leaders, but focuses rather on the role that Paul entrusts to Timothy, which is to safeguard and faithfully hand on the Gospel Paul has been preaching: "Take as your norm the sound words that you heard from me, in the faith and love that are in Christ Jesus. Guard this rich trust with the help of the holy Spirit that dwells within us" (2 Tim 1:13–14); "And what you have heard from me through many witnesses entrust to faithful people who will have the ability to teach others as well" (2:2).[20] While 2 Timothy does not mention presbyters or *episkopoi*, the fact that teaching was one of their tasks suggests that the "faithful people who will have the ability to teach others" were such local church leaders. They constitute an important link in a succession of teachers that begins with Paul. Paul describes himself as "appointed preacher, apostle and teacher" (1:11); he has handed on the "sound words" to Timothy. In turn Timothy is to entrust what he has heard to people who, being "faithful," will safeguard what they have received and teach others as well. Corresponding to the theme of the succession of teachers is the theme of the "deposit" to be safeguarded and handed on intact. The Greek word that the NAB translates as "trust" in 2 Timothy 14 is *paratheke,* which means "property entrusted to another as a deposit to be kept safe and returned." The same word appears at the close of 1 Timothy, where Paul's final exhortation begins: "O Timothy, guard what has been entrusted to you" (1 Tim 6:20).

Safeguarding the sacred deposit of gospel truth will involve refuting the false doctrine spread by teachers of error. Here the authors of these letters have Paul foreseeing the dangers from false teaching, which no doubt were realized at the time the letters were written: "Now the Spirit explicitly says that in the last times some will turn away from the faith by paying attention to deceitful spirits and demonic instructions through the hypocrisy of liars with branded consciences" (1 Tim 4:1–2); "For the time will come when people will not tolerate sound doctrine but, following their own desires and insatiable curiosity, will accumulate teachers and will stop listening to the truth and will be diverted to myths" (2 Tim 4:3– 4). Hence, a man chosen as church leader must be known for "holding fast to the true message as taught so that he will be able both to exhort with sound doctrine and to refute opponents" (Titus 1:9).

In two passages of the New Testament Paul predicts his own imminent death; both show him as entrusting his message and his ministry to others who will carry on his work when he is gone. Above, we have commented on the farewell speech Luke has Paul address to the presbyter/ overseers of Ephesus (Acts 20:17–35). There he clearly counts on these local church leaders to defend the flock from "savage wolves" and from "men who will come forward perverting the truth" (20:29– 30). In the final chapter of 2 Timothy, Paul looks to Timothy to carry on his ministry when he is gone. He gives him a solemn charge:

> I charge you in the presence of God and of Christ Jesus...proclaim the word; be persistent whether it is convenient or inconvenient; convince, reprimand, encourage through all patience and teaching....But you, be self-possessed in all circumstances; put up with hardships; perform the work of an evangelist; fulfill your ministry. For I am already being poured out like a libation, and the time of my departure is at hand. (2 Tim 4:1–6)

THE THIRD LETTER OF JOHN

2 and 3 John are written by a person who calls himself "the Presbyter," without adding his personal name. Scholars have given at least five explanations for this use of the term "presbyter." I follow the one that Raymond Brown thinks most probable, namely, "a disciple of the disciples of Jesus and thus a second-generation figure who served as a transmitter of the tradition that came down from the first generation."[21] Such a use of "presbyter" is also found in the writings of Irenaeus.[22] The contents of these two letters characterize "the Presbyter" as a person whose authority as a witness to tradition is recognized by Christians in a number of churches, but who does not have juridical authority over them. He also sends out missionaries from his church, which seems to have been a major Christian center, such as Ephesus.

3 John is addressed to an individual Christian, Gaius by name, who is commended as a "coworker for the truth" for having provided hospitality to the missionaries sent out by the Presbyter's church. The Presbyter then complains:

> I wrote to the church, but Diotrephes, who loves to dominate, does not acknowledge us. Therefore, if I come, I will draw attention to what he is doing, spreading evil nonsense about us. And not content with that, he will not receive the brothers, hindering those who wish to do so and expelling them from the church. (9–10)

Clearly, Diotrephes exercises authority in the church to which the Presbyter has previously written, and rejects the kind of authority others evidently recognize the Presbyter to have. Diotrephes can effectively exclude the Presbyter's emissaries from his church and can expel those who welcome them. Brown suggests that Diotrephes applies in his church the advice the Presbyter gave in 2 John: "If anyone comes to you and does not bring this doctrine, do not receive him in your house or even greet him; for whoever greets him shares in his evil works" (2 John 10–11). For reasons unknown, Diotrephes evidently had a negative opinion of the doctrine the Presbyter's emissaries would introduce into his church.

Some scholars see in Diotrephes the earliest known example of a "monarchical bishop." However, his exercise of such authority would be easily understandable if he were simply the authoritarian leader of a house-church, especially if he were the owner of the house in which the Christian community gathered. Brown suggests that Diotrephes challenged the right of the Johannine tradition bearers to supervise gospel proclamation in churches in which they did not live.[23] He also notes the difference between St. Paul's response to such a challenge and that of the Presbyter. Paul threatened the Corinthians: "[I]f I come again I will not be lenient" (2 Cor 13:2). The Presbyter could say only: "[I]f I come, I will draw attention to what he is doing" (3 John 10). Paul could act with apostolic authority in a church he had founded; the Presbyter could only appeal to Diotrephes' community to take action against him. However, he evidently expected to be able to address the community, despite Diotrephes' hostile attitude toward him.

This briefest of the New Testament books raises more questions than it answers, but it gives a fascinating glimpse, however obscure, into the troubled history of the Christian churches that followed the tradition represented by the "Johannine school."

SUCCESSORS TO THE APOSTLES?

Having surveyed what the later writings of the New Testament say about ministry during the subapostolic period, we can explore what conclusions might be drawn from this evidence. First, it is obvious that the ministry to which the apostles devoted their lives did not cease with their deaths. Paul fully expected his ministry to continue after his departure, and indeed it was carried on. As seen above, his ministry was twofold: founding churches by preaching the Gospel to those who had not heard it and then exercising pastoral care over the churches he had founded. His many coworkers shared both of these tasks with him during his lifetime, and the Pastoral Letters witness to their continuation by the two most faithful of those coworkers after his death. The ministry described in these letters was the pastoral care of churches they had helped Paul to found; however, the letters still presented them as missionaries, and one of Paul's final commands to Timothy is: "[P]erform the work of an evangelist; fulfill your ministry" (2 Tim 4:5).

The Pastoral Letters witness to the belief of the subapostolic church that Timothy not only continued Paul's work, but that he received his authorization to do so from Paul himself, and therefore shared the mandate Paul had received from the risen Christ. We are surely justified in seeing Timothy and Titus as successors of the apostle Paul in his apostolic mission and ministry. But, as noted above, the authentic letters witness to the fact that Paul had many more coworkers than these two. It seems altogether reasonable to presume that after Paul's death many of these others continued the work he had entrusted to them. If one asks, then, who were the successors to the apostle Paul, the first answer should be: Timothy,

Titus and other coworkers who shared Paul's ministry while he lived and carried it on after he died.

What about Peter and others of the Twelve? Did they also have coworkers who carried on their missionary task after they died? The New Testament gives hardly any information on which to base a reply. We know from St. Paul (Gal 2:9) that Peter and John understood their mission as directed primarily to the circumcised, and we can reasonably presume that the rest of the Twelve did so as well. But our knowledge about missionary work carried on by the Twelve is limited to the little we know about Peter.[24] Two coworkers of Peter are named at the close of 1 Peter (Silvanus and Mark, 1 Pet 5:12–13). Given the probability that Peter, John and others of the Twelve had the help of coworkers, we can reasonably conjecture that their coworkers, like Paul's, carried on their missionary task after the apostles had gone to their reward.

In the pastoral care Paul exercised over the churches he had founded, he received help not only from his missionary coworkers, but also from the local church leaders he mentions in several of his undisputed letters. The farewell address put on his lips in Acts 20:17–35 makes it evident that Luke saw the presbyter/overseers of Ephesus as the successors to Paul in the pastoral care of that church. Foreseeing his own imminent death, Paul entrusted to them the care of the "flock" and the responsibility for safeguarding the Gospel he had preached to them.[25] This farewell speech also clearly shows that Paul left no one as "bishop" in charge of the church at Ephesus; rather, he left a group of leaders, whom Luke called "presbyters" and had Paul call "overseers." We do not know what role Paul had in the choice and appointment of these men, but the farewell address witnesses to the idea that Paul entrusted the care of this community to them and passed on to them a share of the mandate that he had received from Christ. One can hardly doubt that this farewell address reflects the understanding of the subapostolic church that such men as the presbyter/overseers of Ephesus were successors to St. Paul in the pastoral care of churches he had founded.

I conclude that the later writings of the New Testament provide us with sufficient evidence to affirm that after the death of St. Paul two groups of men—his missionary coworkers and the local leaders of churches he had founded—having shared in different aspects of his ministry while he lived, can rightly be seen as his successors in those aspects of his ministry. Those who had been his coworkers continued to evangelize, found churches and provide for ministry in those churches; the presbyter/overseers in each local church continued to "tend the flock" and guard it from false teachers.

We know that at least some of those local church leaders were called *episkopoi;* on the other hand we have no clear evidence in the New Testament that any one of them was a "bishop" in the historic sense of the term, that is, as the residential pastor of a local church with authority over the group of presbyters as well as over the rest of the community. Timothy and Titus are presented as having had authority over groups of presbyters, but they were still missionaries, not residential pastors. We must conclude that the New Testament provides no basis for the notion that before the apostles died, they ordained one man as bishop for each of the churches they had founded. The only person in the New Testament whose role resembles that of a bishop is James the "brother of the Lord," who was most likely designated for his position of leadership in the Jerusalem church by his relationship with Jesus and the special appearance with which he was favored by the risen Christ. It seems extremely unlikely that he was "ordained" as bishop of Jerusalem by St. Peter. Nor does the New Testament evidence support the idea that Peter, Paul or any other apostle became the bishop of any one local church or ordained one man as bishop of any local church. One looks in vain to the New Testament for a basis for the idea of "an unbroken line of episcopal ordination from Christ through the apostles down through the centuries to the bishops of today."

As mentioned above,[26] the Vatican Response to the Final Report of ARCIC I put this forth as the "Catholic" notion of apostolic succession. I believe that this study of ministry in the subapostolic period justifies the comment made earlier: The New Testament provides very little, if any, support for such a theory of apostolic succession. On the other hand, I believe the New Testament does provide a solid basis for a theory of apostolic succession: a theory that respects the evidence serious exegesis really finds there and accepts the fact that the New Testament does not provide all the evidence needed to justify the theory. The following chapters shall consider the evidence found in Christian writings of the postapostolic period.

5
THE *DIDACHE* AND *I CLEMENT*

THE *DIDACHE*

The only surviving manuscript of the early Christian writing now commonly known as the *Didache* gives the work two titles: "The Teaching *[didache]* of the Twelve Apostles," and "The teaching of the Lord to the Gentiles by the twelve apostles." The Byzantine scholar Philotheos Bryennios discovered this manuscript in 1873; prior to that date the work's existence had been known only from references to it in early Christian literature. The church historian Eusebius referred to it as among writings that were neither accepted in the canon of the New Testament nor rejected as heretical;[1] Athanasius also described it as non-canonical, but recommended it for reading by recent converts.[2]

Since its publication by Bryennios in 1883, the work, especially the question of when it was written, has been the object of intense discussion among scholars. While some have placed its origin as late as the third century, most commentators now date the final redaction of the work toward the end of the first century. J. P. Audet favors an earlier date (50–70),[3] while Kurt Niederwimmer suggests a later date (110–20),[4] and the consensus points to a date somewhere between those limits. Another discussion focuses on the place of origin; some have placed it in Egypt, but the more common view now is that it was written in Syria or Palestine.

This work can be described as a manual of instructions intended for Christian communities that must have been rather recently established, judging from the basic nature of the instructions given them. It consists of four parts of quite different literary genres: (1) baptismal catechesis on "the two ways"; (2) instructions on liturgy; (3) instructions on church order; and (4) predictions about "the last days." It is known from other sources that the tractate on "the two ways" was originally used for the moral instruction of Gentile converts to Judaism; the writer of the *Didache* adapted it as a catechesis for candidates for Christian baptism. The fourth part resembles the apocalyptic discourse of Jesus in Matthew 24:1–31, and some scholars have thought that it depended on that Gospel. However, it more probably rests on an apocalyptic tradition that both Matthew and the writer of the *Didache* used independently of each other.[5]

Because my concern is with the information the *Didache* gives about ministry in the early postapostolic period, I shall limit the discussion to parts two and three of this work, focusing on what it tells about the ministers of baptism and Eucharist; about apostles, prophets and teachers; and about *episkopoi* and *diakonoi*. Each portion of the text will be followed by my comments.[6]

Instruction on Baptism

7. (1) Now concerning baptism, baptize as follows: after you have reviewed all these things, baptize "in the name of the Father and of the Son and of the Holy Spirit," in running water. (2) But if you have no running water, then baptize in some other water, and if you are not able to baptize in cold water, then do so in warm. (3) But if you have neither, then pour water on the head three times "in the name of the Father and Son and Holy Spirit." (4) And before the baptism, let the one baptizing and the one who is to be baptized fast, as well as any others who are able. Also, you must instruct the one who is to be baptized to fast for one or two days beforehand.

Comment

In the first line, the word "baptize" is in the plural, indicating that the instruction is addressed to the community. But in the following lines, the instructions address an individual, presumably the "one baptizing" of sentence 4. There is therefore a minister of baptism in the community, who is to fast before the baptism. An individual (the one baptizing?) also gives instructions to the candidate about fasting. The verbs in the singular point to a recognized minister of baptism in the community, but no further information is given about this person.

Instruction about the Eucharist

9. (1) Now concerning the Eucharist, give thanks as follows. (2) First, concerning the cup: "We give you thanks, our Father, for the holy vine of David your servant, which you have made known to us through Jesus, your servant; to you be the glory forever." (3) And concerning the broken bread: "We give you thanks, our Father, for the life and knowledge which you have made known to us through Jesus, your servant; to you be the glory forever. (4) Just as this broken bread was scattered upon the mountains and then was gathered and became one, so may your church be gathered together from the ends of the earth into your kingdom; for yours is the glory and the power through Jesus Christ forever." (5) But let no one eat or drink of your Eucharist except those who have been baptized into the name of the Lord, for the Lord has also spoken concerning this: "Do not give what is holy to dogs."

10. (1) And after you have had your fill,[7] give thanks as follows: (2) "We give you thanks, Holy Father, for your holy name which you have caused to dwell in our hearts, and for the knowledge and faith and immortality which you have made known to us through Jesus your servant; to you be the glory forever. (3) You, almighty Master, created all things for your name's sake, and gave food and drink to men to enjoy, that they might give you thanks; but to us you have graciously given spiritual food and drink, and eternal life through your servant. (4) Above all we give you thanks because you are mighty, to you be the glory forever. (5) Remember your church, Lord, to deliver it from all evil and to make it perfect in your love; and gather it, the one that has been sanctified, from the four winds into your kingdom, which you have prepared for it, for yours is the power and the glory forever. (6) May grace come, and may this world pass away. Hosanna to the God of David. If anyone is holy, let him come; if anyone is not, let him repent. Maranatha! Amen." (7) But permit the prophets to give thanks however they wish.

Comment

The word translated as "give thanks" in these prayers is *eucharistein,* the verb form of *eucharistia* that is found in 9:1, 5. *Eucharistia* undoubtedly meant a blessing or thanksgiving before it came to be used more and more exclusively of the prayer of thanksgiving par excellence, which we know as the Eucharist. The use of the word here does not necessarily mean that the prayer given in *Didache* 10 is what we would now call a eucharistic prayer. There have been many theories about it, but there is a growing consensus that the words "And after you have had your fill" in 10:1 mean that the prayer given in 10:2–6 is a blessing and thanksgiving that concludes the *agape* meal. The words in 10:6, "If anyone is holy, let him come" are understood as an invitation to come to the celebration of the Eucharist that took place after the meal. Some have suggested that the prayer of blessing that preceded the Eucharist can be seen as its "vigil" or "preface."

While these prayers are of primary importance for the history of the eucharistic liturgy, I am most concerned here with the instruction in 10:7: "But permit the prophets to give thanks *[eucharistein]* however they wish." Following immediately upon the prayers given in 9–10, the word "But" *(de)* indicates a difference between what prophets do and what others do. It would seem that the prayers in the text are proposed for use by those who do not have the gift of inspired prayer that prophets have. The latter can improvise; others are not expected to do so. In any case, it is clear that prophets were considered qualified by their charismatic gift to pronounce blessings and prayers of thanksgiving on behalf of the community, and this included presiding at the Eucharist. If others besides prophets also presided at the Eucharist, we are not told at this point who those others were. This question is answered later on, in 15, where the community is instructed to choose for itself "overseers" and deacons, who carry out the ministry of prophets and teachers.

Instruction about Teachers, Apostles and Prophets

11. (1) So, if anyone should come and teach you all these things that have just been mentioned above, welcome him. (2) But if the teacher himself goes astray and teaches a different teaching that undermines all this, do not listen to him. However, if his teaching contributes to righteousness and knowledge of the Lord, welcome him as you would the Lord. (3) Now concerning the apostles and prophets, deal with them as follows in accordance with the rule of the gospel. (4) Let every apostle who comes to you be welcomed as if he were the Lord. (5) But he is not to stay for more than one day, unless there is need, in which case he may stay another. But if he stays three days, he is a false prophet. (6) And when the apostle leaves, he is to take nothing except bread until he

finds his next night's lodging. But if he asks for money, he is a false prophet.

Comment

"...[I]f anyone should come and teach you all these things that have just been mentioned above, welcome him." The communities to which the *Didache* was addressed evidently were accustomed to being taught by itinerants who "came" to them, as well as by resident teachers. "[A]ll these things" would refer to the tractate on the "two ways," as well as to the instruction on prayer and the Eucharist.

"But if the teacher himself goes astray...." The word translated as "the teacher" is not *didaskalos,* but the participial form of the verb: "the one teaching." This does not necessarily refer to a person recognized as a *didaskalos,* as others might also teach. The welcome to be given to such an itinerant teacher would depend on the effect of his teaching: whether it tends to "destruction" or to "righteousness and knowledge of the Lord."

"...in accordance with the rule of the gospel....[l]et...[him] be welcomed as if he were the Lord." Compare this to Matthew 10:40: "Whoever receives you receives me, and whoever receives me receives the one who sent me."

[An apostle who comes to you] "is not to stay for more than one day...." The *Didache* uses the term "apostle" to refer to missionaries who carried on the work of evangelization after the death of the original apostles. Most likely well-established Christian churches sent them out to spread the Gospel to towns and villages where it had not yet been preached. One can recognize such missionaries in the "brothers" whom the Presbyter of 3 John urges Gaius to help continue their journey, "for they have set out for the sake of the Name, and are accepting nothing from the pagans" (3 John 7). While "the Presbyter" does not call them "apostles," in other respects the message is the same: Missionaries should be welcomed in Christian communities and be given what they need for their journey, but they are expected to move on. Other early Christian sources called such missionaries evangelists rather than apostles.[8] The author of the *Didache* did not share the tendency of Luke and others to restrict the term "apostle" to the Twelve; on the other hand, he used the word in a broader sense than most other early Christian writers.

"...[I]f he stays three days, he is a false prophet." "...[I]f he asks for money, he is a false prophet." While one does find a few examples in early Christian writings of the term "false apostle" (cf. 2 Cor 11:13), it is quite rare; the term "false prophet" on the contrary was commonly used of anyone who falsely claimed to speak in the name of God. The term as used here, therefore, most probably has this generic meaning. The "falsity" is

manifested by the visitor's asking more than a genuine apostle was entitled to receive. The gospel rule was even stricter: "Take nothing for the
journey...no food, no sack, no money..." (Mark 6:6–8). The rest of section 11 explains how prophets should be treated.

> (7) Also, do not test or evaluate any prophet who speaks in the
> spirit, for every sin will be forgiven, but this sin will not be for-
> given. (8) However, not everyone who speaks in the spirit is a
> prophet, but only if he exhibits the Lord's ways. By his conduct,
> therefore, will the false prophet and the prophet be recognized.
> (9) Furthermore, any prophet who orders a meal in the spirit
> shall not partake of it; if he does, he is a false prophet. (10) If any
> prophet teaches the truth, yet does not practice what he teaches,
> he is a false prophet. (11) But any prophet proven to be genuine
> who does something with a view to portraying in a worldly
> manner the symbolic meaning of the church (provided that he
> does not teach you to do all that he himself does) is not to be
> judged by you, for his judgment is with God. Besides, the
> ancient prophets also acted in a similar manner. (12) But if any-
> one should say in the spirit, "Give me money," or anything else,
> do not listen to him. But if he tells you to give on behalf of
> others who are in need, let no one judge him.

Comment

"...[D]o not test or evaluate any prophet who speaks in the
spirit....However, not everyone who speaks in the spirit is a prophet, but
only if he exhibits the Lord's ways." These statements would seem contra-
dictory, unless one understands "any prophet" in the first statement to
mean "any prophet who has been proven genuine by his conduct." In
other words, the community rightly judges, on the basis of his conduct,
whether a person is a prophet or a false prophet; once they recognize him
as a prophet, the community cannot pass judgment on what he says or
does "in the spirit." However, it is evident that one cannot judge, from
the mere fact that he speaks or acts "in the spirit," that he is a genuine
prophet. Speaking "in the spirit" meant speaking as one inspired, but
Christians knew that there was more than one spirit by which a person
could be "inspired." They also knew that a person who had prophesied in
the Lord's name could hear from him: "Depart from me, you evildoers"
(Matt 7:23).

"...[A]ny prophet who orders a meal in the spirit shall not partake of
it...." "...[I]f anyone should say in the spirit, 'Give me money,' or anything
else, do not listen to him." These prescriptions are based on the conviction

that a genuine prophet will not seek his own advantage from what he says or does "in the spirit."

"If any prophet teaches the truth, yet does not practice what he teaches, he is a false prophet." This indicates that teaching is one of the "ministries of the Word" for which a prophet is gifted by the Spirit. Addressing the prophets at Corinth, Paul said: "[Y]ou can all prophesy one by one, so that all may learn and all be encouraged" (1 Cor 14:31). However, the fact that a person teaches the truth is not enough to prove him a genuine prophet; he must also practice it.

"...[W]ho does something with a view to portraying in a worldly manner the symbolic meaning of the church"—this mysterious expression may refer to a prophet's being accompanied by a virgin with whom he lives in a "spiritual marriage." He is not to be judged for doing this, provided he does not teach others to do the same. The appeal to the fact that "the ancient prophets also acted in a similar manner" (perhaps referring to Hosea's marriage to Gomer) indicates that Christian prophets were seen as analogous to those of the Old Testament. Further instruction about the treatment of prophets is given in section 13.

> 13. (1) But every genuine prophet who wishes to settle among you "is worthy of his food." (2) Likewise, every genuine teacher is, like "the worker, worthy of his food." (3) Take, therefore, all the first fruits of the produce of the wine press and threshing floor, and of the cattle and sheep, and give these first fruits to the prophets, for they are your high priests. (4) But if you have no prophet, give them to the poor. (5) If you make bread, take the first fruit and give in accordance with the commandment. (6) Similarly, when you open a jar of wine or oil, take the first fruit and give it to the prophets. (7) As for money and clothes and any other possessions, take the "first fruit" that seems right to you and give in accordance with the commandment.

Comment

A prophet who has been proven genuine while a guest may choose to remain permanently in a community; if so, the community should support him. "Likewise, every genuine teacher...." Most commentators take this to mean that prophets and teachers were different persons. However, the patristic scholar, André de Halleux sees them as the same persons, interpreting the text to mean: "The prophet, inasmuch as he is a genuine teacher, is, like the worker, worthy of his food."[9] We have seen above that one of the functions of the prophet was to teach. If prophets were also the teachers, this would explain why, in the rest of the paragraph, only prophets are mentioned as receiving the first fruits.

"...[G]ive these first fruits to the prophets"—note that "prophets" is in the plural, indicating that a community may have had more than one. "...[F]or they are your high priests"—this clearly means that the role of prophets in a Christian community was understood as similar to that of the high priests in Israel. However, one has to be cautious about drawing the conclusion that at the time of the *Didache* prophets were thought to be priests because of their role in offering eucharistic prayer.

"...[I]f you have no prophet"—evidently a community could lack a residential prophet. "[G]ive them to the poor"—no provision is made in this case for the support of teachers. This would seem to confirm de Halleux's view that the prophets were also the teachers.

The Sunday Celebration of the Liturgy

14. (1) On the Lord's own day gather together and break bread and give thanks having first confessed your sins so that your sacrifice may be pure. (2) But let no one who has a quarrel with a companion join you until they have been reconciled, so that your sacrifice may not be defiled. (3) For this is the sacrifice concerning which the Lord said: "In every place and time offer me a pure sacrifice, for I am a great king, says the Lord, and my name is marvelous among the nations."

Comment

The Didachist now returns to the Eucharist as part of his instruction on good order in the community. The stress here is on the confession of sins and reconciliation with the neighbor "so that your sacrifice may not be defiled." We are also told that the community gathered for liturgy every week.

"On the Lord's own day gather together and break bread"—the "Lord's day" was the day of his resurrection: the first day of the week (cf. 1 Cor 16:2; Acts 20:7); to "break bread and give thanks *[eucharistesate]*" referred to eating the *agape* meal and celebrating the Eucharist. The verbs here are in the plural; the whole gathered community breaks bread and gives thanks. This of course does not exclude, but rather requires that someone preside and pronounce the blessing prayers.

"...[H]aving first confessed your sins so that your sacrifice may not be defiled"—the tractate on "the two ways" (4:14) also contains an exhortation to the public confession of sins: "In the assembly you shall confess your transgressions, and you shall not approach your prayer with an evil conscience." Now it is specified that to "approach with an evil conscience" means without being reconciled with a companion after a quarrel. The rule Jesus had laid down to "leave your gift there at the altar" (Matt 5:24) referred directly to offerings made in the temple; now this is applied to Christian worship. The quotation from Malachi 1:11 and 14 is the earliest known application of this text to the Christian Eucharist. Scholars have arrived at no consensus as to the precise sense in which the Eucharist was then understood as a sacrifice, but evidently it was seen as the fulfillment of the prophecy of Malachi about the "pure sacrifice that would be offered in every place."

Instruction about the Choice of Ministers

15. (1) Therefore choose[10] for yourselves bishops and deacons worthy of the Lord, men who are humble and not avaricious and true and approved, for they too carry out for you the ministry of the prophets and teachers. (2) You must not, therefore, despise them, for they are your honored men, along with the prophets and teachers.

Comment

The word "therefore," with which this paragraph begins, suggests that it was with a view to the weekly gathering for the Eucharist that the community should choose *episkopous kai diakonous* for itself. The meaning of these words, which St. Paul also used (Phil 1:1), indicates that some were chosen as leaders (overseers) and others as helpers (ministers). Willy Rordorf attributes this paragraph to a second author, writing at a later period when itinerant charismatics were no longer on the scene and Christian communities had to appoint resident leaders to supply for the lack of visiting prophets and charismatic teachers.[11] However, as seen above, the blessing prayer given in 9 and 10 indicates that not only prophets, but others who did not have their gift of inspired speech already presided at the Eucharist.

André de Halleux argues that there is good reason to interpret the *Didache* as describing a community that knew the ministry both of prophets and of appointed leaders.[12] However, the exhortation not to despise the latter, but to honor them along with the prophets and teachers, suggests that Christians tended to esteem charismatic leaders more highly than they did those whom they themselves chose and appointed. However, the virtues of the men *(andras)* chosen by the community are like those that distinguish genuine prophets (cf. *Did.* 11). The reason for demanding the same moral qualities is that "they too carry out for you the ministry *[leitourgian]* of the prophets and teachers." The last word here indicates that the leaders chosen by the community were also expected to teach. We have seen that this was the case also in the later period of the New Testament. At least some of the presbyters at Ephesus were engaged in teaching, as we know from Acts 20:29–31 and 1 Timothy 5:17. What is clearer in the *Didache* than in the New Testament is that these appointed leaders also presided at the community's Eucharist.

An example of the coexistence of charismatic and appointed ministers in the same church appears in 1 Peter, where persons with charisms for service are encouraged to employ them for the common good (1 Pet 4:10), while the pastoral care of the community lies in the hands of a group of presbyters (5:1–4). The *Didache* does not mention presbyters, but it has *episkopous* in the plural. For that reason the word is best translated as "overseers," as there is no indication that the local church of the *Didache* was led by a single bishop.

Given the evidence that both prophets and leaders chosen by the community presided at the Eucharist, a modern reader might ask whether they were ordained to do this. As far as prophets are concerned, one can presume that the Church of that period would have seen no need to lay hands on anyone recognized as having received a charism for ministry directly from the Holy Spirit.

Would the community have asked a prophet to lay hands on those whom they chose as overseers and deacons? There is no mention of this, but it does not seem unlikely, as this was a gesture of prayer, calling down the Spirit on those chosen for ministry. One can recall that at Antioch, the other prophets laid hands on Barnabas and Saul when they were sent out as missionaries (Acts 13:3). The fact that these same prophets are described as "worshiping the Lord and fasting" suggests that they presided at the Eucharist. The prophet's gift of inspired speech would have been an important qualification for leading the community in its great prayer of thanksgiving. However, the lack of a prophet did not mean that a community would be unable to celebrate its weekly Eucharist. Worthy men, who would "carry out the ministry of the prophets and teachers" and be honored as they were, could be chosen.

THE LETTER OF THE ROMANS TO THE CORINTHIANS (*I CLEMENT*)

In contrast to the many uncertainties that remain concerning the date, place of origin and author of the *Didache,* there is general agreement that the letter commonly known as *I Clement* was sent from the church of Rome to the church of Corinth about the year 96, and that a leading member of the Roman church named Clement wrote it. The author's name does not appear in the letter, but Dionysius, bishop of Corinth, writing to Soter, bishop of Rome, about the year 170, refers to an earlier letter from Rome to Corinth as "written to us by Clement."[13] Some scholars have proposed an earlier date, arguing that the letter must have been written before the destruction of the Jerusalem temple in 70, and others have proposed a later date, but the consensus holds for middle of the last decade of the first century.

The occasion that prompted the letter is described in its first chapter as "the detestable and unholy schism...which a few reckless and arrogant persons have kindled" (1:1). As a result of this "schism," some of the presbyters of the church of Corinth had been unjustly deposed from their ministry. The church of Rome wrote this letter to exhort the Corinthians to end the strife and restore the unity and harmony they had lost. In the past, Catholic writers have interpreted this intervention as an early exercise of Roman primacy, but now it is generally recognized as the kind of exhortation one church could address to another without any claim to authority over it.

This letter is extremely important for our topic because of information it provides about the ministry in the church of Corinth toward the end of the first century, and its claim that the apostles established this ministry and also provided for its permanence by decreeing the orderly appointment of successors in generations to come. As before, I shall give the text of pertinent passages of the letter, followed by some comments.

Leaders of the Christian Community

Raymond Brown and others believe that the Letter to the Hebrews was addressed to the Roman church. As we have seen, the writer of Hebrews referred to the leaders of the Christian community, both past and present, with the generic word *hegoumenoi* (Heb 13:7, 17, 24). Writing on behalf of the Roman church, Clement also used this term, as in the following texts:

1:3 For you did everything without partiality, and you lived in accordance with the laws of God, submitting yourselves to your leaders *[tois hegoumenois umon]* and giving to the older men *[presbyterois]* among you the honor due them. You instructed the young to think temperate and proper thoughts....

21:6 Let us respect our leaders *[tous prohegoumenous hemon]*; let us honor our elders *[presbuterous]*, let us instruct our young with instruction that leads to the fear of God.

Comment

Clement more often referred to the leaders of the Corinthian church as *presbuteroi*, but here he may have chosen to use *hegoumenoi*, for in the same sentences he planned to use *presbuteroi* with its literal meaning of "older men" in contrast to "the young." In any case, here is an indication that the vocabulary for those engaged in ministry was still fluid, allowing for the use of such generic terms as *hegoumenoi* and *prohegoumenoi*. We are also reminded that the term "presbyter" could still be used to mean simply an older man.

The Jerusalem Temple Liturgy as an Example of Good Order

Clement addressed a lengthy exhortation to the Corinthians to restore good order to their community, invoking examples of such good order from a variety of sources, such as the orderly course of nature and the discipline of an army. In the following passage, he drew his argument from the prescriptions laid down in the Mosaic Law for the orderly conduct of the temple liturgy.

40. (1) Since, therefore, these things are now clear to us and we have searched into the depths of the divine knowledge, we ought to do, in order, everything that the Master has commanded us to perform at the appointed times. (2) Now he has commanded the offerings *[prosphoras]* and services *[leitourgias]* to be performed diligently, and not to be done carelessly or in disorder, but at the designated times and seasons. (3) Both where and by whom he wants them to be performed, he himself has determined by his supreme will, so that all things, being done devoutly according to his good pleasure, might be acceptable to his will. (4) Those, therefore, who make their

offerings at the appointed times are acceptable and blessed: for those who follow the instructions of the Master cannot go wrong. (5) For to the high priest the proper services have been given, and to the priests the proper office has been assigned, and upon the Levites the proper ministries have been imposed. The layman is bound by the layman's rules.

41. (1) Let each of you, brothers, in his proper order give thanks to God, maintaining a good conscience, not overstepping the designated rule of his ministry *[leitourgias]* but acting with reverence. (2) Not just anywhere, brothers, are the continual daily sacrifices offered, or the freewill offerings, or the offerings for sin and trespasses, but only in Jerusalem. And even there the offering is not made in every place, but in front of the sanctuary at the altar, the offering having been first inspected for blemishes by the high priest and the previously mentioned ministers. (3) Those, therefore, who do anything contrary to the duty imposed by his will receive death as the penalty. (4) You see, brothers, as we have been considered worthy of greater knowledge, so much the more are we exposed to danger.

Comment

These two paragraphs are best read in the light of the exhortation addressed to the Corinthians in 41:1, which urges each of them to observe "the designated rule of his ministry." The rules God prescribed for the ministries connected with the offering of sacrifices in the temple of Jerusalem are then proposed by way of an analogy, whose point is brought out in the final sentence of 41: "[A]s we have been considered worthy of greater knowledge, so much the more are we exposed to danger." The analogy is developed as a warning to those in the Corinthian church who have been "overstepping the designated rules of [their] ministry" by getting duly appointed presbyters removed and ruling in their place.

In view of the fact that the letter describes the liturgy of the temple in Jerusalem, with its daily sacrifices and animal victims, for which Christian worship had no parallel, it would be a mistake to conclude from 40:5 that in Clement's day the Christian community also had its "high priest, priests, and Levites." The word "layman" *(laikos)* appears here for the first time in Christian literature, but in the context it does not refer to the Christian "laity." The fact that Clement refers to worship in the temple of Jerusalem here in the present tense has led some to conclude that the work must have been written before the year 70, but most scholars do not agree with this conclusion.

The analogy from the ministry in the temple of Jerusalem stresses the importance of observing the rules God has laid down for good order in the community. The following section shows how this applies to the Christian church.

Divine Provision for Good Order in the Church

42. (1) The apostles received the gospel for us from the Lord Jesus Christ; Jesus the Christ was sent forth from God. (2) So then Christ is from God, and the apostles are from Christ. Both, therefore, came of the will of God in good order. (3) Having therefore received their orders and being fully assured by the resurrection of our Lord Jesus Christ and full of faith in the Word of God, they went forth with the firm assurance that the Holy Spirit gives, preaching the good news that the kingdom of God was about to come. (4) So, preaching both in the country and in the towns, they appointed their first fruits, when they had tested them by the Spirit, to be bishops *[episkopous]* and deacons *[diakonous]* for the future believers. (5) And this was no new thing they did, for indeed something had been written about bishops and deacons many years ago; for somewhere thus says the Scripture: "I will appoint their bishops in righteousness and their deacons in faith."

Comment

Writing to the Corinthians about thirty years after the death of the founder of their church, Clement declares that the apostles, after preaching the Gospel, "appointed their first fruits, when they had tested them by the Spirit, to be bishops *[episkopous]* and deacons *[diakonous]* for the future believers." Can we rely on this statement of Clement as an historical account of what the apostles did to provide for ministry in the churches they founded? One answer is based on the fact that in the year 96 there must have been at least some Corinthians who knew firsthand what St. Paul had done and would therefore have rejected an account that did not correspond to the facts as they knew them. It is not likely that Clement would risk such a negative reaction in a letter intended to persuade the Corinthians to change their ways. On the basis of this argument, Brown and others have concluded that this account can hardly be a pure fabrication. They think it more plausible that Clement has generalized an apostolic practice that was occasional but not consistent or universal.[14]

I presume that the reason for saying it was not consistent or universal rests in the lack of evidence for this in the New Testament. Knowledge about the practice of the apostles in this regard is limited to what is known about St. Paul. The only instance of his appointing local church leaders is found in Acts 14:23, which says that he and Barnabas appointed presbyters in each of the churches they had founded in Asia Minor. However, many have questioned the historicity of this report. On the other hand, as we have seen above, there is good evidence in Paul's authentic letters that there were local leaders in each of his churches and that he put his own apostolic authority behind theirs, urging the community to be "subordinate to such people" as Stephanas and his household, whom he described as the "first-fruits" of his mission in Achaia (1 Cor 16:15–16). Furthermore, we know that he referred to the local leaders in Philippi as *episkopoi* and *diakonoi* (Phil 1:1). Still, we have no certain knowledge from the New Testament that Paul himself appointed such local church leaders.[15]

On the other hand, I have argued that one cannot conclude from the fact that in Acts 20:28 Luke has Paul say that the Holy Spirit made them overseers, that no human agency was involved in their appointment.[16] While the New Testament does not confirm Clement's account of the apostolic practice of appointing local church leaders, it does not contradict it, nor does it make it seem implausible. At the same time, the New Testament also makes clear that there were local church leaders qualified for their ministry by the charismatic gifts of the Spirit. We can presume that the apostles recognized the leadership exercised by such people without feeling any need to appoint them for it.

At the end of this section Clement invokes scriptural authority for the appointment of *episkopoi* and *diakonoi,* citing a text from the Book of Isaiah. The Septuagint or LXX version of Isaiah 60:17 does mention *episkopoi,* but no known Greek version of Isaiah has *diakonoi* in this verse. The couplet is found in the New Testament, both in Philippians 1:1 and in 1 Timothy 3:1–13, but it is typical of Clement's approach that he would look to the Scriptures for confirmation that these appointments were divinely sanctioned.

Provision for an Orderly Succession in Ministry

In the following section, Clement again invokes a scriptural example to illustrate his next point, namely, that the apostles also provided for an orderly succession in the ministry they established. He cites how Moses ensured that no dispute about the right of the tribe of Aaron to the priesthood in Israel would arise. He then continues:

44. (1) Our apostles likewise knew, through our Lord Jesus Christ, that there would be strife over the bishop's office. (2) For this reason, therefore, having received complete fore-knowledge, they appointed the officials mentioned earlier and afterwards they gave the offices a permanent character, that is, if they should die, other approved men should succeed to their ministry. (3) Those, therefore, who were appointed by them or, later on, by other reputable men with the consent of the whole church, and who have ministered to the flock of Christ blamelessly, humbly, peaceably, and unselfishly, and for a long time have been well spoken of by all—these men we consider to be unjustly removed from their ministry. (4) For it will be no small sin for us, if we depose from the bishop's office those who have offered the gifts blamelessly and in holiness. (5) Blessed are those presbyters who have gone on ahead, for they need no longer fear that someone might remove them from their established place. (6) For we see that you have removed certain people, their good conduct notwithstanding, from the ministry which has been held in honor by them blamelessly.

Comment

44:1 "[b]ishop's office"—This translates the Greek *tes episkopes,* which could also be translated: "the ministry of oversight." *I Clement* contains no reference to a bishop in the later sense of a single pastor of a local church. At Corinth, several *episkopoi* have been removed from their office.

44:2 "...they gave the offices a permanent character"—This translation depends on accepting a textual emendation proposed by J. B. Lightfoot. However, other scholars who do not accept this emendation take the phrase to mean "they added a further decree." In either case, it means that the apostles provided for an orderly succession in the ministry they established.

44:2 "...if they should die, other approved men should succeed to their ministry"—This could possibly mean: "If the apostles should die, others should succeed to their ministry." But, in the light of 44:3, it is better understood to mean: "If those appointed by the apostles should die, other approved men should succeed to their ministry." The word translated "approved" means "tested and approved"; an example of its New Testament use appears in 1 Timothy 3:10 where it refers to the test-ing of candidates for the diaconate.

44:3 "Those, therefore, who were appointed by them [i.e., by the apostles] or, later on, by other reputable men"—here there is question of two groups of successors. Those appointed "later on" are the successors to the first generation of *episkopoi;* they are appointed by "reputable men" who succeed the apostles in their role of appointing local church leaders. In the New Testament we find such "reputable men" in the persons of Timothy and Titus, who are seen in the Pastoral Letters as successors to Paul and have the task of appointing local church leaders.

44:3 "…with the consent of the whole church…and have for a long time been well spoken of by all"—This highlights the role of the whole community, both in the appointment of its leaders and in judging their performance in office.

44:3 "…these men we consider to be unjustly removed from their ministry"—Because they "have ministered to the flock of Christ blamelessly, humbly, peaceably, and unselfishly," it is unjust to remove them from their ministry. This makes it clear that the community could justly remove from office those who proved themselves unworthy of it. Office holders were not immune from such judgment and removal.

44:4 "…if we depose from the *episkope* those who have offered the gifts blamelessly and in holiness."—From this it is evident that those with the office of "oversight" were to "offer the gifts." Hebrews used this expression *(prospherein ta dora)* several times to describe the role proper to priests (see Heb 8:3–4). As used here by Clement it is generally understood to refer to the offering of gifts in the context of the Eucharist. It is not certain in what sense the Eucharist was then understood as sacrificial worship, but there is no doubt about the fact that the expression to "offer the gifts" normally referred to the offering of sacrifice. We recall also that the *Didache,* which was contemporary with *I Clement,* saw the fulfillment of the prophecy of Malachi in the offering of the Eucharist.

The Leaders of the Corinthian Church are Called "Presbyters"

44:5 "Blessed are those presbyters who have gone on ahead…."—Here we find the term Clement will use consistently in the rest of the letter to refer to the leaders of the Corinthian church. Clement used the words *episkopoi* and *diakonoi* only when speaking about appointments made by the apostles themselves. He did this perhaps because he knew that Paul had used these terms (Phil 1:1). Otherwise, Clement normally referred to the leaders of the church as "presbyters," as he did here referring to those who had already died. In the following passages, the current leaders of the Corinthian church are called "presbyters."

47. (6) It is disgraceful, dear friends, yes, utterly disgraceful and unworthy of your conduct in Christ, that it should be reported that the well-established and ancient church of the Corinthians, because of one or two persons, is rebelling against its presbyters. (7) And this report has reached not only us, but also those who differ from us, with the result that you heap blasphemies upon the name of the Lord because of your stupidity, and create danger for yourselves as well.

54. (1) Now then who among you is noble? Who is compassionate? Who is filled with love? (2) Let him say: "If it is my fault that there are rebellion and strife and schisms, I retire, I will go wherever you wish, and will do whatever is ordered by the people. Only let the flock of Christ be at peace with its duly appointed presbyters." (3) The one who does this will win for himself great fame in Christ, and every place will receive him, for the earth is the Lord's, and all that is in it."

Comment

54:2 "...[w]hatever is ordered by the people"—The word for "people" is *plethous*, literally: "the multitude." This gives another indication of the significant role played by the whole community in making decisions. We have already seen its role in giving its consent to the appointment of church leaders, in 44:3.

"...[T]he flock of Christ"—This image for the church occurs four times in *I Clement:* 16:1, 44:3, 54:2 and 57:2.

"...[A]t peace with its duly appointed presbyters"—Clement insists that the presbyters were appointed to their office, no doubt in contrast to those who have usurped their position.

57. (1) You, therefore, who laid the foundation of the revolt, must submit to the presbyters and accept discipline leading to repentance, bending the knees of your heart. (2) Learn how to subordinate yourselves, laying aside the arrogant and proud stubbornness of your tongue. For it is better for you to be found small but included in the flock of Christ than to have a preeminent reputation and yet be excluded from his hope.

Comment

57:1 "...submit to the presbyters and accept discipline leading to repentance"—This indicates not only that the presbyters have authority in the community, but also that they exercised a key role in dealing with the guilty and leading them to repentance.

An Exercise of Authority by the Roman Church?

Some Catholic scholars have seen in this *Letter of the Romans to the Corinthians* an exercise of primatial authority by the church of Rome. They have found this especially in the call to obedience that appears in the following passages.

> 59. (1) But if certain people should disobey what has been said by him through us, let them understand that they will entangle themselves in no small sin and danger. (2) We, however, will be innocent of this sin....

> 63. (1) Therefore it is right for us, having studied so many and such great examples, to bow the neck and, adopting the attitude of obedience, to submit to those who are the leaders of our souls, so that by ceasing from this futile dissension we may attain the goal that is truly set before us, free from all blame. (2) For you will give us great joy and gladness, if you obey what we have written to you through the Holy Spirit and root out the unlawful anger of your jealousy, in accordance with the appeal for peace and harmony which we have made in this letter. (3) We have also sent trustworthy and prudent men who from youth to old age have lived blameless lives among us, who will be witnesses between you and us.

Comment

In the first of these passages, it is important to note that disobeying what has been said "by him," that is, by Christ, through the letter of the Roman church would entangle certain people in sin. The confidence that Christ had spoken to the Corinthians through the Romans resembles the confidence of the apostles and presbyters when they wrote: "It is the decision of the holy Spirit and of us..." (Acts 15:28). The second passage urged the Corinthians to "obey what we have written to you through the holy Spirit." Here again, some have seen an exercise of Roman primacy, but most scholars nowadays, including Catholics, interpret this rather as an expression of confidence that the Holy Spirit has spoken through what they have written.

63:1 "...submit to those who are the leaders *[archegois]* of our souls"— Clement has used this Greek word in 60:2 and 60:4 to refer to "our rulers and governors on earth," to whom Christians should also render obedience.

This may also explain why he has used the same word here, but qualifying it with "of our souls."

63:3 "...men who from youth to old age have lived blameless lives among us"—This fits well with the dating of the letter to the mid-90s, when there could be members of the Roman church who had been Christians from youth to old age. The three men, named in 65:2, are expected to bring back to Rome the report of the letter's reception and its favorable results.

AGREEMENT AND DISAGREEMENT
OF SCHOLARS ABOUT *I CLEMENT*

Since this letter provides good evidence that the church of Rome was well informed about the current situation in the church of Corinth, scholars generally agree that the information it provides about the ministry in the Corinthian church during the last decade of the first century is reliable. It reveals that a group of presbyters who had been appointed to their ministry led the Corinthian church. They had a role of authority in the community, and one of their functions was to "offer the gifts." While the presbyters were also called *episkopoi,* no one "bishop" was in charge of the Corinthian church at this time. The whole community had an important role in making decisions: It gave its consent to the appointment of presbyters and could remove them from office if they were found blameworthy; it would also determine what the leaders of the revolt should do if they repented.

There is general agreement among scholars that the structure of ministry in the church of Rome at this time would have resembled that in Corinth: with a group of presbyters sharing leadership, perhaps with a differentiation of roles among them, but with no one bishop in charge. As we shall see, the work known as *The Shepherd of Hermas* has been taken to mean that this was still the case in the Roman church well into the second century.

Disagreement among scholars focuses on Clement's account of the apostolic origin of this structure of ministry. According to him, the apostles not only appointed *episkopoi* and *diakonoi* in the churches they founded, but they also established a rule of succession in that ministry, whereby other "reputable men" would appoint the next generation of local church leaders. Protestant scholars reject this account as a fiction, invented to give apostolic, and ultimately divine, authority to a development that, in their view, was simply natural and historical, following the sociological laws that apply to any developing society.[17]

A few Catholic scholars, notably Hans Küng and Gotthold Hasenhüttl, tend to agree with the Protestants on this issue. However, most Catholic writers reject the claim that Clement's account is "pure fiction." With varying emphases and nuances, they defend the view that ministry in the postapostolic period can be traced back to the founding apostles, at least in the sense that they did not leave their churches without local leaders and that they supported them with their own apostolic authority. The authentic letters of St. Paul support this claim.

Secondly, the Pastoral Letters tell us about apostolic coworkers who would carry on the work of Paul after his death and who, like the "reputable men" of *I Clement,* appointed presbyters for the next generation. True, the New Testament says nothing about what other apostles did in this regard, but one can hardly imagine that after founding churches, they took no thought to provide for their ongoing pastoral care. In any case, if, as most scholars believe, *I Clement* was written only thirty years after the martyrdom of the apostles Peter and Paul, there must have been some older members of the Corinthian church who could judge whether what Clement wrote corresponded to the facts or not.

I Clement certainly does not support the theory that before the apostles died, they appointed one man as bishop in each of the churches they had founded. This letter witnesses rather to the fact that in the last decade of the first century, the collegial ministry of a group of presbyters, like that seen in the later writings of the New Testament, was still maintained in the Pauline church of Corinth. This was most likely the case also in the church of Rome at this period. *I Clement* is an important voice on the question of apostolic succession in the ministry, but he does not provide an answer to the question why, after the middle of the second century when each church was being led by one bishop, it was the bishops, rather than the presbyters, who were recognized as the successors to the apostles.

THE *DIDACHE* AND *I CLEMENT* COMPARED

At the close of this chapter on the *Didache* and *I Clement,* a few remarks about the differences between them are in order. The most striking of these is the prominent role the *Didache* attributes to prophets, of whom *I Clement* makes no mention. Likewise, for Clement, apostles are the founders of churches and are clearly of a past generation, whereas for the author of the *Didache* they are missionaries who might come to enjoy the hospitality of a Christian community, but must not stay more than two days. For Clement, the apostles appointed the first generation of local leaders and their successors were appointed by other "reputable men"; in the *Didache* the community chose them. How can these differences be explained, if these two writings are more or less contemporary?

Considering the rather basic and rudimentary nature of the instructions given in the *Didache*, I conclude that the churches for which they were written must have been only recently established. Toward the end of the first century, there were surely regions being evangelized for the first time and Christian communities being founded. Here one might still find the kind of charismatic ministry that marked the early phase in the life of churches founded by St. Paul. On the other hand, by the last decade of the century, the church of Corinth had gone through more than forty years of development and had become accustomed to the regular succession of appointed presbyters. We have to keep in mind that at the same period of time local churches could be at different stages of development. The next chapter will show that this was still true in the first half of the second century.

6
IGNATIUS OF ANTIOCH

THE CHURCH OF ANTIOCH

Antioch, the capital of Syria and third-largest city of the Roman Empire, was the first city to have a Christian community made up of both Jews and Gentiles and the first place where the members of this community were known as "Christians" (Acts 11:19–26). At the time St. Paul undertook his first missionary journey (probably in the late 40s), the church at Antioch was led by a group of prophets and teachers, who are described as "worshiping the Lord" and who laid their hands on Barnabas and Saul and "commended [them] to the grace of God" for the mission to which the Holy Spirit had called them (Acts 13:1–3; 14:26).

We know from Paul's Letter to the Galatians that St. Peter resided for a time with the Christian community in Antioch (cf. Gal 2:11–14), a fact that later gave rise to the idea of the "chair of Peter" at Antioch. While the notion that Peter had presided as bishop of Antioch is legendary, there is good reason to believe that the Antiochene church attributed a primary role to Peter as the "rock" on which Jesus built his church and to whom he gave the keys of the kingdom of heaven, with power to "bind" and "loose" (cf. Matt 16:18–19). This, of course, depends on the commonly held view that Matthew's Gospel had its origin in the church of Antioch.

Scholars who hold this view also look to Matthew for hints regarding the ministry in the Antiochene church in the 80s, when it is generally believed that this Gospel was written. John P. Meier has seen in the "prophets and wise men and scribes" of Matthew 23:34 an "alias" of the "college of prophets and teachers" who formed the leadership in the Antioch of Matthew's day.[1] Raymond Brown, however, observes that

we do not know whether there were offices (presbyter-
bishops, deacons) in the Matthean community or only authoritative charisms. The mention in the gospel of apostles,
prophets, wise men and scribes (see 23:34) has been thought
to favor the latter, but do wise men and scribes exhibit
charisms?...Matthew's failure to mention presbyters and bishops proves nothing, for that would be the type of blatant
anachronism that Matthew avoids in his gospel. "Shepherd"
was a set image in the late first century for presbyter-bishops
(Acts 20:28; I Peter 5:2–4; perhaps John 21:15–17) and Matt
18:12–14 does speak of the responsibility of shepherds.[2]

As Brown says, we do not know whether by the mid-80s the church of
Antioch was being led by a group of presbyters. However, we have evidence that at that same period the church of Ephesus had a presbyteral
structure of ministry (Acts 20:17–35).

As will be shown, we also have reliable information from the letters of
Ignatius of Antioch that by the year 115 the church of Ephesus and the
church of Antioch each had a single bishop as well as a college of presbyters. I think it improbable that the church of Antioch would have had a
single bishop over the presbyterate by the year 115 if it had not adopted
the presbyteral structure by the mid-80s. I argue to this conclusion from
the evidence in *I Clement* that the church of Corinth, in the mid-90s, was
still being led by a college of presbyters. Only in the second century did
Corinth begin to have a single bishop. In other words, it took some time
for the monepiscopal structure to develop out of the presbyteral. It is a
reasonable conjecture that the church of Antioch, like those of Corinth
and Ephesus, must have been led by a college of presbyters for at least several decades before it had its first bishop. It is not certain that Ignatius was
in fact its first bishop, but his letters leave no doubt about the fact that he
was a real bishop.

THE LETTERS OF IGNATIUS OF ANTIOCH

In his *Ecclesiastical History* (3.36), the fourth-century church historian
Eusebius describes Ignatius as the second bishop of Antioch,[3] who, while
being taken under arrest to Rome where he would suffer martyrdom,
wrote seven letters: five of them to churches in Asia Minor, one to the
bishop of Smyrna, and one to the church of Rome. Eusebius evidently had
these letters, as he quotes several passages from them. However, the manuscripts in which the letters have come down to us offer three different

recensions, commonly referred to as the short, middle and long. The short recension, preserved only in Syriac, has only three of the letters mentioned by Eusebius, along with a paragraph of a fourth. The middle recension, preserved in Greek and in a Latin translation, has the seven letters mentioned by Eusebius. The long recension has an expanded version of these seven, along with six additional letters.

Two eminent scholars, working independently in the 1870s and '80s, concluded that the seven letters of the middle recension were the authentic letters of Ignatius.[4] Most scholars accepted their judgment until 1979, when it was challenged, again by two scholars working independently: Robert Joly and J. Ruis-Camps.[5] However, William R. Schoedel, who has written the commentary on the letters of Ignatius for the prestigious Hermeneia series, has demonstrated, to the satisfaction of most reviewers, that the seven letters of the middle recension are indeed those written by Ignatius on his way to martyrdom during the last years of the reign of the emperor Trajan (115–17).[6]

Five of the churches to which Ignatius wrote were located in the Roman province of Asia, whose principal city was Ephesus. In that province the soldiers taking him to Rome made a brief stop in Philadelphia and a longer one in Smyrna. In each of these cities, Ignatius was able to meet the local community and its bishop. While in Smyrna, he received delegations from the churches of Ephesus, Magnesia and Tralles and wrote letters to those churches; he also wrote to the church at Rome. The group next stopped at Troas, where Ignatius learned that peace had been restored to his church of Antioch and where he wrote letters to the churches of Philadelphia and Smyrna, and to Polycarp, the bishop of Smyrna. This last is the only letter addressed to a bishop; all the others are addressed to the whole local church. (In referring to the letters, I shall use the following abbreviations: Eph., Mag., Trl., Rom., Phd., Smr., Pol.)

There has been much speculation recently about the nature of the trouble at Antioch. Previously it was thought that restoration of peace there marked the end of persecution by the Roman authorities that had condemned Ignatius and sent him to Rome for execution. However, Percy N. Harrison has argued that the church of Antioch must have been troubled by a schism at the time Ignatius departed for Rome.[7] Schoedel agrees with this conjecture, seeing in it an explanation for the expressions of self-effacement that occur in the letters. These would reflect the loss of self-esteem Ignatius would have suffered if he were to see the disunity of his church as a sign of his failure as its bishop.[8] Ignatius was certainly aware of the danger of schism in the churches he visited, and the major theme of his letters to them deals with maintaining unity with the local bishop. So it is not unlikely that these exhortations reflected his own experience of schism.

The letters of Ignatius of Antioch are very much worth reading in their entirety; however, the theme of this book and its limits demand the citation of only those passages in which Ignatius speaks of the ministry. As in the previous chapter, each citation will be followed by brief comments.

The Letter to the Ephesians

While Ignatius was in Smyrna he was visited by the bishop of Ephesus, Onesimus, along with the deacon Burrhus and several others of that church. He speaks of them in his letter to that community.

> 1:3 Since, therefore, I have received in God's name your whole congregation in the person of Onesimus, a man of inexpressible love who is also your earthly bishop, I pray that you will love him in accordance with the standard set by Jesus Christ and that all of you will be like him. For blessed is he who has graciously allowed you, worthy as you are, to have such a bishop. (2:1) Now concerning my fellow servant Burrhus, who is by God's will your deacon, blessed in every respect, I pray that he might remain with me both for your honor and the bishop's.

Comment

Onesimus is also the name of a slave Paul wrote about in his Letter to Philemon; however, it seems unlikely that this bishop is the same person. In using the term "earthly bishop" Ignatius implies that the church also has a heavenly bishop. Referring to the church of Antioch, Ignatius says that in his absence, God will be its shepherd and Christ will be its bishop (Rom. 9:1).

The term "fellow servant" means literally "fellow slave"—a term Ignatius used only in reference to deacons and St. Paul used to refer to his coworker Epaphras (Col 1:7). Ignatius seems to have felt an especially close bond with deacons, perhaps because they put themselves in a special way at the service of the bishop. This is reflected in his request that Burrhus be allowed to remain with him, on loan from the church of Ephesus.

> 2:2 May I always have joy in you, if, that is, I am worthy. It is proper, therefore, in every way to glorify Jesus Christ, who has glorified you, so that you, joined together in a united obedience

and subject to the bishop and the presbytery, may be sanctified in every respect.

Comment

This is one of several places where Ignatius associates the presbyters with the bishop as the leaders to whom the community owes obedience. As Schoedel remarks, "there is a strong collegial element in Ignatius's view of ministry, and the presbyterate is still very much alive."[9]

> 3:2 Since love does not allow me to be silent concerning you, I have therefore taken the initiative to encourage you, so that you may run together in harmony with the mind of God. For Jesus Christ, our inseparable life, is the mind of the Father, just as the bishops appointed throughout the world are in the mind of Christ.
>
> 4:1 Thus it is proper for you to act together in harmony with the mind of the bishop, as you are in fact doing. For your presbytery is attuned to the bishop as strings to a lyre. Therefore in your unanimity and harmonious love Jesus Christ is sung.

Comment

Most scholars now doubt whether in the time of Ignatius, bishops like him had been appointed "throughout the world." For instance, in his letter to the Philippians, written later than those of Ignatius, Polycarp speaks of the presbyters at Philippi, but makes no mention of a bishop. Schoedel comments that Ignatius "tends to shape the world about him in his own image."[10]

Note that the harmony of the presbytery with the bishop is clearly a key to the unity of the whole community. This is one of many passages in which Ignatius insists on the close association of the presbyters with the bishop.

> 5:1 For if I in a short time experienced such fellowship with your bishop, which was not merely human but spiritual, how much more do I congratulate you who are united with him, as the church is with Jesus Christ and as Jesus Christ is with the Father, that all things might be harmonious in unity. (2) Let no one be misled: if anyone is not within the sanctuary, he lacks the bread of God. For if the prayer of one or two has such power, how much more that of the bishop together with the whole church! (3) Therefore whoever does not meet with the congregation thereby demonstrates his arrogance and has separated himself, for it is written: "God opposes the arrogant." Let

us, therefore, be careful not to oppose the bishop, in order that
we may be obedient to God.

Comment

The word translated "sanctuary" is *thusiasterion,* the biblical word for
"altar" or place where sacrifice was offered. The context of the phrase
"within the sanctuary" suggests that the congregation gathered with the
bishop is being described as a sanctuary, where alone the "bread of God"
can be had. It seems likely that Ignatius was referring to the gathering of
the congregation with the bishop for the Eucharist. The use of the word
thusiasterion could suggest that the celebration of the Eucharist was seen
as the offering of sacrifice. We have already seen hints of this in the
Didache and in *I Clement.*

> 6:1 Furthermore, the more anyone observes that the bishop is
> silent, the more one should fear him. For everyone whom the
> Master of the house sends to manage his own house we must
> welcome as we would the one who sent him. It is obvious,
> therefore, that we must regard the bishop as the Lord himself.

Comment

Ignatius also refers to the "silence" of the bishop of Philadelphia (Phd.
1). He may have meant the gentleness and forbearance with which these
two bishops dealt with those who opposed them. Henry Chadwick suggests that the silent bishop should be all the more feared because he must
be regarded "as the Lord himself," and, for Ignatius, silence is an attribute
of God (cf. Mag. 8:2; Eph. 19:1).[11]

Here Ignatius applies to bishops a theme that in the Gospels refers to
the sending of the apostles, namely, that they are to be received as the one
who sent them (Matt 10:40; John 13:20). This shows that for Ignatius,
bishops are "sent" by the Lord. However, he nowhere explains this as
meaning that bishops participate in the mission given to the apostles, by
apostolic succession. In his view, bishops receive their mission directly
from the Lord.

The Letter to the Magnesians

While Ignatius was staying in Smyrna, he received a delegation from
the church of Magnesia, consisting of its bishop Damas, two presbyters
and a deacon. He refers to them in his letter to that community.

2:1 So, then, I was permitted to see you in the persons of Damas, your godly bishop, your worthy presbyters Bassus and Apollonius, and my fellow servant, the deacon Zotion; may I enjoy his company, because he is subject to the bishop as to the grace of God, and to the presbytery as to the law of Jesus Christ.

Comment

Here again Ignatius refers to a deacon as his "fellow slave." Like the rest of the community, the deacon is subject not only to the bishop but also to the presbyters (cf. Eph. 2:2). In being subject to them, he is really being subject to God and to Jesus Christ; their authority comes from above. He brings this out more explicitly in what follows.

3:1 Indeed, it is right for you also not to take advantage of the youthfulness of your bishop, but to give him all the respect due him in accordance with the power of God the Father, just as I know that the holy presbyters likewise have not taken advantage of his youthful appearance, but yield to him as one who is wise in God, yet not really to him, but to the Father of Jesus Christ, the Bishop of all.

Comment

The term "presbyter" literally means "an older man," and it seems likely that many Christian presbyters had the prestige of age as well as the authority of office. Hence it is remarkable that a young man should be the bishop to whom the elders must "yield." One would like to know by what process a young man would attain the office of bishop, but Ignatius does not enlighten us. He does, however, make it clear that the bishop receives his authority from the Father, the "Bishop of all."

6:1 Since, therefore, in the persons mentioned above I have by faith seen and loved the whole congregation, I have this advice: Be eager to do everything in godly harmony, the bishop presiding in the place of God and the presbyters in the place of the council of the apostles and the deacons, who are most dear to me, having been entrusted with the service of Jesus Christ, who before the ages was with the Father and appeared at the end of time.

Comment

This is one of two passages in which Ignatius describes the threefold ministry, linking the bishop with God, the presbyters with the apostles, and the deacons with Christ. (The other is Trl. 3:1.) That Ignatius describes the Father of Jesus Christ as the "Bishop of all" explains why he sees the bishop as the image of the Father. He apparently compares the presbyters with the apostles because of their structure as a council or college. There is no hint that he saw them as successors to the apostles. The association of the deacons with Christ can be explained by the fact that Jesus referred to himself as "one who serves" (*ho diakonon*: Luke 22:27; cf. Mark 10:45) and that St. Paul described Christ as the "minister *[diakonos]* of the circumcised" (Rom 15:8). The final clause provides a good example of Ignatius's "high christology," with its reference to Jesus Christ as having been with the Father "before the ages" prior to his appearing "at the end of time."

> Mag. 6:2 Let there be nothing among you which is capable of dividing you, but be united with the bishop and with those who preside, as an example and a lesson of incorruptibility. (7:1) Therefore, as the Lord did nothing without the Father, either by himself or through the apostles (for he was united with him), so you must not do anything without the bishop and the presbyters.

Comment

Twice in this passage Ignatius links the bishop with the presbyters; he undoubtedly refers to them when he writes of "those who preside."[12] Here we have another indication of the collegial element in the ministry as Ignatius described it and presumably also practiced it. It can hardly have been many decades since the churches of Syria and Asia Minor had been led by presbyters without any bishop presiding over them. It would seem that the transition to episcopal leadership had not deprived the presbyters of a considerable share of authority.

The Letter to the Trallians

During his stay in Smyrna, Ignatius had received a visit from the bishop of Tralles, Polybius, in whom he says that he had seen the entire Trallian congregation (1:1). He then wrote them a letter, exhorting them to unity with the bishop and the presbytery.

> 2:2 It is essential, therefore, that you continue your current practice and do nothing without the bishop, but be subject also to the presbytery as to the apostles of Jesus Christ, our

hope, in whom we shall be found, if we so live. (3) Further-more, it is necessary that those who are deacons of the "mysteries" of Jesus Christ please everyone in every respect. For they are not merely "deacons" of food and drink, but ministers of God's church. Therefore they must avoid criticism as though it were fire.

3:1 Similarly, let everyone respect the deacons as Jesus Christ, just as they should respect the bishop, who is a model of the Father, and the presbyters as God's council and as the band of the apostles. Without these no group can be called a church.

Comment

Once again he urges the community to be subject both to the bishop and to the presbyters. This is the only place where Ignatius speaks of the duties incumbent on deacons. His description of them as "deacons of the mysteries of Jesus Christ" probably refers to their role at the Eucharist.[13] This could explain his urging the Trallians to respect the deacons as Jesus Christ, just as they should respect the bishop as the image of the Father and the presbyters as the band of the apostles. There follows a distinctive thesis of Ignatian ecclesiology: "Without these no group can be called a church." He had no doubt about the structure a church ought to have, but there is reason to doubt that all the Christian churches of his day actually realized it.

The Letter to the Romans

This letter differs greatly from the others Ignatius wrote. While the others deal mainly with the unity of the local church under the leadership of its bishop and presbyters, Ignatius makes no mention of a bishop or presbyters in the letter to the Romans, nor does he include any exhortation to unity. Rather, he makes an impassioned appeal to the Roman community to do nothing to hinder his attaining the goal of martyrdom. Ignatius evidently thought some members of the Roman church had enough influence to get his sentence reversed, and he wrote to dissuade them from any such intervention on his behalf.

This is by far the best known of the letters of Ignatius, famous especially for his description of himself as "God's wheat, being ground by the teeth of wild beasts, that I might prove to be pure bread" (4:1). However, given its special theme, it does not have much to offer concerning the topic of the present book. We can draw no conclusions from the absence of any mention of a bishop of Rome in this letter, as the letter does not mention presbyters either, and it is hardly likely that Ignatius would have imagined that the church of Rome had no presbytery.

The salutation with which Ignatius began this letter has occasioned much debate about whether it means Ignatius attributed a primatial role to the church of Rome. While he began each of his letters with a greeting expressing his esteem of the church to which he was writing, the other letters have nothing resembling the language he used in greeting the Roman church.

> Ignatius, who is also called Theophorus, to the church that has found mercy in the majesty of the Father Most High and Jesus Christ his only Son, [church] beloved and enlightened through the will of him who willed all things that exist, in accordance with faith in and love for Jesus Christ our God, [church] which also presides in the place of the district of the Romans, worthy of God, worthy of honor, worthy of blessing, worthy of praise, worthy of success, worthy of sanctification, and presiding over love, observing the law of Christ, bearing the name of the Father, which I also greet in the name of Jesus Christ, Son of the Father; to those who are united in flesh and spirit to every commandment of his, who have been filled with the grace of God without wavering and filtered clear of every alien color: heartiest greetings blamelessly in Jesus Christ our God.

Comment

The debate has focused on Ignatius's use of the word *prokathemai* (to preside), which occurs twice: the church of Rome "presides in the place of the district of the Romans" and "presid[es] over love." Older Catholic scholars have seen here a recognition of the primacy of the church of Rome over the church throughout the Roman world; however, the word translated "district" *(chorion)* means a limited area such as a city or town. Love *(agape)* was sometimes used as a synonym for "communion," which in turn could mean the Christian community; hence some Catholic writers took "presiding over love" to mean "presiding over the whole church." However, scholars now generally agree that Ignatius attributes to the church of Rome a preeminence in charitable activity rather than a juridical primacy.

In his scholarly history of papal primacy, Klaus Schatz, S.J., sees in the extraordinary language Ignatius used in the salutation of his letter to the Romans testimony to the unique religious and spiritual significance the church of Rome was even then recognized to possess.[14] He sees this as the first step in the development of what eventually became a juridical primacy. It is also important to note the absence of any hint that Ignatius saw the preeminence he attributed to the church of Rome as in any way due to the status of the city of Rome as the capital of the Roman Empire.

The letter to the Romans is the only one in which Ignatius refers to himself as a bishop. The passage is as follows:

> 2:2 Grant me nothing more than to be poured out as an offering to God while there is still an altar ready, so that in love you may form a chorus and sing to the Father in Jesus Christ, because God has judged the bishop of Syria worthy to be found in the West, having summoned him from the East. It is good to be setting from the world to God, in order that I may rise with him.

Comment

When St. Paul was in danger of death, he had also spoken of the possibility of his being "poured out as a libation" (Phil 2:17). By saying: "while there is still an altar ready" Ignatius may have meant: "as long as nothing prevents my attaining to the goal of martyrdom."

"The bishop of Syria"—the Lightfoot translation has "from Syria," but the Greek has the genitive: "of Syria." Ignatius speaks of the church of Syria in the letters written from Smyrna (Eph. 21:2; Mag. 14; Trl. 13:1; Rom. 10:2). Only in the letters written from Troas, after he had learned that peace had been restored to his church, does he speak of it as the church in Antioch (Phd. 10:1; Smr. 11:1; Pol. 7:1). Schoedel suggests that his previous reticence may have been due to the painful memory of the state of schism in which he had left his church.[15]

The fact that Ignatius referred to himself as "the bishop of Syria" raises the question whether the church of Antioch was the only one in Syria with a bishop at this time. Ignatius hints at others in his statement that the "neighboring churches" (literally "the closest") had sent bishops to Antioch after peace had been restored there (Phd. 10:2).

The following passage of his letter to the Romans mentions the teaching role that church had exercised.

> 3:1 You have never envied anyone; you taught others. And my wish is that those instructions which you issue when teaching disciples will remain in force.

Comment

This may well refer to *I Clement*, which was a good example of how the Roman church "taught others." That letter had also blamed envy for the death of many Christians, including Peter and Paul (*I Clement* 5–6).

4:3 I do not give you orders like Peter and Paul; they were apostles, I am a convict; they were free, but I am even now still a slave. But if I suffer, I will be a freedman of Jesus Christ, and will rise up free in him. In the meantime, as a prisoner, I am learning to desire nothing.

Comment

This passage shows that Ignatius knew the tradition about the ministry of Peter and Paul in Rome, on which the prestige of that church primarily rested. It also attests to Ignatius's profound respect for the apostles, which he expressed elsewhere in his letters, for example, when he said: "I did not think myself qualified for this, that I, a convict, should give you orders as though I were an apostle" (Trl. 3:3).

9:1 Remember in your prayers the church in Syria, which has God for its shepherd in my place. Jesus Christ alone will be its bishop—as will your love. (2) But I myself am ashamed to be counted among them, for I am not worthy, since I am the very last of them, and an abnormality. But I have been granted the mercy to be someone, if I reach God.

Comment

The phrase "will be its bishop" translates the verb *episkopesei:* "will oversee it." This "oversight" will be exercised by the Father, by Christ, and by the *agape* of the Roman church. They will express their love through their prayers, which he requests; he hardly expects any direct intervention of the church of Rome in the affairs of Antioch.

Schoedel and other scholars attribute the very strong expressions of self-abasement Ignatius uses here to his sense of shame on account of the divided state in which he left his church. They interpret his eagerness for martyrdom as based on the conviction that through "reaching God" in this way he will be "someone" again.

The Letter to the Philadelphians

Before arriving at Smyrna, where he wrote the four letters just discussed, Ignatius had stopped for a briefer period in Philadelphia. There he engaged in controversy with some people causing division in that church by preaching Judaism. When he arrived in Troas, where he learned that peace had been restored to the church in Antioch, he wrote to the church of Philadelphia, exhorting it to maintain unity with its bishop, presbyters and deacons. Although in the body of the letter he speaks of the "division caused by certain people" (7:2), he begins his letter with a salutation that describes this church as "firmly established in godly harmony."

> Ignatius, who is also called Theophorus, to the church of God the Father and of Jesus Christ at Philadelphia in Asia, one that has found mercy and is firmly established in godly harmony and unwaveringly rejoices in the suffering of our Lord, fully convinced of his resurrection in all mercy, which I greet in the blood of Jesus Christ, which is eternal and lasting joy, especially if they are at one with the bishop and the presbyters and deacons who are with him, who have been appointed by the mind of Jesus Christ, whom he, in accordance with his own will, securely established by his Holy Spirit.

Comment

Ignatius more often speaks of deacons as worthy of respect; here he joins them with the bishop and presbyters as those with whom the community should maintain unity. He goes on to insist that all of these officials have been appointed in accordance with the mind and will of Christ and established by the Holy Spirit. Ignatius speaks only of the divine source of their office and authority; he makes no mention of the human process by which they were chosen or appointed.

> 1:1 I know that the bishop obtained a ministry (which is for the whole community) not by his own efforts nor through men nor out of vanity, but in the love of God the Father and the Lord Jesus Christ. I am impressed by his forbearance; he accomplishes more through silence than others do by talking.

Comment

Ignatius insists that the bishop (whom he does not name) has obtained his ministry *(diakonian)* from God rather than from men or through his own efforts. He uses language such as Paul used of his call to be an apostle (Gal 1:1). However, Paul was called directly by Christ; one presumes that there must have been some human involvement in the process by which a man came to be a bishop, but Ignatius gives us no information about how this happened. Could it have been simply that the community recognized someone as having the charism of leadership (cf. 1 Cor 12:28; Rom 12:8)?

Ignatius praises the bishop of Philadelphia for his forbearance and his silence. In the body of the letter it becomes evident that Ignatius himself would deal with opposition differently; he would "speak out with a loud voice" against "people who wanted to deceive him" (7:1).

> 3:2 All those who belong to God and Jesus Christ are with the bishop, and all those who repent and enter into the unity of the church will belong to God, that they may be living in accordance with Jesus Christ. (3) Do not be misled, my brothers: if anyone follows a schismatic, he will not inherit the kingdom of God. If anyone holds to alien views, he dissociates himself from the Passion.

Comment

Here we have an early expression of the doctrine usually attributed to Cyprian: "No salvation outside the church." Only in the unity of the church can one "belong to God and Jesus Christ." Schismatics will not inherit the kingdom of God; heretics will not profit from the Passion.

> 4 Take care, therefore, to participate in one Eucharist (for there is one flesh of our Lord Jesus Christ, and one cup which leads to unity through his blood; there is one altar, just as there is one bishop, together with the presbytery and the deacons, my fellow servants), in order that whatever you do, you do in accordance with God.

Comment

The sequence "one Eucharist, one altar, one bishop" shows that for Ignatius the unity of the church is profoundly rooted in the "one flesh and one cup" of the Eucharist and in the person of the bishop who presided at it. In his letter to the Smyrnaeans Ignatius will insist that only that Eucharist over which the bishop, or one designated by him, presides is valid (Smr. 8:1). In the reference to the "one altar" (*thusiasterion,* "place where sacrifice is offered"), we have another indication that the celebration of the Eucharist was seen as sacrificial worship; however, Ignatius uses no priestly terms in referring to the bishop. Here again he associates the presbyters and deacons with him.

> 5:1 My brothers, I am overflowing with love for you, and greatly rejoice as I watch out for your safety—yet not I, but Jesus Christ. Though I am in chains for his sake, I am all the more afraid, because I am still imperfect. But your prayer to God will make me perfect, that I may attain the lot by which I have received mercy, since I have taken refuge in the gospel as the flesh of Jesus and in the apostles as the presbytery of the church.

Comment

The word here translated as "lot" is *kleros,* whose original meaning is the lot one casts, and then came to mean the portion one obtained by lot and hence one's assigned destiny. (The Lightfoot translation has "fate" here.) Ignatius looks upon martyrdom as the "lot" the Lord has assigned to him.

Ignatius's assertion that he has received mercy because he has "taken refuge" in the Gospel and the apostles refers to the controversy he had at Philadelphia with Christians who were "expounding Judaism." Ignatius expressed his esteem also for the Hebrew prophets because "they anticipated the gospel in their preaching, and set their hope on Christ and waited for him, because they also believed in him" (5:2). His description of the Gospel as "the flesh of Christ" suggests his insistence on the reality of Christ's human body, passion and death, against the heresy of docetism.[16] The "gospel" is the "good news about Jesus Christ," which tells us that he really came "in the flesh" and truly died for us. More puzzling is the expression "in the apostles as the presbytery of the church." As we have seen, Ignatius several times associates the presbyters with the apostles, and I have suggested that he does so because they both constitute a "college" or "council." The description of the apostles as the "presbytery of the church" may mean that Ignatius sees the apostles in glory as exercising a permanent role as a council, caring for the welfare of the church on earth. That he "has taken refuge in them" could mean that he puts his trust in their heavenly guidance of the church.

> 7:1 For even though certain people wanted to deceive me, humanly speaking, nevertheless the Spirit is not deceived, because it is from God, for it knows from where it comes and where it is going, and exposes the hidden things. I called out when I was with you, I was speaking with a loud voice, God's voice: "Pay attention to the bishop and the presbyters and deacons." (2) To be sure, there were those who suspected that I said these things because I knew in advance about the division caused by certain people. But he for whose sake I am in chains is my witness, that I did not learn this from any human being. No, the Spirit itself was preaching, saying these words: "Do nothing without the bishop. Guard your bodies as the temple of God. Love unity. Flee from divisions. Become imitators of Jesus Christ, just as he is of his Father."

Comment

Here Ignatius claims to have had supernatural knowledge about the division in the church at Philadelphia; he did not learn about this from "human flesh" (cf. Matt 16:17: "flesh and blood has not revealed this to you"). He says he felt inspired to speak out in a prophetic way against those responsible for it: he spoke "with...God's voice" and "the Spirit itself was preaching." Speaking in a loud voice was also associated with prophetic speech (cf. Luke 1:41–42: "Elizabeth, filled with the Holy Spirit, cried out in a loud voice...").

So here we have an example of a bishop who manifested charismatic gifts. In this connection, one should also note that in writing to the Ephesians he spoke of his intention to write them a second letter in which he would further explain "the divine plan with respect to the new man Jesus Christ"..."especially if the Lord reveals anything to me" (Eph. 20:1–2). Did his charismatic gifts have a role to play in his appointment as bishop of Antioch? Might such gifts also explain how a young man, instead of one of the elders, was chosen as bishop of Magnesia? Ignatius gives us no help in answering these questions.

> 8:1 I was doing my part, therefore, as a man set on unity. But God does not dwell where there is division and anger. The Lord, however, forgives all who repent, if in repenting they return to the unity of God and the council of the bishop.

Comment

While schism would have been considered a grave sin, Ignatius assures the schismatics that repentance will bring them forgiveness from the Lord, if they "return to the unity of God." This no doubt means the unity of the church, which he has elsewhere described as a flock whose shepherd is God (cf. Rom. 9:1). The "council *[sunedrion]* of the bishop" is the presbytery, which Ignatius elsewhere says must be respected as *sunedrion theou:* "council of God" (Trl. 3:1). The call to return to the "council of the bishop," and not simply to the bishop, also indicates the collegial element in the leadership of the church as it is portrayed in these letters.

The Letter to the Smyrnaeans

The band of soldiers taking Ignatius to Rome allowed him to stay as a guest of the Smyrnaean church and its bishop for a considerable period, during which he wrote the first four of these letters. During the next, briefer stay at Troas he wrote a letter to the Smyrnaean community and another to

Polycarp, its bishop. While at Smyrna he had encountered people who "hold heretical opinions about the grace of Jesus Christ" and who "abstain from the Eucharist and prayer, because they refuse to acknowledge that the Eucharist is the flesh of our Savior Jesus Christ" (6:2). As one would expect, he exhorts the community to follow the bishop.

> 8:1 Flee from divisions, as the beginning of evils. You must all follow the bishop as Jesus Christ followed the Father, and follow the presbytery as you would the apostles; respect the deacons as the commandment of God. Let no one do anything that has to do with the church without the bishop. Only that Eucharist which is under the authority of the bishop (or whomever he himself designates) is to be considered valid.

Comment

We have already seen two passages (Mag. 6:1 and Trl. 3:1) in which Ignatius associates the bishop with God the Father, the presbyters with the apostles and the deacons with Christ. It remains unclear why the letter here says the deacons are rather to be respected "as the commandment of God."

That nothing "that has to do with the church [is to be done] without the bishop" obviously applies above all to the Eucharist, at which one would expect the bishop to preside. The Greek reads simply: "which is under the bishop," which no doubt means "over which he presides." The new note introduced here is that the bishop can also delegate someone else to preside. From the fact that Ignatius does not specify who could be delegated, James F. McCue has argued that we cannot be sure that only presbyters would have been eligible for this.[17] On the other hand, Ignatius does associate presbyters with the bishop as those who preside over the church (Mag. 6:2), and H. Legrand, from his study of the presidency of the Eucharist in the early church, has concluded that one who presided over the community would also preside over its Eucharist.[18]

> 8:2 Wherever the bishop appears, there let the congregation be; just as wherever Jesus Christ is, there is the catholic church. It is not permissible either to baptize or to hold a love feast without the bishop. But whatever he approves is also pleasing to God, in order that everything you do may be trustworthy and valid.

Comment

Here we have the first instance of the word "catholic" in extant Christian literature. The word *katholikos* in the Greek of that period meant "universal" in a variety of senses, and here the "catholic church," as contrasted with the local congregation, must be seen as the "whole church" or "universal church." The local church must be in union with its bishop, as the whole church is in union with Christ. The emphasis is on union with the bishop, apart from whom it is not permissible to baptize or to hold the *agape*. This was a congregational meal, associated with the celebration of the Eucharist (cf. 1 Cor 11:17–34). It seems that at Smyrna a faction led by a person with a "high position" (Smr. 6), (i.e., of leadership) may have celebrated separate celebrations of the *agape* and the Eucharist. Against such, Ignatius insists that what the bishop approves is pleasing to God and valid, thus applying the kind of divine sanction Jesus applied to decisions taken by the apostles (cf. Matt 16:19; 18:18) to approval by the bishop.

The Letter to Polycarp

During his stay at Smyrna, Ignatius came to know and esteem its bishop, Polycarp. He wrote this letter to him (the only one addressed to an individual) from Troas. He evidently expected Polycarp to read this letter to his congregation; in fact, much of the final section (6–8) addresses the whole community.

In the first five sections of this letter, Ignatius offers his advice to Polycarp as to how he should perform his duties as bishop. One gets the impression that Ignatius looked on Polycarp as less experienced than himself in dealing with the problems a bishop had to face, and he did not hesitate to tell him how he should perform his task. For this reason, this letter sheds a good deal of light on the ministry of a bishop as Ignatius understood it.

> 1:2 I urge you, by the grace with which you are clothed, to press on in your race and to exhort all people, that they may be saved. Do justice to your office with constant care for both physical and spiritual concerns. Focus on unity, for there is nothing better. Bear with all people, even as the Lord bears with you; endure all in love, just as you now do. (3) Devote yourself to unceasing prayers; ask for greater understanding than you have. Keep on the alert with an unresting spirit. Speak to the people individually, in accordance with God's example. Bear the diseases of all, as a perfect athlete. Where there is more work, there is much gain.

Comment

The exhortations to "[b]ear with all," "endure all," and "[b]ear the diseases of all" suggest the troubles Polycarp has had with those causing division in his church. The image of the bishop as a "physician" treating illness is developed more fully in the following section.

> 2:1 If you love good disciples, it is no credit to you; rather with gentleness bring the more troublesome ones into submission. "Not every wound is healed by the same treatment"; "relieve inflammations with cold compresses." (2) "Be as shrewd as snakes" in all circumstances, yet always "innocent as doves." You are both physical and spiritual in nature for this reason, that you might treat gently whatever appears before you, but ask, in order that the unseen things may be revealed to you, that you may be lacking in nothing and abound in every spiritual gift.

Comment

The repeated advice to treat people gently suggests that Ignatius had found Polycarp less than gentle in dealings with the "troublesome ones." His advice is expressed in well-known medical maxims, as well as in the gospel saying about imitating both serpents and doves (Matt 10:16). The last bit of advice here shows that Ignatius believed in praying for spiritual gifts, so that one might lack nothing and abound in every charism.

> 4:1 Do not let the widows be neglected. After the Lord, you be their guardian. Let nothing be done without your consent, nor do anything yourself without God's consent, as indeed you do not. Stand firm. (2) Let meetings be held more frequently; seek out everybody by name. (3) Do not treat slaves, whether male or female, contemptuously, but neither let them become conceited; instead, let them serve all the more faithfully to the glory of God, that they may obtain from God a better freedom. They should not have a strong desire to be set free at the church's expense, lest they be found to be slaves of lust.

Comment

This provides a fascinating glimpse into the pastoral ministry of a bishop in Ignatius's day. One major responsibility consisted of caring for the widows in the community. This also involved supervision of the community's funds to support needy widows. Evidently Christian slaves sometimes wanted some of these funds to pay for their freedom. Ignatius discouraged such a practice. It would also seem that Polycarp did not have community meetings as often as Ignatius thought appropriate; no doubt Ignatius saw them as a good way of strengthening the church's unity. The advice that Polycarp should "greet everyone by name" suggests that the community was not large; this would follow if the meetings were held in a private house, as was most likely the case.

> 5:1 Flee from wicked practices, better yet, preach sermons about them. Tell my sisters to love the Lord and to be content with their husbands physically and spiritually. In the same way command my brothers in the name of Jesus Christ to love their wives, as the Lord loves the church. (2) If anyone is able to remain chaste to the honor of the flesh of the Lord, let him so remain without boasting. If he boasts, he is lost, and if it is made known to anyone other than the bishop, he is ruined. And it is proper for men and women who marry to be united with the consent of the bishop, that the marriage may be in accordance with the Lord and not due to lustful passions. Let all things be done for the honor of God.

Comment

The advice to married persons echoes that of the Pauline Letter to the Ephesians (5:21–33). St. Paul had also recommended celibacy, so that one might be anxious "about the things of the Lord" and not "about the things of the world" (1 Cor 7:25–38). For Ignatius the motive is to "honor the flesh of the Lord," which perhaps meant to imitate Jesus' own celibacy. Ignatius was evidently much concerned that the practice of celibacy could lead to pride; perhaps he had witnessed the spiritual ruin to which boasting about it could lead.

In the letter to the Smyrnaeans, Ignatius had said: "Let no one do anything that has to do with the church without the bishop" (Smr. 8:1). Here he says to their bishop that those who marry should do so with the consent of the bishop. The logical conclusion is that marriage was considered to have something to do with the church. What the Roman world considered a merely secular event now received religious significance. It needed the consent of the bishop to assure that it was "in accordance with the Lord."

> 7:1 Since (as I have been informed) the church at Antioch in Syria is at peace through your prayer, I too have become more encouraged in a God-given freedom from anxiety—provided, of course, that through suffering I reach God, that I may prove to be a disciple by means of your prayer. (2) It is certainly

appropriate, Polycarp, (how blessed by God you are!) to convene a council that will be most pleasing to God and to appoint
someone whom you consider to be especially dear and resolute,
who is qualified to be called God's courier, commission him to
go to Syria, that he may glorify your resolute love, to the glory
of God.

Comment

In each of the letters he wrote from Troas, Ignatius urged that dele-
gates be sent to the church of Antioch, now that he knew that peace had
been restored there. Here he suggests how this should be done.
Polycarp should "convene a council" to "appoint someone whom you
[plural] consider to be especially dear and resolute...." This indicates
the collegial element in the exercise of authority in these churches. The
convening of a council and the use of the plural "you" make it clear that
the sending of a delegate is not an action of the bishop alone. While
Ignatius called the presbytery the "council *(sunedrion)* of the bishop"
(Phd. 8:1), the "convening" of a council *(sumboulion)* would suggest a
broader participation of the church in choosing the delegate and giving
him his commission.

I CLEMENT AND THE LETTERS OF IGNATIUS COMPARED

At this point it seems useful to compare the information about ministry gleaned from the letters of Ignatius of Antioch with that from the
letter of Clement of Rome to the Corinthians. We have to keep in mind
that, if the dates generally accepted by scholars are correct, Ignatius
wrote about twenty years after Clement did. The churches with which
they were familiar were located in different parts of the world: Clement
knew those of Rome and Corinth, while Ignatius knew those in Syria
and western Asia Minor. At a period when structures of ministry in the
Christian churches were developing, it is not surprising that, given the
differences in time and region, there would be differences between
the church of Corinth and the churches addressed by Ignatius of
Antioch. In recalling these differences, we must also note what they
have in common. I begin with the ministers who are found in the
churches of both of these regions.

Presbyters

At the time Clement wrote to the church of Corinth, it was led by a group of presbyters. In each of the churches to which Ignatius wrote there was also a council of presbyters, whom he described as "those who preside" and to whom he urged the deacons and the rest of the community to be subject. As noted several times, the role Ignatius attributed to the presbyters showed a strong collegial element in church leadership.

An important difference here is that Clement attributed to the apostles the appointment of the first local church leaders and saw the current presbyters as their successors, according to a rule laid down by the apostles themselves. In other words, for Clement, the presbyters' authority was ultimately based on the mission given by Christ to the apostles and handed down in regular succession.

In contrast to this, Ignatius nowhere invoked the principle of apostolic succession to explain the authority of presbyters. While several times he compared the presbyters with the apostles, just as he spoke of the apostles as the "presbytery of the church," the point of the comparison would seem to be the collegial structure they had in common. Ignatius gives no hint as to how local church leaders entered upon their office, whereas Clement says that initially they were appointed by the apostles and subsequently "by reputable men with the consent of the whole church."

Bishops

A major difference between Clement and Ignatius is that Corinth had no bishop presiding over the local church. Although Clement speaks of the church leaders appointed by the apostles as *episkopoi,* the word is in the plural, and there is no indication that Clement meant that the apostles had appointed one "bishop" for each church. On the other hand, he says that at Corinth several men who had "offered the gifts blamelessly" had been deposed from the office of *episkope.* From the rest of the letter it is clear that at Corinth, the group of presbyters, and not any one bishop, exercised the office of oversight. Most modern scholars think that in Clement's day the same would have been true of the church at Rome.

One reason a number of scholars have questioned the authenticity of the letters of Ignatius of Antioch is that they do not think that the episcopate could have been as well established as he describes by the second decade of the second century. Ignatius speaks of himself as the bishop of Syria and mentions the bishop of all the churches to which he writes, with the notable exception of Rome. For Ignatius, the episcopal structure of ministry was so essential that he could say that no group lacking a bishop could be called a church. He even described bishops as "appointed throughout the world" (Eph. 3:2).

Schoedel and other scholars who defend the authenticity of the letters admit that these last statements of Ignatius probably did not correspond to the reality of the church throughout the world in his day. Furthermore, they see in the urgency with which he exhorted the Christian communities to unity with their bishop an indication that the episcopal structure was not yet as firmly established as Ignatius wanted. On the other hand, they do not think it improbable that in Antioch and the region about Ephesus the episcopate could have been in place by the year 110.

Following scholarly opinion on the authenticity and dating of these letters, I accept their testimony that at least in part of the Roman world, by the second decade of the second century, each Christian church was led by a bishop, assisted by a council of presbyters. This structure certainly differs from that described in *I Clement*. But there is an even greater difference, in that for Clement, church leaders obtained their authority by being appointed in a succession going back to the apostles, whereas the notion of apostolic succession seems to have played no role in the thinking of Ignatius of Antioch. Rather, as he understood it, a bishop received his authority directly from God. He leaves us in the dark as to how a particular member of a church would come to be its bishop.

An intriguing fact is that a young man might be the bishop to whom the elders were expected to yield. Perhaps a person's charismatic gifts would single him out; Ignatius himself manifested gifts of knowledge and prophecy. In any case, we have to reckon with the fact that while Ignatius of Antioch is a major witness to the early development of the episcopate, he offers no support for the thesis that bishops receive their authority from Christ as successors to the apostles. He did not exclude it, but neither did he invoke it as an argument for what he so passionately promoted: the unity of the local church under the authority of its bishop.

7

POLYCARP, HERMAS, JUSTIN
AND HEGESIPPUS

THE LETTER OF POLYCARP, BISHOP
OF SMYRNA, TO THE PHILIPPIANS

We have met Polycarp as the Bishop of Smyrna whom Ignatius came to know during his stay in that city and to whom he wrote a letter from Troas. Like Ignatius, Polycarp suffered martyrdom, but many years later, about the year 156, when he was eighty-six years old. Irenaeus, the Bishop of Lyons, when writing his great work against the heresies around 185, tells us that in his youth he had met Polycarp, whom he venerated as a man who had known the apostles and had been appointed bishop of Smyrna by them.[1]

After leaving Troas, the soldiers taking Ignatius to Rome stopped briefly in Philippi, where the Christian community welcomed him. While there, Ignatius told them that peace had been restored to the church of Antioch and asked them to write a letter to his church, as he had asked the churches in Asia Minor to write and send delegations. Some time after Ignatius had left Philippi on the way to Rome (a journey that would take about six weeks), the Philippians wrote Polycarp a letter and sent it to him along with their letter to the church of Antioch, which they asked him to forward for them. In their letter to Polycarp, they also asked his advice as to how they should deal with a presbyter guilty of misusing community funds. We have his reply.

However, some have raised the question whether we have one letter or a combination of two letters: one composed of chapters 13 and 14, written only a short time after Ignatius had stopped in Philippi, and the other written about twenty years later, comprising chapters 1 through 12. The main argument for two letters is that in chapter 9 Polycarp speaks of Ignatius and his companions as already "with the Lord," but in chapter 13 he seems to speak of them as still living. Percy Harrison has also argued from the contents of chapters 1 through 12 that they must have been written no earlier than 135.[2]

A number of scholars accepted his thesis, but more recent commentators have not found it convincing. They solve the apparent contradiction between chapters 9 and 13 by observing that when Polycarp wrote, he could have presumed that Ignatius had reached Rome and been executed, but could still have been waiting for definite word about it.[3] Following this view, I shall treat it as one letter, written within the second decade of the second century. As before, I shall cite only passages that shed light on the ministry. The letter begins with the following salutation:

> Polycarp and the presbyters with him to the church of God which sojourns at Philippi: may mercy and peace from God Almighty and Jesus Christ our Savior be yours in abundance.

Comment

Polycarp associates the presbyters of his church with himself in writing this letter. He does not speak of himself as a bishop, but neither does he say "Polycarp and his fellow presbyters" *(sunpresbuteroi)*. In any case, Ignatius wrote to Polycarp as to a bishop like himself. The fact that Polycarp included the presbyters in his salutation suggests the persistence of the collegial element in local church leadership, which the letters of Ignatius also indicate.

Polycarp addressed his letter to the church that "sojourns" at Philippi. The Greek word *paroikousa* means "living in a place as a stranger, without citizenship," suggesting the idea that Christians "have their citizenship in heaven." He addressed himself to the whole community, without mention of its leaders. As we shall see, in the course of his letter he speaks of the deacons and presbyters of Philippi, but says nothing about a bishop.

> 3:1 I am writing these comments about righteousness, brothers, not on my own initiative but because you invited me to do so.

Comment

Evidently Polycarp thought it unfitting to give advice to another church unless invited to do so—in this respect he differed from Ignatius, whose letters abound in exhortations to other churches. We can reasonably surmise that the invitation came from the presbyters of Philippi, one of whom no

doubt must have been deputed to write the letter. The request for help indicates the fraternal relationship among churches, an expression of their
koinonia. Polycarp was invited to write "about righteousness"; the problem
at Philippi was not so much one of false teaching as of immoral conduct on
the part of a presbyter.

> 5:1 Knowing, therefore, that "God is not mocked," we ought to
> live in a manner that is worthy of his commandment and glory.
> (2) Similarly, deacons must be blameless in the presence of his
> righteousness, as deacons of God and Christ and not of men: not
> slanderers, not insincere, not lovers of money, self-controlled in
> every respect, compassionate, diligent, acting in accordance with
> the truth of the Lord, who became a "servant of all."

Comment

In the phrase "as deacons of God and Christ" the word *diakonoi* has its
original meaning as "servants"; so also "the Lord became servant
(diakonos) of all." That deacons should not be lovers of money suggests
that they have care of the funds used to provide for the widows and other
needy members of the community. The passage makes no reference to a
role of deacons in the liturgy.

> 5:3 Similarly, the younger men must be blameless in all things,
> they should be concerned about purity above all, reining
> themselves away from all evil. For it is good to be cut off from
> the sinful desires in the world, because every "sinful desire
> wages war against the spirit," and "neither fornicators nor
> male prostitutes nor homosexuals will inherit the kingdom of
> God," nor those who do perverse things. Therefore one must
> keep away from all these things and be obedient to the pres-
> byters and deacons as to God and Christ. The young women
> must maintain a pure and blameless conscience.

Comment

Whereas Ignatius called on Christians to be subject to the bishop as to
God and Christ and to the presbyters as to the apostles, Polycarp calls for
obedience to the presbyters and the deacons as to God and Christ. One
could hardly explain his not mentioning the bishop here if there were a
bishop at Philippi at that time.

> 6:1 The presbyters, for their part, must be compassionate, mer-
> ciful to all, turning back those who have gone astray, visiting all
> the sick, not neglecting a widow, orphan, or poor person, but

"always aiming at what is honorable in the sight of God and of men," avoiding all anger, partiality, unjust judgment, staying far away from all love of money, not quick to believe things spoken against anyone, nor harsh in judgment, knowing that we are all in debt with respect to sin. Therefore if we ask the Lord to forgive us, then we ourselves ought to forgive, for we are in full view of the eyes of the Lord and God, and we must "all stand before the judgment seat of Christ," and "each one must give an account of himself." So, then, let us serve him with fear and all reverence, just as he himself has commanded, as did the apostles, who preached the gospel to us, and the prophets, who announced in advance the coming of our Lord. Let us be eager with regard to what is good, and avoid those who tempt others to sin and false brothers and those who bear the name of the Lord hypocritically, who lead foolish men astray.

Comment

If one compares this description of the ministry of the presbyters with the exhortation Ignatius addressed to Polycarp concerning his ministry, one will see that here the presbyters have the same kind of responsibilities Ignatius attributed to Polycarp. Their ministry is clearly pastoral, and the description contains several indications that their role includes passing judgment on faults in the community. They are to avoid unjust judgment; they must not be quick to believe things spoken against anyone, nor be harsh in judgment; rather they must be compassionate, merciful, turning back those who have gone astray, ready to forgive. That the presbyters must "stay far away from all love of money" suggests that their care for the widows, orphans and the poor would involve being in charge of the common funds. The following passage shows that one of the Philippian presbyters had succumbed to the temptation this could involve.

11:1 I have been deeply grieved for Valens, who once was a presbyter among you, because he so fails to understand the office that was entrusted to him. I warn you, therefore, avoid love of money, and be pure and truthful. Avoid every kind of evil. (2) But how can a man who is unable to control himself in these matters preach self-control to someone else? If a man does not avoid love of money, he will be polluted by idolatry, and will be judged as one of the Gentiles, who are ignorant of the Lord's judgment. "Or do we not know that the saints will judge the world," as Paul teaches?[4] (3) But I have not observed or heard of any such thing among you, in whose midst the

blessed Paul labored, and who were his letters of recommenda-
tion in the beginning. For he boasts about you in all the
churches—those alone, that is, which at that time had come to
know the Lord, for we had not yet come to know him.[5] (4)
Therefore, brothers, I am deeply grieved for him and for his
wife; may the Lord grant them true repentance. You, therefore,
for your part must be reasonable in this matter, and do not
regard such people as enemies, but as sick and straying members, restore them, in order that you may save your body in its
entirety. For by doing this you build up one another.

Comment

"Valens, who once was a presbyter among you" indicates his removal
from his office, evidently as a consequence of his misuse of money belonging to the community. Presumably the rest of the presbyters had passed
this judgment on him, but since Polycarp addresses his letter to the community, it may well be that the whole community was involved in the decision to remove Valens from his office.

The question: "How can a man who is unable to control himself in these
matters preach self-control to someone else?" indicates that such "preaching"
was part of the duty of presbyters. Evidently Valens's wife must have shared
his guilt in the matter, as both are called to repentance. As a consequence of
their sin they have been cut off from the community; however they are to be
regarded not as enemies, but as "sick and straying members" and restored to
the body, so that it may be saved in its entirety. No doubt this advice as well as
his advice to the presbyters reflects Polycarp's own pastoral practice.

Summary

One can hardly avoid drawing the conclusion that the church of
Philippi, at the time Polycarp wrote this letter, was being led by a group of
presbyters, assisted by deacons, but without any bishop over the whole
community. If the absence of a bishop were merely temporary, as it was at
that time in Antioch, one would surely expect Polycarp to make some reference to this situation. Hence, it seems reasonable to conclude that in
the second decade of the second century, the structure of ministry at
Philippi resembled that of Corinth two decades earlier. From this we can
also conclude that the development of the episcopate took place sooner in
the churches of Syria and Asia Minor than in churches of Europe. We do
not know when the churches of Corinth and Rome began to be led by a
bishop, but we have good reason to believe that this did not happen there
any sooner than it did in Philippi.

THE MARTYRDOM OF POLYCARP

An authentic, eyewitness account of the martyrdom of Polycarp, which occurred around the year 156, is preserved in the form of a letter from the church of Smyrna to the church of Philomelium, written not long after the event. While I recommend reading the whole of this moving account, I shall cite only two passages, both of which refer to the reputation Polycarp enjoyed as a bishop: one expressed by his enemies, the other by his friends. The first is by his enemies.

> 12:1 As he [Polycarp] spoke these and many other words, he was inspired with courage and joy, and his face was filled with grace, so that not only did he not collapse in fright at the things that were said to him, but on the contrary the proconsul was astonished, and sent his own herald into the midst of the stadium to proclaim three times: "Polycarp has confessed that he is a Christian." (2) When this was proclaimed by the herald, the entire crowd, Gentiles as well as Jews living in Smyrna, cried out with uncontrollable anger and with a loud shout: "This is the teacher of Asia, the father of the Christians, the destroyer of our gods, who teaches many not to sacrifice or worship." Saying these things, they shouted aloud and asked Philip the Asiarch to let a lion loose upon Polycarp. But he said that it was not lawful for him to do so since he had already brought to a close the animal hunts. (3) Then it occurred to them to shout out in unison that Polycarp should be burned alive. For it was necessary that the vision which he received concerning his pillow be fulfilled, when he saw it on fire while praying, and turned and said prophetically to the faithful who were with him, "It is necessary that I be burned alive."

Comment

The expression "teacher of Asia" (referring to the Roman Province of Asia) shows that Polycarp was recognized, even by pagans and Jews, as the outstanding Christian teacher of that whole region. His teaching was undoubtedly heard not only by Christians, but also by others who were moved by it to renounce pagan worship and presumably embrace Christianity. Polycarp's pastoral role within the church is beautifully expressed by the term "the father of the Christians."

> 16:1 When the lawless men eventually realized that his body could not be consumed by the fire, they ordered an executioner

to go up to him and stab him with a dagger. And when he did this, there came out a large quantity of blood, so that it extinguished the fire; and the whole crowd was amazed that there should be so great a difference between the unbelievers and elect. (2) Among them most certainly was this man, the most remarkable Polycarp, who proved to be an apostolic and prophetic teacher in our own time, bishop of the holy [catholic] church in Smyrna. For every word which came from his mouth was accomplished and will be accomplished.

Comment

This passage highlights how Polycarp was esteemed by the members of his own church. Again the stress is on his role as teacher, with the added qualities of "apostolic" and "prophetic." "Apostolic" most likely refers to his fidelity to the teaching of the apostles, and perhaps to the fact that, having lived as a youth in the time of the apostles and their immediate successors, he was a preeminent witness to the apostolic tradition. His admirers also described him as "prophetic," which would seem to refer to his gift of prophecy, an instance of which is seen in his prediction of his martyrdom by fire.

In the phrase "bishop of the church in Smyrna," some manuscripts have "holy," others have "catholic." If "catholic" is the original reading, it would be the first known instance of this term being used in reference to a particular church. Because the word means "universal," its use here would probably mean that the church of Smyrna is in communion with "all the communities of the holy and catholic church sojourning in every place," which the writer greets in the opening sentence of this account.

THE SHEPHERD OF HERMAS

Hermas, a lay member of the Roman church who claimed to have had visions and received instructions from heavenly messengers, wrote this work to share what he had learned with his fellow Christians. The work consists of five visions, twelve mandates and ten similitudes (or parables). The heavenly messenger for the visions is the church, in the form of a lady who first appeared as elderly and became progressively younger. The messenger for the rest is a shepherd, hence the title for the whole. The primary message of the work is a call to conversion in an ecclesial context, that is, to a communal, ecclesial examination of conscience.[6]

While some scholars have attributed the writing of *The Shepherd* to several authors, most now generally agree that the work was written in Rome by one author during the first half of the second century and most probably over an extended period of that time. The *Muratorian Canon* (the earliest known list of New Testament and other Christian writings, composed about 200) indicates that Hermas wrote *The Shepherd* while his brother Pius was bishop of Rome (ca. 140–54). Most scholars think it likely that Visions 1 through 4 were written some time before the rest of the work, perhaps early in the second century. The great Alexandrian teachers, Clement and Origen, considered the book divinely inspired, and St. Athanasius recommended its usefulness for catechesis. While Tertullian strongly criticized it, many other patristic writers described it as an edifying but noncanonical work. I shall limit its examination to passages that throw some light on ministry at this period in Rome.

In Vision 2 Hermas says that the elderly lady had given him a little book to copy; later on the meaning of what he had copied was revealed to him. It included the following message:

> Vis. 2:2.5 For the Master has sworn by his own glory regarding his elect, that if sin still occurs, now that this day has been set as a limit, they will not find salvation, for repentance for the righteous is at an end; the days of repentance for all the saints are over, although for the heathen there is the possibility of repentance until the last day. (6) So speak, therefore, to the officials of the church, in order that they may direct their ways in righteousness, in order that they might receive the promises in full with much glory.

Comment

The Greek word rendered "officials" is *prohegoumenois,* which also appeared in *I Clement* 21:6. Literally it means "those who go before and lead the way"; both here and in *I Clement* it refers to the leaders of the local church. In both texts the word is in the plural; there was no one bishop at Corinth when Clement wrote, nor is there any indication of a single bishop in the church for which Hermas was writing.

> Vis. 2:4.1 As I slept, brothers, a revelation was given to me by a very handsome young man, who said to me, "Who do you think the elderly woman from whom you received the little book was?" I said, "The Sybil." "You are wrong," he said. "She is not." "Then who is she?" I said. "The Church," he replied. I said to him, "Why, then, is she elderly?" "Because," he said, "she was created before all things; therefore she is elderly, and for her sake the world was formed." (2) Afterwards I

saw a vision in my house. The elderly woman came and asked me if I had already given the little book to the elders. I said that I had not given it. "You have done well," she said," "for I have words to add. So when I finish all the words, they will be made known to all the elect through you. (3) Therefore you will write two little books, and you will send one to Clement and one to Grapte. Then Clement will send it to the cities abroad, because that is his job. But Grapte will instruct the widows and orphans. But you yourself will read it to this city, along with the elders who preside over the church."

Comment

A "high Christology" begins with the preexisting eternal Logos; here we have a "high ecclesiology" that begins with the church in the mind and purpose of God and views the eschatological church as the goal for whose sake the world was created.

The word rendered "elders" is *presbuteroi;* they are further described as "presiding *(proistamenon)* over the church." In each case the plural form is used; there is no indication of any individual presiding over the church. The role ascribed here to Clement corresponds to the role played by the author of the Letter of the Romans to the Corinthians; if Visions 1 through 4 were written early enough in the second century, it could be the same person. The message given to Hermas is intended for all the churches. Grapte is a woman who had the task of instructing the widows and orphans; one can recall that in Titus 2:3–4, older women were to "teach[ing] what is good" and "train younger women." Hermas is evidently not one of the presbyters, but is to read it along with those who preside over the church "in this city," generally understood to mean Rome. The structure of leadership here is clearly collegial, as we have seen it was in Corinth in the last decade of the first century.

In the third Vision, Hermas is shown an image of the church in the form of a great tower being built out of various kinds of stones. In answer to his request, the elderly lady explained the significance of these stones.

Vis. 3:5.1 "Now hear about the stones that go into the building. The stones that are square and white and fit at their joints, these are the apostles and bishops and teachers and deacons who have walked according to the holiness of God and have ministered to the elect of God as bishops and teachers and deacons with purity and reverence; some have fallen asleep, while others are still living. And they always agreed with one another, and so they had peace with one another and listened to one another. For this reason their joints fit together in the building of the tower."

Comment

The consistent use of the past tense in this section indicates that these "perfectly joined stones" are seen mainly as belonging to the past. This is clearly the case with all the apostles, as only some of those who have ministered as bishops, teachers and deacons are still alive. The Greek that is rendered "ministered as" uses the verb forms "who have exercised oversight, have taught and have ministered." The rest of this work contains only one other reference to bishops and one to deacons. Hermas several times refers to apostles and teachers of the past who preached the word of the Lord to the world (Sim. 9.15.4, 16.5, 17.1, 25.2). He also refers to teachers of his own day, some of whom he castigates as "teachers of wickedness"(Sim. 9.19.2), and as those who "wish to be teachers in spite of their folly"(Sim. 9.22.2). He also has some very harsh words to say about the "leaders of the church and those who occupy the first seats."

> Vis. 3:9.7–10 "…Now, therefore, I say to you officials of the church, and occupants of the seats of honor: do not be like the sorcerers. For the sorcerers carry their drugs in bottles, but you carry your drug and poison in your heart. (8) You are calloused and don't want to cleanse your hearts and mix your wisdom together in a clean heart, in order that you may have mercy from the great King. (9) Watch out, therefore, children, lest these divisions of yours deprive you of your life. (10) How is it that you desire to instruct God's elect, while you yourselves have no instruction? Instruct one another, therefore, and have peace among yourselves, in order that I too may stand joyfully before the Father and give an account on behalf of all of you to your Lord.…."

Comment

The elderly lady who personifies the church rebukes those who are called *prohegoumenois tes ekklesias* (the leaders of the church) and *protokathedritais* (those who occupy the first seats). The first of these terms carries no negative overtones, but the second recalls the *protokathedria* Jesus castigated the scribes and Pharisees for seeking (Matt 23:6; Mark 12:39.) It would seem that the leaders are guilty of divisions among themselves, which deprive them of peace. Part of their leadership role requires them to "instruct God's elect"; the term *paideuein* means not merely to teach doctrine, but to train, to educate. Presumably these officials are the same persons that Hermas has elsewhere spoken of as the "presbyters who preside over the church." This passage recalls the likelihood that within such a group there could be rivalry about the first place; it also points to the role of the leaders as educators of the faithful.

The shepherd who is the heavenly messenger in the second part of the book also has some very harsh words to say about certain deacons who abused their trust.

> Sim. 9:26.1 "And from the ninth mountain, which was desert, which had on it reptiles and wild beasts that destroy men, are believers such as these: (2) the ones with the spots are deacons who carried out their ministry badly and plundered the livelihood of widows and orphans, and profited themselves from the ministry which they received to carry out. If, therefore, they persist in the same evil desire, they are dead and there is no hope of life for them. But if they turn about and fulfill their ministry purely, they will be able to live."

Comment

This is the second of the two references to deacons in *The Shepherd*. It shows that deacons had the care of widows and orphans, and therefore of the funds with which the church supported them. In the letter of Polycarp to the Philippians we have seen how a presbyter also succumbed to the temptation this offered. In both cases, there was the possibility of repentance and forgiveness.

Having seen some negative comments by Hermas about presbyters and deacons, I conclude with a positive one about bishops. Here again the shepherd speaks.

> Sim. 9:27.1–3 "And from the tenth mountain, where the trees were sheltering some sheep, are believers such as these: (2) bishops, hospitable men, who were always glad to welcome God's servants into their homes without hypocrisy. And the bishops always sheltered the needy and the widows by their ministry without ceasing, and conducted themselves in purity always. (3) All these, then, will be sheltered by the Lord forever. The ones, therefore, who have done these things are glorious in God's sight, and their place is already with the angels, if they continue serving the Lord to the end."

Comment

This is the second of the two passages in *The Shepherd of Hermas* that mentions *episkopoi*. In both texts the word is in the plural and would be better translated as "overseers." As seen above, Hermas also used the plural when speaking of the *prohegoumenoi* of the church and of "the presbyters who preside over the church." "Leaders" and those who "preside" can also be described as exercising "oversight," so it is not improbable that these same persons may have also been called *episkopoi*. In any case, *The Shepherd of Hermas* has no reference to any one *episkopos* being in charge of the church for which he wrote, which scholars generally agree was Rome.

From the absence of any reference to one bishop and the several references in the plural to leaders and presbyters, most scholars now conclude that during the period this work was written, the church of Rome still had collegial leadership. Although the *Muratorian Canon* indicates that it was written while Hermas's brother Pius was bishop of Rome, *The Shepherd of Hermas* includes nothing that would confirm this assertion, whose reliability in any case has been questioned by a number of scholars.[7]

THE *FIRST APOLOGY* OF JUSTIN, MARTYR

St. Justin was born of Gentile parents in Samaria. As a young man he studied the Greek philosophers and became particularly attracted to Platonism. However, when he came to learn about Christianity, he recognized it as the true wisdom he had been seeking. Deeply impressed also by the heroism of the martyrs who willingly died rather than renounce their faith, he became a Christian himself and spent the rest of his life teaching this faith to others, especially in Rome, where he founded a school. He wrote his *First Apology*, or defense of his fellow Christians against the false accusations being made against them, in the form of a plea addressed to the emperor Antoninus Pius, about the year 155. He suffered martyrdom at Rome in the persecution of Marcus Aurelius, about 165.

One of the accusations made against Christians was that during their worship services they sacrificed an infant and ate its body. Because this was obviously a slanderous account of the Eucharist, Justin refuted it by giving a factual account of what happened when Christians gathered for worship. The following passage of his *First Apology* gives the earliest known description of the celebration of the Eucharist. Particularly important for this study of early ministry is what Justin says about the person who presided at the Eucharist. He described two celebrations of the Eucharist: one that followed the baptism of a new convert and the regular Sunday worship of the community.[8]

65. We, however, after thus washing the one who has been convinced and signified his assent, lead him to those who are called brethren, where they are assembled. They then earnestly offer common prayers for themselves and the one who has been illuminated and all others everywhere, that we may be made worthy, having learned the truth, to be found in deed good citizens and keepers of what is commanded, so that we may be saved with eternal salvation. On finishing the prayers we greet each other with a kiss. Then bread and a cup of water and mixed wine are brought to the president of the brethren and he, taking them, sends up praise and glory to the Father of the universe through the name of the Son and of the Holy Spirit, and offers thanksgiving at some length that we have been deemed worthy to receive these things from him. When he has finished the prayers and the thanksgiving, the whole congregation present assents, saying "Amen." "Amen" in the Hebrew language means "So be it." When the president has given thanks and the whole congregation has assented, those whom we call deacons give to each of those present a portion of the consecrated bread and wine and water, and they take it to the absent.

66. This food we call Eucharist, of which no one is allowed to partake except one who believes that the things we teach are true, and has received the washing for forgiveness of sins and for rebirth, and who live as Christ handed down to us. For we do not receive these things as common bread or common drink; but as Jesus Christ our Savior being incarnate by God's word took flesh and blood for our salvation, so also we have been taught that the food consecrated by the word of prayer which comes from him, from which our flesh and blood are nourished by transformation, is the flesh and blood of that incarnate Jesus. For the apostles in the memoirs composed by them, which are called Gospels, thus handed down what was commanded them: that Jesus, taking bread and having given thanks, said, "Do this for a memorial, this is my body"; and likewise taking the cup and giving thanks he said, "This is my blood"; and gave it to them alone. This also the wicked demons in imitation handed down as something to be done in the mysteries of Mithra; for bread and a cup of water are brought out in their secret rites of initiation, with certain invocations which you either know or can learn.

67. After these services we constantly remind each other of these things. Those who have more come to the aid of those who lack, and we are constantly together. Over all that we receive we bless the Maker of all things through his Son Jesus Christ and through the Holy Spirit. And on the day called Sunday there is a meeting in one place of those who live in cities or the country, and the memoirs of the apostles or the writings of the prophets are read as long as time permits. When the reader has finished, the president in a discourse urges and invites us to the imitation of these noble things. Then we all stand up together and offer prayers. And, as said before, when we have finished the prayer, bread is brought, and wine and water, and the president similarly sends up prayers and thanksgivings to the best of his ability, and the congregation assents, saying the Amen; the distribution, and reception of the consecrated elements by each one, takes place and they are sent to the absent by the deacons. Those who prosper, and who so wish, contribute, each one as much as he chooses to. What is collected is deposited with the president, and he takes care of orphans and widows, and those who are in want on account of sickness or any other cause, and those who are in bonds, and the strangers who are sojourning among us, and, briefly, he is the protector of all those in need. We all hold this common gathering on Sunday, since it is the first day, on which God transforming darkness and matter made the universe, and Jesus Christ our Savior rose from the dead on the same day. For they crucified him on the day before Saturday, and on the day after Saturday, he appeared to his apostles and disciples and taught them these things which I have passed on to you also for your serious consideration.

Comment

The Greek word translated as "the president" is *proestos*—a participial form of the verb *proistemi* that means "the one presiding." The first reference to him here (no. 65) further designated him as "the president of the brethren." We have previously cited H.-M. Legrand's judgment that in the early Church the one who presided over the community also presided at its Eucharist. Justin's description of the celebration of the Eucharist shows this to have been the case at Rome. The Greek phrase translated as "offers thanksgiving" could be translated literally as "makes Eucharist," as the word translated "thanksgiving" is *eucharistia*. The Greek word translated as "consecrated" (referring to the bread, wine and water) is the passive of the verb *eucharistein,* and literally could be rendered: "over which the prayer of thanksgiving has been said." The liturgical ministry of the deacons consisted of distributing the consecrated elements and taking them to those who are absent. A reader proclaimed the Scripture passages. There is no mention of presbyters.

The description of the Sunday liturgy gives further information about the tasks performed by the "president." After the readings have concluded, he exhorts the community to imitate the noble things they have heard. The collection for the poor is deposited with him, and it is his responsibility to care for all in need: orphans, widows, the sick, prisoners and visiting strangers. Justin concludes this enumeration by saying: "Putting it simply, he is the protector of all in need."

Justin does not use the term *episkopos* of this "president of the brethren," but in several particulars his role corresponds to that of bishops, such as Ignatius and Polycarp. Ignatius insisted that a valid Eucharist is one over which the bishop (or someone delegated by him) presides (Smr. 8:1). In writing to Polycarp, Ignatius described him as the "guardian of widows" (Pol. 4:1). This suggests he would have provided for orphans and other needy persons as well. And it is abundantly clear that Ignatius saw it as the bishop's task to teach the faithful and exhort them to a virtuous Christian life.

There is an interesting possibility that Justin may have actually seen Polycarp when that venerable bishop visited Rome. In a letter St. Irenaeus, bishop of Lyons, wrote to Victor, the bishop of Rome, he speaks of a visit that "the blessed Polycarp" made to Rome some years before, while Anicetus was the bishop there. In what is very likely an eyewitness account, Irenaeus tells of how, at the liturgy, Anicetus conceded the celebration of the Eucharist to Polycarp.[9] Polycarp must have visited Rome only a few years before his martyrdom, for Anicetus became bishop of Rome no earlier than 154 and Polycarp's martyrdom took place around the year 156.

Given the fact that Justin wrote his *First Apology* in Rome around 155, he might have attended the liturgy where Anicetus yielded the role of "presider" to Polycarp. Moreover, it is not unreasonable to think that the person whom Justin describes as "the president of the brethren" could actually have been Anicetus. In any case, it is certain from the letter of Irenaeus to Victor that, while Polycarp of Smyrna was still alive and about ten years before Justin himself was martyred, the Eucharist at Rome was being presided over by a bishop. We find further information about the bishops of Rome at this period in a passage of a work by Hegesippus, which Eusebius has preserved by citing it.

HEGESIPPUS

Hegesippus was a Christian writer concerned about the heresies that had sprung up in the second century. Seeking certainty about the true doctrine, he found the guarantee of sound teaching in the tradition handed down in the churches by the succession of bishops. Eusebius speaks of him as follows.[10]

> Hegesippus, in the five treatises that have come down to us, has left us a very complete record of his own opinion. In these he shows that he traveled as far as Rome and mingled with a great many bishops, and that he received the same doctrine from all. It is well to listen to what he said after some remarks about the epistle of Clement to the Corinthians: "And the church of the Corinthians remained in the true word until Primus was Bishop of Corinth. I associated with them on my voyage to Rome and I spent some days with them in Corinth, during which we were mutually stimulated by the true Word. And while I was in Rome I made a list of succession *[diadochen epoiesamen]* up to Anicetus, whose deacon was Eleutherus, and Soter succeeded Anicetus, and after him Eleutherus. In each succession *[diadoche]* and each city all is as the Law, the Prophets, and the Lord preach."

Rather than offer my own comment on this passage, whose meaning has engendered controversy between Catholic and Protestant scholars, I shall quote that of the eminent Protestant church historian, Hans von Campenhausen.[11]

> In the case of Hegesippus there is no reason to doubt that his pilgrimage for the purpose of ecclesiastical and theological study was very particularly aimed at helping in the fight against heresy. As one result of his investigations he records his conclusion that the Corinthian church has lived "in the right word" up to the time when Primus was bishop, and that the situation was just the same at Rome, where Soter "succeeded" Anicetus, and was himself succeeded by Eleutherus, that is, each took over from his predecessor in the succession of teaching and office. Hence, "in each succession *(diadoche)* and in each city things are as the Law and the Prophets and the Lord preach."[12] For Hegesippus the very fact of this unanimous agreement in doctrine is a sign that the doctrine in question is the original one. In addition, however,

he makes the attempt in some sort to demonstrate historically the existence of a continuous tradition. He refers to the unbroken chain of bishops, which guarantees the undistorted transmission of doctrine in all orthodox churches. In so doing he is not as yet bringing out a juristic or even a sacramental continuity, which might be capable of safeguarding the teaching office as such; he is thinking rather of the actual links between spiritual teacher and taught, by which a continuous tradition is established. That is why he lays particular emphasis as regards Rome on the fact that Eleutherus, who succeeded Soter, had already been Anicetus' deacon in the time of the latter's episcopate; for this shows that there did indeed exist here an unbroken progression in the teaching and handing on of the faith. Nevertheless, we can already discern in this passage how the word *diadoche* is beginning to change its meaning in an ecclesiastical direction. The intellectual continuity of a teaching succession becomes something like succession to the highest teaching office in the church, a succession which is maintained in each congregation, and which must be maintained in order that the existence of a living chain of tradition may be taken as proven.

What Hegesippus has to tell us of his own activities in Rome takes us even further in the same direction. He relates that while there he "made a *diadoche* as far as Anicetus." This sentence was regarded for a long time as hopelessly textually corrupt. To speak of a "succession" not merely existing but being "made" seemed intolerably harsh. Nevertheless, if one rightly reconstructs the historical and dogmatic significance of the concept, then this further extension of its meaning does not seem at all difficult to understand. Hegesippus wants to say not merely that he is asserting that there is a genuine continuity of teaching behind the bishops who hold office in his time, but that he has also proved it by compiling a complete list of the actual series of "transmitting" and "receiving" bishops. This demonstration of the succession or *diadoche* is now, therefore, itself termed a *diadoche,* and in this way the word acquires in this passage something like its later normal sense of "list of bishops." That while at Rome, Hegesippus did in fact do something of this kind, or cause it to be done, seems probable in the light of other indications....How Hegesippus went to work in detail on his task we can no longer say. There are no grounds for suggesting that the list is "faked." The names which he compiled will have been communicated to him by the clergy of the Roman church, and will naturally not have been simply invented for the purpose. They may, for the most part, have belonged to actual people who had at one time played a part in the life of the congregation, and of whom something was still known or thought to be known. That the writer of *I Clement* should be among them is natural enough. The order of the names in the list may, however, derive purely from Hegesippus himself, and the whole compilation is no more reliable than the memory of the Roman church at the time on the subject of the preceding hundred years or more, a memory which was unchecked then and which we certainly have no means of checking now.

Comment

When we combine this testimony with that of Irenaeus concerning the visit of Polycarp to Rome and with Justin's description of the celebration of the Eucharist there, we have good reason to conclude that by the time of Anicetus (155–66), the church of Rome was being led by a bishop whose role resembled that of Ignatius or Polycarp. How long before Anicetus this was the case is uncertain. If the *Muratorian Canon* is reliable on this point, Pius, the brother of Hermas, had been bishop of Rome, and in Irenaeus's list, he directly precedes Anicetus. However, *The Shepherd* gives no indication of the presence of such a bishop of Rome.

Arguing from the fact that the clergy of Rome could provide Hegesippus with the names of men who *at that time were thought of* as having succeeded one another as "bishops" of their church from the beginning, most scholars now conclude that these men must have stood out as the principal leaders and teachers in the Roman church. When the presbyters came together for a community celebration of the Eucharist, one of them must have presided, and most likely this would have been the presbyter recognized as the most competent leader and teacher. At what point in time the "presiding presbyter" began to be called a "bishop" and to be recognized as the chief pastor of the church of Rome, we do not know. It is certain, however, that by the time of Anicetus, that is, not long after the middle of the second century, this development had taken place in Rome, as it had in Corinth and in all the other churches Hegesippus visited on his way from the East to Rome.

Eusebius has not preserved enough of the writings of Hegesippus for us to know whether he described these bishops as "successors to the apostles." There is no doubt, however, that the preeminent Christian theologian of the second century, Irenaeus, the bishop of Lyons, recognized them as such. The next chapter will begin with some passages of his great work *Against the Heresies.*

8

IRENAEUS AND TERTULLIAN

IRENAEUS, BISHOP OF LYONS

From the fact that Irenaeus tells us that in his youth he had seen Polycarp, the bishop of Smyrna, one can conclude that he himself was a native of the Roman province of Asia. Like Hegesippus, he traveled from the East to the West. His writings contain enough ideas and phrases resembling those of Justin to suggest that he may have frequented the school Justin conducted in Rome. Irenaeus was probably in Rome at the time when Polycarp paid his visit to Anicetus, around 155, as his account of that visit suggests the presence of an eyewitness. It may have been at Rome that he became familiar with the teachings of the Gnostics Valentinus and Marcion; he mentions that both of these heretics were active in Rome during the episcopate of Anicetus (155–66).[1]

Irenaeus traveled to Gaul and became a presbyter of the church of Lugdunum (Lyons). While a presbyter, he was commissioned by that church to carry a letter to Eleutherus, bishop of Rome, telling him of the persecution that took place at Lyons in the year 177. On his return to Lyons he was chosen as successor to its martyred bishop, Pothinus. He wrote his work against the Gnostic heresies while Eleutherus was still bishop of Rome, hence no later than 189. From a letter he wrote to Victor, who was bishop of Rome from 189 to 199, we know that Irenaeus was still alive during the last decade of the second century. It is not certain when he died or whether he died as a martyr, although in the church calendar he is venerated as one.

His lasting memorial is the work *Exposure and Refutation of the Knowledge falsely so called*. Only fragments remain of the original Greek text; however, a complete and faithful Latin translation has been preserved, which is usually referred to by the Latin title *Adversus Haereses*.[2] I shall cite some passages of this major work that illustrate his understanding of the role the successions of bishops had played in the preservation and transmission of the genuine apostolic teaching. Against the claim of the Gnostics to possess a secret, more perfect tradition, known only to the elite of their group, Irenaeus appealed to the tradition handed down by the apostles and transmitted in the Christian churches by the bishops who succeeded one another as teachers down to his own day.

The Bearers of the Genuine Apostolic Tradition

III.1 For we learned the plan of our salvation from no others than from those through whom the gospel came to us. They first preached it abroad, and then later by the will of God handed it down to us in Writings, to be the foundation and pillar of our faith....

III.2 But when they [the Gnostics] are refuted from the Writings, they turn around and attack the Writings themselves, saying that they are not correct, or authoritative, and that the truth cannot be found from them by those who are not acquainted with the tradition....[3] But when we appeal again to that tradition which had come down from the apostles and is guarded by the successions of elders in the churches, they oppose the tradition, saying that they are wiser not only than the elders, but even than the apostles, and have found the genuine truth....What it comes to is that they will not agree with either Scripture or tradition. It is such people, my dear friend, that we have to fight with, who like slippery snakes are always trying to escape us. Therefore we must resist them on all sides, hoping that by cutting off their escape we may be able to bring them to turn to the truth. For although it is not easy for a soul which has been seized by error to turn back, still it is not absolutely impossible to put error to flight by putting the truth beside it.[4]

Comment

In contrast to the secret tradition the Gnostics claimed to possess, Irenaeus appealed to the tradition that came down from the apostles and was guarded "by the successions of elders *[per successiones presbyterorum]* in the churches." Irenaeus sometimes used the term "presbyters" when referring to men who had lived during or close to the apostolic period and were especially reliable witnesses to what the apostles had taught.[5] Here, however, the presbyters *by whose successions* the tradition was guarded in the churches are evidently those who have succeeded one another from the time of the apostles up to Irenaeus's own day. The following citation shows how Irenaeus also referred to these bearers of the apostolic tradition as *episcopi*. We shall see other examples of Irenaeus using the term "presbyters" of men whom elsewhere he called bishops.[6]

> III.3.1 The tradition of the Apostles is there, manifest throughout the world in each church, to be seen by all who wish to see the truth. Further we can list those who were appointed by the Apostles to be bishops in the churches and their successors to our own day. What they taught and what they knew had nothing to do with these [Gnostic] absurdities. Still, even if the Apostles had known hidden mysteries which they taught the "perfect" apart from the rest, surely they would have passed on such knowledge above all to those to whom they entrusted the churches. For they wished the men whom they designated as successors and to whom they left their teaching office to be perfect and beyond reproach in all things. So, if these men were to accomplish their task faultlessly, it would be a great gain, but, if not, the greatest disaster.

Comment

The key idea for Irenaeus is that the apostles entrusted the safeguarding and transmission of their message to those to whom they entrusted the care of the churches. The apostles handed on their own teaching office to those whom they left as their successors *[quos et successores relinquebant, suum ipsorum locum magisterii tradentes]*. Here Irenaeus uses the term "bishops" of those appointed by the apostles with this teaching office. Writing as a bishop himself, Irenaeus no doubt was aware of the many pastoral duties incumbent on bishops, but here he focuses on their role as transmitters of the teaching of the apostles.

The Apostolic Tradition of the Church of Rome

> III.3.2 But since it would be extremely long in a book such as this to give the succession lists for all the churches (we shall take just one), the greatest and most ancient church, known to

all, founded and established at Rome by the two most glorious Apostles, Peter and Paul. We shall show that the tradition which it has from the Apostles and the faith which it has preached to men, comes down to us through the successions of bishops. Thus we shall confound all who, in whatever way, either through self-satisfaction or vainglory, blindness or doctrinal error, form communities they should not. For every church, i.e. the faithful who are in all parts of the world, should agree with this church because of its superior foundation. In this church the tradition from the Apostles has been preserved by those who are from all parts of the world.

Comment

Rather than attempting to give the succession lists for all the churches—one can only wonder whether he could actually have done this—Irenaeus focuses on the church of Rome, which he describes as "greatest, most ancient and known to all, founded and established by the two most glorious apostles, Peter and Paul." Here we must acknowledge a bit of rhetoric, as the church of Rome was obviously not so ancient as those of Jerusalem and Antioch, nor was it actually founded by Peter or Paul. However, one could say that these two apostles had established the *greatness* of this church by giving their ultimate witness to Christ by martyrdom at Rome during the persecution of Nero. Thus they bequeathed to it the legacy of apostolic faith that the church of Rome had handed on through the successions of bishops. Note that whereas in a preceding passage he had described this transmission as done *per successiones presbyterorum*, here it is *per successiones episcoporum*. There can be no doubt that Irenaeus used these terms of the same persons.

The final sentence of this paragraph has generated much controversy. We do not have the original Greek; the ancient Latin translation runs as follows: *"Ad hanc enim ecclesiam propter potentiorem principalitatem necesse est omnem convenire ecclesiam, hoc est eos qui sunt undique fideles, in qua semper ab his qui sunt undique conservata est ea quae est ab apostolis traditio."* The English version I am using translates *propter potentiorem principalitatem* as "because of its superior foundation"; the French version in Sources Chrétiennes has *"en raison de son origine plus eccellente."*[7]

The terms "foundation" and "origin" are understood to refer to the apostolic source of Rome's tradition; it is "superior" or "more excellent" because of the preeminence of Peter and Paul among the apostles. Likewise, because the church of Rome has inherited the faith witnessed there by the martyrdom of the two greatest apostles, the faith of every other church must be in agreement with it. The final point states that the tradition from the apostles has been preserved in Rome "by those who are from all parts of the world." This would seem to refer to the fact that the Christian community at Rome was made up of people who had come there from all the provinces of the empire. That the language of the Roman church well into the third century was not Latin but Greek, the common language of the whole Mediterranean world, provides another indication of this.

The List of the Bishops of Rome

III.3.3   The blessed Apostles after founding and providing for the church, handed over the leadership and care of the church to Linus (the same one Paul mentioned in his letters to Timothy, cf. 2 Tim 4:21). Anacletus succeeded him. Next, in the third place from the Apostles, Clement received the episcopate, a man who had seen the Apostles themselves and had talked with them. He still had their preaching resounding in his ears and their teaching before his eyes. He was not the only one, of course. At that time there survived many who had been taught by the Apostles....To this Clement succeeded Evaristus; to Evaristus, Alexander, and then, sixth from the Apostles, Sixtus. After him came Telesphorus who gloriously suffered martyrdom. And then Hyginus; afterwards Pius, and after him, Anicetus. After Soter had succeeded Anicetus, then came Eleutherus who now holds the episcopate, the twelfth from the Apostles. By this order and succession, the tradition of the Apostles in the Church and the preaching of the truth have come down to us. And this is a most complete demonstration that one and the same life-giving faith which is in the Church from the Apostles until now has been preserved and handed down in truth.

Comment

The original Greek text of this passage has been preserved by Eusebius.[8] The phrase translated here as "the leadership and care of the church" is *ten tes episkopes leitourgian,* which literally means "the ministry of oversight" or "the episcopal ministry." According to Irenaeus, Peter and Paul, not Peter alone, appointed Linus as the first in the succession of bishops of Rome. This suggests that Irenaeus did not think of Peter and Paul as bishops, or of Linus and those who followed as successors of Peter more than of Paul. Irenaeus saw a clear distinction between apostles and bishops, even though he understood bishops as the "successors" to whom the apostles handed on their teaching office.

Irenaeus proceeds to give us the names of the twelve bishops who succeeded one another at Rome up to Eleutherus, during whose episcopate Irenaeus wrote his work against the Gnostics. While he does not tell us the source of his list, it may be based on the one Hegesippus had compiled a few years before, after he arrived in Rome during the episcopate of Anicetus. The passage of the work of Hegesippus that Eusebius has preserved for us does not give the names of the bishops prior to Anicetus, but presumably the list he compiled did have them. In any case, if Irenaeus's list is not the same one, no doubt it likewise depends on the memory of the clergy of Rome.

The remarks of Von Campenhausen cited in the previous chapter would apply equally to the list given by Irenaeus.[9] What I said there about Hegesippus's list would also apply to that of Irenaeus, namely, given the fact that toward the end of the second century the clergy of Rome could provide the names of the men who *at that time were thought of* as having been the past bishops of their church, we can conclude that they remembered these men as the principal leaders and teachers among the Roman presbyters. At what point in time the leading presbyters in Rome began to be called "bishops" remains unknown.

Irenaeus's Tribute to Polycarp of Smyrna

III.3.4 And Polycarp also, who not only was taught by the Apostles and lived with many of those who had seen our Lord, but was also made bishop of the Church of Smyrna by the Apostles in Asia, this very man we once saw in our childhood. He lived a long life and as a very old man most gloriously and nobly suffered martyrdom, departing this life. He always taught these things and that they alone are the truth. All the churches in Asia and those who up until now have succeeded Polycarp bear witness to these (teachings). Polycarp was a much greater authority and more faithful witness to the truth than Valentinus and Marcion and all the other teachers of perverse doctrines. For when Polycarp, in the time of Anicetus, came to Rome, by his preaching he brought back many of the heretics to the Church of God, proclaiming that he had received from the Apostles one truth and one only, the very same which he himself passed on to the Church....There is also the church at Ephesus, founded by Paul, where John remained up until the time of Trajan, a true witness to the tradition of the Apostles.

Comment

Whereas Irenaeus had to rely on the memory of the clergy of Rome for the list of their earlier bishops, he relied on his own memory with regard to Polycarp, having actually seen that venerable bishop in Smyrna during his early youth. One wonders why he said Polycarp had been made bishop of Smyrna "by the apostles" rather than saying "by John," as Tertullian would later do.[10] The presbyters who wrote of the martyrdom of Polycarp described him as an "apostolic teacher," but the letter of Ignatius to Polycarp makes no mention of his having been appointed by an apostle. However, having served as bishop of Smyrna through the first half of the second century, he was indeed an extraordinary link with the apostolic period.

Irenaeus also invokes the church of Ephesus, bringing out the idea that the church itself, founded by Paul and holding the memory of John, remains as a "true witness to the tradition of the apostles."

IV.26.2 Wherefore you must listen to those who are elders in the Church, those who hold the succession from the Apostles, as we have shown, who, together with the succession of the episcopate, have received the certain charism of truth in accord with the Father's will. But the rest, those who depart from the original succession and gather apart— these must be considered suspect either of being heretics, or of wrong ideas, or as schismatics, proud and self-satisfied, or as hypocrites working for money or fame. All of these stray from the truth.[11]

Comment

This provides a striking example of how Irenaeus could speak of "elders" (presbyteris) as having the succession of the episcopate. Furthermore, along with the episcopate they have received "the certain charism of truth" (charisma veritatis certum). Some have understood this as a "charismatic gift" by which bishops would be assured of holding to the truth. Others, though, think Irenaeus was describing the gospel truth itself as the charisma certum or "assured gift," which the successors of the apostles were handing on in the church.[12] In any case, Irenaeus insisted that only by listening to those who maintained this "original succession" could one be sure of hearing the truth taught by the apostles.

THE LETTER OF IRENAEUS TO VICTOR, BISHOP OF ROME

While Irenaeus was bishop of Lyons, he wrote a letter to Victor, bishop of Rome from 189 to 199. It is quoted by Eusebius, who also explained the circumstances that led to its composition.[13] Prior to the Council of Nicaea (325) there were two different Christian traditions concerning the day Easter should be celebrated. The churches of the province of Asia (Ephesus, Smyrna, etc.) celebrated Easter on the fourteenth day of the lunar month of Nisan, that is, on the day of the Jewish Passover. Obviously, this day would not always be a Sunday. The church of Rome and most others celebrated Easter on the following Sunday. Thus some Christians would still be fasting, while others were celebrating Easter.

The problem surrounding the date of Easter became acute in the church of Rome, which, as noted above, consisted of people "from everywhere." It seems that within the Christian community at Rome some people from the province of Asia maintained their tradition of celebrating Easter on the 14th of Nisan, thus dividing the church of Rome at Easter time. Bishop Victor not only imposed uniform practice in Rome, but tried to get Easter observed on Sunday everywhere. For this purpose, he urged bishops in other regions to hold synods to discuss this issue and to adopt the Roman custom if they did not already follow it.

According to Eusebius, only the churches of the province of Asia insisted on maintaining their tradition of celebrating Easter on the 14th of Nisan. He quotes a letter that Polycrates, the bishop of Ephesus, wrote to Victor, declaring that the bishops of his region were determined to maintain their tradition about Easter on the grounds that it was equally apostolic as that of Rome. Victor responded by threatening to cut off those churches from communion with Rome. The prospect of a break of communion between the church of Rome and the churches of his native region led Irenaeus to write to Victor, urging him not to take such a drastic step.

The following passage of his letter was quoted by Eusebius.[14] In reading it, one must note that when he said "observe," he meant "observe the 14th of Nisan as the day of Easter." Irenaeus based his argument on the fact that Victor's predecessors had maintained communion with those who insisted on following the tradition of celebrating Easter on the day of the Jewish Passover.

> Among those, too, were the presbyters before Soter, who presided over the Church which you now rule: we mean Anicetus and Pius and Telesphorus and Xystus. Neither did they themselves observe, nor did they enjoin it upon their followers; nevertheless, although not observing it them- selves, they were at peace with those who came to them from dioceses in which it was observed, although to observe it was more objectionable to those who did not do so. Yet, never were any cast out because of this form, and the pres- byters themselves before you sent the Eucharist to those from other dioceses who did; and when the blessed Polycarp sojourned in Rome in the time of Anicetus, although they had small difficulties about certain other matters, they immediately made peace, having no desire for strife among themselves on this outstanding question. Neither was Anicetus able to persuade Polycarp not to observe it, inas- much as Polycarp had always observed it, together with John the disciple of our Lord and the other Apostles with whom he had lived; nor, on the other hand, did Polycarp persuade Anicetus to observe it, for Anicetus said that he was obliged to cling to the practice of those who were pres- byters before him. And under these conditions they com- municated with each other, and in the church Anicetus conceded the celebration of the Eucharist to Polycarp, obvi- ously out of respect for him, and they departed from each other peacefully, for they maintained the peace of the entire Church, both those who observed and those who did not.

Comment

The episode that occasioned Irenaeus's letter has given rise to a great deal of controversy because of its obvious importance for any account of the origin and early history of the Roman primacy. In this book I am obvi- ously concerned with the development of the Roman episcopate, which is a basic premise of the primacy of the bishops of Rome, but it would require a volume of equal or greater length to deal with the development of the primacy itself. Hence, I shall offer only one comment about the action taken by Pope Victor.

As seen above, Irenaeus insisted that every church must agree with the church of Rome because of its "superior foundation" or "more excellent origin." He meant that just as every church must be in agreement with the teaching of Peter and Paul, so every church must agree in faith with the church that has inherited the teaching of those greatest of the apostles and has continued to hand it on in an unbroken succession of teachers. Victor's action in the Easter controversy shows that he also held that "every church must be in agreement with the church of Rome," but for him that evidently meant not only agreement in faith but uniformity in practice as well. Irenaeus insisted such uniformity was unnecessary; Victor's predecessors had not required it, nor should Victor.

Irenaeus's Use of the Term "Presbyter"

It is noteworthy that each time Irenaeus referred to Victor's predecessors in this letter, he spoke of them as "presbyters" rather than as "bishops." The Greek of the first sentence above could more literally be translated: "And those presbyters before Soter who presided over the church of which you now have the leadership...." Irenaeus was referring to a succession of individuals who had presided over the church of Rome, who at least from the time of Anicetus (155–66) were bishops whose leadership was comparable to that exercised by Polycarp in Smyrna. And yet, in this letter Irenaeus called them presbyters. One wonders whether his choice of the term, which literally means "elders," might have been influenced by the fact that he was invoking the example set by past bishops of the church of Rome, whom Victor ought to respect as his "elders." A similar reason might account for the fact that while Irenaeus certainly thought of Polycarp as a bishop, he could also refer to him as "that blessed and apostolic presbyter."[15]

In any case, Irenaeus, writing late in the second century, still thought it acceptable to refer to bishops as "presbyters." Yet by his time there was certainly a difference between them. Irenaeus himself had been a presbyter of the church of Lyons before he became its bishop. The fact that he still spoke of the bishops of Rome as "presbyters" would seem to confirm the hypothesis that Clement and the others in the earlier part of Irenaeus's list had really been members of the college of presbyters, but were remembered as the outstanding leaders and teachers of their time. Toward the end of the century it was normal enough to think of them as bishops from the beginning, but the fact that Irenaeus still called them presbyters fits in with what we have learned from Clement and Hermas about the earlier collegial leadership of the Roman church.

TERTULLIAN

Q. Septimius Florens Tertullianus was born between 155 and 165 of well-to-do pagan parents in Carthage, North Africa. He received a good education in Latin and Greek literature, most likely in the schools of Carthage, although he may also have studied at Rome. His writings manifest a knowledge of Roman law, but not such as one might expect of a professional jurist. He became a Christian around the year 194, possibly influenced by the courage of Christian martyrs, and his writings date from 196 to 220. He is the first Christian known to have written his works in Latin. According to St. Jerome, Tertullian was ordained a presbyter, but this can hardly be correct, for Tertullian includes himself among the laity who share in the common priesthood.[16]

Tertullian's writings are divided between those of his fully Catholic period (196–206) and those showing the influence of his adherence to the "New Prophecy" or Montanism. This movement began around 173 in Phrygia, Asia Minor, where a certain Montanus and two women disciples of his began to utter prophecies in a state of ecstasy. Claiming to be spokespersons for the Paraclete, they predicted an imminent end of the world and called for more rigid standards of morality than currently observed in the Christian churches of their day. In particular they declared that the Paraclete restricted the forgiveness of grave sins to God, denying to the Church or its bishops the power to absolve them.

From the time of his conversion to Christianity Tertullian manifested a tendency to rigorism, and this probably attracted him to the "New Prophecy." In his later writings he became more and more critical of the Catholic bishops for claiming to absolve those repenting of such sins as adultery and fornication. He also castigated Catholic clergy who fled during times of persecution and who failed in other respects to live up to a strict code of morality. It must be noted, however, that Tertullian remained orthodox in regard to the basic Christian dogmas, and while he rejected some claims made by the Catholic bishops, there is no evidence that he ever left the Catholic Church to join or found a schismatic one.

Tertullian on Apostolic Tradition

We shall begin the discussion of his writings by quoting some passages from two of his works against heretics: one from his Catholic period, and the other from his Montanist period. In both of these he argued that genuine apostolic tradition was only that which had been handed down in the apostolic churches.

De Praescriptione Haereticorum

The first work discussed here has the title: "On the Prescription against the Heretics." "Prescription" is a legal term, of which the closest modern equivalent is "demurrer." It is a preliminary objection that denies to an opponent the right to introduce a certain kind of evidence in presenting his case. In this work of his Catholic period, Tertullian argued against the Gnostics, who claimed to support their tenets from the Scriptures. His "preliminary objection" held that the heretics have no right to argue their case from the Scriptures; the Scriptures are the exclusive property of the apostolic churches, in which the teaching of the apostles has been faithfully handed on by a succession of bishops who are the rightful successors of the apostles. As one can see, the argument is essentially the same one used by Irenaeus, but Tertullian has his own distinctive way of presenting it.

> 15.3–4 Here, then, is where I draw the line: these people are not to be admitted to any discussion of the Scriptures in the first place. If the Scriptures are their strong point, as long as they can get at them, we must look into the question of who properly possess the Scriptures, lest some who have no right be allowed access to them.[17]

> 21 On this basis, therefore, we draw up our prescription: if the Lord Jesus Christ sent the apostles to preach, no others ought to be received as preachers than those whom Christ appointed, for "no one knows the Father save the Son, and he to whom the Son will reveal Him." Nor does the Son seem to have revealed Him to any other than the apostles, whom He sent forth to preach just that which he revealed to them. Now, what that was which they preached—in other words, what it was that Christ revealed to them—can, as I must likewise pre-scribe, properly be proved in no other way than by those very churches which the apostles founded in person, by declaring the gospel to them directly themselves, both *viva voce*, as the phrase is, and subsequently by their epistles. If, then, these things are so, it is in the same degree manifest that all doctrine which agrees with the apostolic churches—those molds and original sources of the faith—must be reckoned for truth, as

undoubtedly containing that which the churches received from the apostles, the apostles from Christ, Christ from God. Whereas all doctrine must be prejudged as false which savours of contrariety to the truth of the churches and apostles of Christ and God. It remains, then, that we demonstrate whether this doctrine of ours, of which we have now given the rule, has its origin in the tradition of the apostles, and whether all other doctrines do not *ipso facto* proceed from falsehood. We hold communion with the apostolic churches because our doctrine is in no respect different from theirs. This is our witness to the truth.[18]

Comment

It seems likely that Tertullian was familiar with the Letter of Clement to the Corinthians. In any case, his sequence: "God–Christ–the apostles–apostolic churches" is obviously reminiscent of Clement's: "God–Christ–apostles–bishops."[19] However, it is noteworthy that Tertullian emphasizes the apostolic churches as reliable witnesses to what the apostles taught, rather than bishops as successors to the apostles. His proof that the Catholic churches of his day remained faithful to apostolic doctrine consisted of the assertion that they were in communion with churches known to have been founded by the apostles.

> 32   If any heresies claim to plant themselves in the age of the apostles in order to make it seem that their ideas were handed down by the apostles because they existed under the apostles, we can say: Let them show the origins of their churches, let them unroll the list of their bishops, (showing) through a succession coming from the very beginning, that their first bishop had as his authority and predecessor someone from among the number of the apostles or apostolic men and, further, that he did not stray from the apostles. In this way the apostolic churches present their earliest records. The church of Smyrna, for example, records that Polycarp was named by John; the church of the Romans, that Clement was ordained by Peter. In just the same way, the other churches show who were made bishops by the apostles and who transmitted the apostolic seed to them. Let the heretics try to invent something like that. But after their blasphemy, nothing is beyond them. Even if they can come up with something, it will do them no good. Their very teaching, when compared with that of the apostles, from its diversity and internal contradictions, will show itself for

what it is—that it has no apostle or apostolic man at its origins because just as the apostles did not contradict each other in their teachings, so the next generation taught nothing contrary to what the apostles had preached, unless, of course, you believe that they preached something different from what they had learned from the apostles. This is how they will be challenged by those churches which cannot historically claim as founder either an apostle or an apostolic man because they came much later. New churches are still being founded every day. Since they are in agreement on the faith, they are to be considered no less apostolic because of their kinship in doctrine. Thus let all heresies challenged by our churches to furnish this two-fold proof show for what reasons they consider themselves apostolic. But in fact they are not apostolic. They are not received into peace and communion by churches that are in any way apostolic, because the diversity of their teaching proves that they are in no way apostolic.[20]

Comment

Tertullian's argument took for granted that the apostles and "apostolic men" who founded churches had left bishops in charge of them and that the bishops of his day were the successors of those original bishops. It seems evident that he did not consider this a matter of controversy. Rather, he wished to prove that the Catholic churches of his day could rightly claim to be apostolic on the grounds that they could do what the heretical sects could not do: namely, "unroll the list of their bishops, showing through a succession coming from the very beginning, that their first bishop had as his authority and predecessor someone from among the number of the apostles or apostolic men."

Here again his argument focused on the apostolicity of the Catholic churches, proven by the fact that they could provide a list of their bishops going back from the present incumbent to one appointed by an apostle or by an "apostolic man." The fact that three times in this section Tertullian refers to "apostolic men," along with apostles, as founders of apostolic churches would seem to confirm what we have said earlier about the coworkers of the apostles as their immediate successors in the task of founding churches and overseeing their further growth. One might also compare Tertullian's "apostolic men" with the "eminent men" who, according to Clement, appointed the second generation of church leaders.

Tertullian, of course, was aware of the fact that some Catholic churches could not trace their list of bishops back to apostolic times, simply because they had been founded more recently. However, these also had a valid claim to apostolicity: They shared the same faith with the churches founded by apostles and were in full communion with them. Here was another proof the heretics could not match. He now goes on to mention some of the more important of the apostolic churches.

> 36   Well then, if you wish to make better use of your curiosity in the business of your salvation, go to visit the apostolic churches, those places where the chairs of the apostles even now preside in their places, where their authentic letters are still read, bringing back to us how they sounded and how they looked. If Achaea is close by, you have Corinth. If you are not far from Macedonia, you have Philippi. If you can go to Asia, there is Ephesus. If you are in the vicinity of Italy, you have Rome, whence [apostolic] authority came also to us.[21] Blessed is that church upon which the apostles poured out their entire teaching along with their blood. This is where Peter suffered like his Lord; where Paul was crowned with John (the Baptist's) death and where John the Apostle, after having been plunged into boiling oil but suffering no ill effects, was exiled to an island.

Comment

"[W]here the chairs of the apostles even now preside"—In the ancient world teaching was done sitting down, and a ruler would be seated on a throne; hence the chair was the symbol of teaching and presiding. Tertullian's reference to the "chairs of the apostles" as "even now presiding" would seem to mean that the teaching and ruling authority of the apostles has been inherited by the bishops who now preside in apostolic churches.

"Blessed is that church upon which the apostles poured out their entire teaching along with their blood."—Here Tertullian echoes Irenaeus in ascribing the preeminence of the church of Rome to the fact that the apostles had not only taught there but had confirmed their teaching with the ultimate witness of martyrdom. Both Irenaeus and Tertullian based the greatness of Rome on its association not with Peter alone but with both Peter and Paul; Tertullian adds the witness of John the apostle as well.[22]

Adversus Marcionem

In his work *Against Marcion*, Tertullian again appealed to the authority of the apostolic churches and once more invoked the special authority of the church of Rome. He wrote this during his Montanist period and despite his adherence to the "New Prophecy," he did not change his conviction that the truth of the Gospel had been faithfully handed down in the church of Rome and the other churches that could trace their origin back to the apostles. We can see in the following passage how he developed this argument against the Gnostic Marcion, who had rejected three Gospels and retained only a mutilated version of the Gospel of Luke.[23]

> *Adv. Marc.* IV.5 In fine, if it is a fact that what is earlier has a greater claim to be the truth, and that which comes from the beginning is necessarily the earlier, what was from the beginning comes from the Apostles. So it will be agreed that what has been held most sacred in the churches founded by the Apostles is that which has been handed down from the Apostles themselves. Let us see what milk the Corinthians were given to drink by Paul, to what rule the Galatians were recalled, what the Philippians, Thessalonians and Ephesians read, what the Romans who are nearest (of all these) to us have to say, they to whom Peter and Paul bequeathed their Gospel signed in their own blood. We also have churches founded by John; for although Marcion repudiates the Apocalypse, the list of their bishops traced backwards will be found to have John at the beginning. Just so is the pedigree of all the others known. Thus I say among them—not just those founded by Apostles but among all those united in the communion of the mysteries, that the Gospel of Luke has existed since its first appearance, whereas Marcion's Gospel is unknown to most, but those who know it, condemn it....The same authority of the apostolic churches will support the other Gospels as well....We use this type of summary argument when we defend the Gospel faith against heretics, using the temporal prescription argument against late-coming counterfeits, and the authority of the churches which protects the tradition of the Apostles; because the truth of necessity comes before falsity, and it comes from those by whom it was handed down.

Comment

Even in his Montanist period, Tertullian consistently appealed to the tradition handed down not only in the churches of apostolic origin, but in all the churches in communion with them. Again he singled out the church of Rome, nearest of the apostolic churches to Carthage and doubly apostolic by the fact that both Peter and Paul had sealed their witness there by the shedding of their blood. Here he did not mention the story about John being plunged into boiling oil in Rome, but invoked him as the origin of the episcopate in the churches mentioned in the Apocalypse.

We have now seen how Tertullian, in arguing against Gnostic heretics, had appealed to the faith of the churches that could trace their origins back to the apostles. In this argument, he took as indisputable the fact that the apostles or "apostolic men" who founded churches had left bishops in charge of them and that these had been followed by a line of successors down to the present day. Writing both as a Catholic and as a Montanist, Tertullian provides an important witness to the fact that by the end of the second century each church was led by a bishop and that these bishops were understood to be the successors of the apostles. However, Tertullian emphasizes the reliability of the faith handed on in the apostolic churches more than the role of the bishops as its official teachers. In fact, in these works against the Gnostics, he says little about the ministry of the bishops or other clergy. We can learn something about this, however, from his description of the disorderly way the heretics conducted their communities.

Tertullian on Ministry

Toward the end of his *Prescription against Heretics* Tertullian added the following proof of the falsity of their claims.[24]

> 41   I will not end without describing the heretical lifestyle, how pointless, how worldly and merely human it is. There is no seriousness, no authority, no discipline—it all fits right in with their faith. First of all, you are never sure who is a catechumen and who is already baptized. They are all there; they all hear and pray together. If some pagan should drop by, they will cast what is holy to the dogs and cast their pearls (false ones!) before swine. The subverting of discipline they prefer to call simplicity; concern about discipline they call affectation. They grant peace and communion to anyone at all. Differences in doctrine are no problem for them provided they agree in attacking the truth. They are all proud; they all promise knowledge. Their catechumens are baptized before they have received instruction. Their women are irrepressible; they have no scruples about teaching, debating, conducting exorcisms, promising cures, perhaps even baptizing. Their ordinations are done without forethought or investigation and do not last. Sometimes they take the newly baptized, sometimes

men too closely tied to worldly business, sometimes even people who have abandoned our Church, perhaps hoping that honors will bind them in a way the truth could not. Nowhere is it easier to gain advancement than in the rebel camp; just being there is reason for promotion. And so, one person is the bishop today; someone else tomorrow. Today's deacon is tomorrow's reader; a priest one day becomes a layman the next. For they impose priestly duties even on the laity.

Comment

From this caustic description of the lack of "discipline" in the churches of the heretics, one can infer Tertullian's esteem for the order and discipline characterizing the Catholic Church for which he was writing. One can conclude, by contrast, that the Catholic churches were doing the opposite of what the heretical churches did. Thus, for instance, in the Catholic churches catechumens and those already baptized did not worship together, nor were pagans admitted to their services. Catechumens were carefully instructed before being baptized. Women were not allowed to teach, to conduct exorcisms or baptize. Ordinations were preceded by careful investigation of the candidate. In the Catholic churches there was no doubt about who was a bishop, who a deacon, who a priest, who a layman and what their duties were.

All of this makes it clear that when Tertullian wrote this work (around 203), the Catholic churches of North Africa had a well-developed ministerial structure, with bishop, priests, deacons and readers. Also evident is a definite distinction between the ordained and the laity and that priestly functions were not imposed on the laity.

Tertullian's use of the terms *sacerdos* and *sacerdotalis* (priest and priestly) shows that by his day, at least in North Africa, bishops, presbyters and deacons were understood to belong to the *ordo sacerdotalis*, which the church clearly distinguished from the laity or *plebs*. The following passage of Tertullian's work *On Baptism*, written while still fully Catholic, brings out the differing roles of the clergy and the laity in administering baptism.

> *De Baptismo* 17. To round off our slight treatment of this subject it remains for me to advise you of the rules to be observed in giving and receiving baptism. The supreme right of giving it belongs to the high priest, which is the bishop; after him, to the presbyters and deacons, yet not without commission from the bishop, on account of the Church's dignity; for when this is safe, peace is safe. Except for that, even laymen have the right: for that which is received on equal terms can be given on

equal terms; unless perhaps you are prepared to allege that our Lord's disciples were already bishops or presbyters or deacons; that is, as the word ought not to be hidden by any man, so likewise baptism, which is no less declared to be "of God," can be administered by all. Yet how much rather are the rules of humility and restraint incumbent upon laymen, seeing they apply to greater persons, who must not arrogate to themselves the function of the bishop. Rivalry for the episcopate is the mother of schisms. The holy apostle has said that all things are lawful but all things are not expedient; which means it is enough that you should use this right in emergencies, if ever conditions of place or time or person demand it. The boldness of a rescuer is acceptable when he is constrained to it by the necessities of the man in peril, since he will be guilty of a man's destruction if he forbears to give the help he is free and able to give. But the impudence of that woman who assumed the right to teach is evidently not going to arrogate to her the right to baptise as well—unless perhaps some new serpent appears, like that original one, so that as that woman abolished baptism, some other should of her own authority confer it.[25]

Comment

This is the only place where Tertullian refers to the bishop as "high priest." M. Bévenot suggests that in using it here, he may have been alluding to the passage in *I Clement,* which we have seen above,[26] where the Jewish priesthood is presented as a model for the orderly structure of Christian ministry.[27] The letters of Ignatius of Antioch have indicated that either the bishop or someone designated by him could celebrate the Eucharist.[28] It seems most likely that this person would be a presbyter, but Ignatius does not say so. Here we see that in the churches of North Africa, the bishop had to authorize presbyters and deacons to administer baptism. They were "greater persons" than laymen, but "must not arrogate to themselves the function of the bishop." Needless to say, for Tertullian the laity must not arrogate to themselves the function of the clergy, except in a case of necessity. And for Tertullian, it would seem, in that case, that baptism could be given by a layman, but not by a laywoman.

Celebration of the Eucharist by a Layman

In a later work, written during his "Montanist" period, Tertullian claimed that in a case of necessity, a layman could not only baptize, but celebrate the Eucharist as well. In this work, *Exhortation to Chastity,* Tertullian argued that the rule forbidding a priest to marry again after the death of his wife ought to apply to the laity as well. He justifies this by arguing that, in a case of necessity, a layman could celebrate the Eucharist and therefore ought always to be fit to do this. This included observing the rule laid down for the clergy, who at that time were not bound to celibacy but to "monogamy."

> *De Exhort. Cast. 7* To Christ was reserved, as in all other points so in this also, the "fulfilling of the law." Thence therefore the Apostle more fully and strictly prescribes that those who are chosen into the sacerdotal order must be men of one marriage.[29] This rule is so strictly observed, that I remember some removed from their office for marrying a second time. But you may say: "Then this must be permitted to those whom he exempts." We would certainly be foolish if we thought that what was not permitted to priests was permitted to laity. For are not we laity also priests? It is written: "He has made us a kingdom and priests for God and his Father" (Rev 1:6). It is the authority of the Church that instituted the distinction between clergy and laity and the honor shown the ranks of the clergy made holy for God. Where there is no duly constituted clergy, you offer, you baptize, you are your own priest, for where there are three, this is a church, albeit of laity. For, as the Apostle says, each one "lives by his faith; there is no respect of persons with God," (Heb 2:4; Rom 1:17) since "not the hearers, but the doers, of the Law are justified" (Rom 2:11). Therefore if, in time of necessity, you yourself have the right to be a priest, it is necessary that you also maintain a priestly discipline even when it is not necessary for you to act as a priest. Do you, a remarried man, baptize? Do you offer? How much greater a sin is it for a remarried layman to act as a priest when the right to priestly ministry is withdrawn from a real priest who marries again. But, you may object, necessity knows no law. There can be no excuse for such an unnecessary "necessity." The simple solution is: do not remarry and, when a genuine necessity arises, you will have no problem. God wishes all of us to be ready at all times to administer the sacraments.[30]

Comment

The requirement that the laity observe the rule of "monogamy" was part of the rigid code of morality Tertullian believed the Paraclete revealed in one of the Montanist prophecies. Catholic commentators have also tended to describe his idea that a layman could offer the Eucharist as a Montanist aberration. It is important to keep in mind that, even as a Montanist, Tertullian held that in normal circumstances a layman could offer the Eucharist only through the ministry of a priest. In this same work he scoffs at the layman who remarried after the death of his first wife and comes accompanied by his second one to have a priest offer the Eucharist for his two wives.[31]

It is not certain that his adherence to Montanism led Tertullian to think that in a case of necessity a layman could celebrate the Eucharist. Even in his Catholic period he may have thought that the authority of the Church instituted the distinction between clergy and laity. One does not find in his writings the notion that priestly ordination confers a "sacred power" to celebrate the Eucharist: a power the laity lack, and on that account cannot validly celebrate the Eucharist. This has been Catholic doctrine for a long time now, but it may not have been the way Tertullian thought about it even in his Catholic period. It would seem more likely that for him the restriction to the clergy of priestly functions, whether baptizing or offering the Eucharist, was a matter of church discipline and not of "sacred power."

The Question of the Power of Bishops to Absolve from Grave Sins

Early in the third century, this question of "sacred power" became a major point of controversy, especially as it applied to the power of bishops to grant absolution, after suitable penance, to those guilty of such sins as adultery and fornication. Tertullian was convinced that these sins were beyond the power of the bishops to forgive. The "New Prophecy" may not have been the source of his belief about this, but it certainly confirmed it, as we can see in the following passages of his work *On Purity*.[32]

> *De Pudicitia* 1.5–9 But now the condition of our own virtues is in decline. The foundations of Christian purity are shaken, that purity which draws from heaven all that it has—its nature from the laver of regeneration, its schooling from the ministry of preaching, its rigor from verdicts pronounced in both Testaments, firmly sanctioned by the fear of an eternal fire and the desire of an eternal kingdom. I even hear that an Edict has been issued, indeed a peremptory one (nor could I permit it to

pass unnoticed) which opposes this rigor. The Pontifex Maximus, forsooth—I mean the "bishop of bishops"!—issues this pronouncement: *"I forgive sins of adultery and fornication to those who have performed penance."* Oh Edict, upon which one cannot write: *Good deed.* And where shall this indulgence be posted? There, I fancy, on the very doors and under the very titles of debauchery. Penitence such as this should be promulgated where the sin itself will be committed. There one should read the pardon where one enters with its hope. But instead of this it is read in church and it is promulgated in church—and the Church is a virgin! Far, far from the bride of Christ be such a proclamation! She who is faithful and pure and holy ought to preserve even her hearing from defilement. She has none to whom she can make such a promise, and even if she should have them, she will not make it, for with less difficulty could the temple of God on earth be called by the Lord a *den of thieves* than a den of adulterers and fornicators.

Comment

Tertullian was attacking a statement recently issued by an important Catholic bishop, whose name he does not give. The identity of this bishop has been much disputed; the most likely candidates are Callistus, bishop of Rome (217–22), and Agrippinus, bishop of Carthage about the same time. The sarcastic reference to him as "Pontifex Maximus" (the title of the president of the guild of pagan priests at Rome) does not necessarily point to Callistus, as this title was not applied to the bishops of Rome until much later. The "edict" may not have been expressed with the imperial tone Tertullian gives to it, but it evidently offered the possibility of absolution, after suitable penance, to those guilty of adultery.

St. Cyprian, bishop of Carthage from 248 to 258, says that at an earlier period the bishops of his own province had been divided on this issue, some refusing to grant absolution for the sin of adultery and others granting it.[33] This could well explain why an earlier bishop of Carthage might have declared his readiness to grant such absolution. Tertullian, by now a convinced Montanist, found this totally unacceptable. He even went so far as to say: "The church has none to whom she could make such a promise," which means that, in his view, a person guilty of adultery would no longer belong to the church, and therefore not be eligible for its ministry of penance and absolution. However, as is seen in the following passage, Tertullian's principal argument was that the Catholic bishops lacked the power to grant absolution for such grave sins.[34]

De Pud. 21.1–6 And now, at length, I come to that point in my argument where I make a distinction between the doctrine of the apostles and their power. Doctrine gives direction to a man; power marks him out with a special character. The power of the Spirit is a thing apart, for the Spirit is God. What, then, did he teach? "There must be no fellowship with works of darkness."[35] Observe his commandment! And who had power to forgive sins? This no one can do but He Himself: "For who forgives sins but God alone?"[36] This means, of course, mortal sins committed against Him and against His temple. For as far as you yourself are concerned, you are commanded in the person of Peter to forgive offenses committed against yourself even seventy times seven times. Therefore if it were proved that the blessed apostles themselves showed indulgence to any sin of such a character that it could be pardoned by God alone and not by man, they would have done this because power was given them and not because doctrine allowed it. Moreover, the apostles raised the dead to life, something which God alone can do. They healed the sick, something which no one but Christ can do. They even inflicted punishments, something which Christ did not wish to do, for it was not fitting that He should strike who came to suffer. Ananias was smitten and Elymas also, Ananias with death and Elymas with blindness; this itself proves that Christ, too, had the power to do these things.

So it was with the prophets also. They pardoned murder—and adultery, which was joined with it—to those who were penitent; this was justified by the fact that they also gave proof of their severity.[37] Now then, apostolic man, show me samples of your prophetic works so that I may recognize your divine authorization; after this, claim for yourself the power to forgive such sins. If, however, you have been entrusted with no office beyond that of teaching moral doctrine, and if your presidential authority is that of a servant and not of a master, then who do you think you are, or how exalted, that you grant pardon for sin? You show yourself neither prophet nor apostle; therefore you lack the power in virtue of which pardon is granted.

Comment

"I make a distinction between the *doctrine* of the apostles and their *power.*" "If...you have been entrusted with no office beyond that of teaching moral doctrine...."—Tertullian did not question the bishops' role as the official teachers of apostolic doctrine; their role as reliable transmitters of the apostolic faith had been a key argument in his works against the heretics.

Furthermore, he did not question the authority of bishops to grant pardon for "lesser sins." Earlier in this same work Tertullian had spoken of penitence performed by the baptized, which could obtain pardon for lesser sins from the bishop. What he rejected was the bishops' claim to have inherited from the apostles the power to grant absolution for graver sins such as adultery, which according to Tertullian could obtain pardon only from God.[38] Here his argument was thoroughly Montanist: If apostles and prophets had such power, God had given it to them as part of their unique role as apostles and prophets; it was not something they could pass on to others. In order to claim the power to pardon grave sins, one would have to demonstrate the other charismatic gifts of an apostle or prophet.

"Now then, apostolic man...."—Tertullian addresses the Catholic bishop as *apostolice,* no doubt a sarcastic reference to his claim to have received his power as a successor of the apostles. Some have taken this as referring to the bishop of Rome, but the claim could have been made by the bishop of Carthage just as well. "Your presidential authority is that of a servant and not a master" *(nec imperio praesidere sed ministerio)*— Tertullian does not question the bishop's right to preside, but insists that it must remain within the limits set for it by God.

> *De Pud.* 21.7–8 "But the Church," you say, "has power to forgive sins." I know this better than you do and I regulate it better, because I have the Paraclete Himself saying in the person of the new prophets: "The Church can forgive sin, but I will not do it lest others also sin." But what if a false prophetic spirit said this? This cannot be the case, since the Destroyer would rather have commended himself by his clemency and he would have set others in the way of sin. Or if, here too, he tried to ape the Spirit of Truth, then the Spirit of truth can, indeed, grant pardon to fornication, but will not do it when it brings harm to many.

Comment

"'The Church' you say 'has power to forgive sins.'"—This, no doubt, was the teaching of the Catholic bishop with whom Tertullian was arguing. Tertullian seems to admit this here and even quotes the Paraclete as saying: "The Church can forgive sins...." However, as we shall see a bit further on, for Tertullian the church that can forgive sins is not the church of the bishops, but the Church he identifies with the Spirit Himself. In any case, Tertullian accepts as authentic the prophecy according to which

the Spirit will not use such power, on the grounds that it would lead
others to sin.

> *De Pud*. 21:9–10 And now I put a question to you about this
> opinion of yours: Where do you get this right which you claim
> for your Church? If it is because the Lord said to Peter: *Upon
> this rock I will build my Church; I have given you the keys of the
> kingdom of heaven; or Whatsoever you shall bind or loose on
> earth, will be bound or loosed in heaven,* then you presume that
> the power of binding and loosing has devolved upon you also,
> that is, upon every church which is akin to Peter. Who are you
> to pervert and to change completely the manifest will of
> Christ, who grants this to Peter personally? *Upon you,* he says,
> *I will build my Church;* and *I will give the keys to you,* not to the
> Church; and *Whatsoever you shall loose or bind,* not what they
> shall loose or bind.

Comment

"[T]hen you presume that the power has devolved upon you also, that
is, upon every church which is akin to Peter."—This has often been taken
as proof that the author of the "edict" was Callistus, the bishop of Rome.
However, the Latin phrase *ad omnem ecclesiam Petri propinquam* suggests
that the author of the "edict" based his claim to have the power to forgive
sin on the grounds that *every* church related by kinship to Peter had inherited his power to loose and bind. One can recall how Tertullian had said
that churches that had not been founded by an apostle were still apostolic
"by kinship of doctrine."[39] Every church united in the same apostolic faith
could be said to be related by kinship to Peter, as the chief of the apostles.
From Tertullian's argument here one can infer that Catholic bishops were
taking the promises made to Peter to apply not only to the bishop of
Rome, but to the bishop of every church that could rightly call itself
"apostolic."

> *De Pud*. 21.16–17 What, then, does this have to do with the
> Church, and I mean yours, you Sensualist? For this power is
> Peter's personally and, after that, it belongs to those who have
> the Spirit—to an apostle or a prophet. For the Church is itself,
> properly and principally, the Spirit Himself, in whom there is a
> trinity of one divinity, Father, Son and Holy Spirit. He unites
> in one congregation that Church which the Lord said consists
> of three persons. And so, from this time on, any number of
> persons at all, joined in this faith, is recognized as the Church

by Him who founded and consecrated it. Therefore it is true that the Church will pardon sins, but this is the Church of the Spirit, through a man who has the Spirit; it is not the Church which consists of a number of bishops. For it is the Lord and not the servant who has this sovereign right. It belongs to God Himself, not to a priest.

Comment

"[Y]ou Sensualist"—Tertullian's word is *psychice*. He uses it here the way that St. Paul used it in 1 Corinthians 2:14, where *psychikos* is contrasted with *pneumatikos* (2:15). It could also, and perhaps better, be translated "you unspiritual man." In Tertullian's view, the fact that the Catholic bishops did not manifest charismatic gifts showed that they lacked the Spirit, without which they had no power to absolve the kind of sins whose pardon, he believed, was reserved to God alone.

"[T]he Church of the Spirit...not the Church which consists of a number of bishops"—this should probably not be taken to mean that Tertullian was thinking of a Montanist church and the Catholic Church, as if they were two churches structurally separated from one another. He had not rejected the authority of the Catholic bishops to preside and teach or to grant pardon for lesser sins; however, he insisted that the power to forgive such sins as adultery had to come directly from the Spirit as a charismatic gift and not through ordination to the priesthood.

IRENAEUS AND TERTULLIAN COMPARED

These two men were almost contemporaries, in the sense that Tertullian began his career as a Christian writer (ca. 196) at just about the time that Irenaeus's life ended, perhaps by martyrdom. What makes their testimony concerning church leadership at the end of the second century particularly valuable is the fact that it is substantially concordant, despite the many differences between them. Irenaeus was a bishop, thoroughly orthodox and devoted to the Catholic Church; Tertullian was a layman, who in his later years became a Montanist and a severe critic of Catholic bishops. They were acquainted with different regions of the Church: Irenaeus with Asia Minor, Rome and Gaul and Tertullian with North Africa. This summary shall briefly recall what is common in their testimony and in what respects they differ.

First of all, they both bear witness to the fact that in their day, the church in each city was being led by a single bishop and that these bishops were recognized as the successors to the apostles. Both of them affirm that the first bishops had been appointed by the apostles (or by "apostolic men"). Both of them appeal to the orderly succession of bishops as evidence that the genuine teaching of the apostles had been handed on in their churches. Both appeal also to the fact that all of these churches had the same rule of faith as proof for the authentic apostolic doctrine. Both invoked the church of Rome as an especially reliable bearer of the apostolic tradition, being the church where the greatest of the apostles had given their ultimate witness to the faith.

While both used the argument from apostolic succession in refuting the Gnostic heretics, each of them developed it differently. Irenaeus focused on the bishops as the inheritors of the apostles' teaching office *(locum magisterii)*, and thus stressed their role in handing on the apostolic tradition as teachers in the churches. Thus it was important for him to name the bishops who had succeeded one another in the church of Rome, beginning with the one who had been appointed to the episcopate by Peter and Paul. He appealed to this unbroken series of official teachers as guaranteeing the fidelity of the church of Rome to the teaching of the apostles.

Tertullian, on the other hand, put his stress on the apostolic churches themselves as bearers of the apostolic tradition. As he developed the argument, the fact that a church could name the predecessors of its current bishop back to one who had been appointed by an apostle or "apostolic man" provided clear proof of its claim to be an apostolic church. Other churches, founded more recently, could also be called "apostolic" by virtue of their "kinship of doctrine" with those founded by the apostles.

Tertullian also tells us more about the pastoral ministry of bishops than Irenaeus does. Irenaeus focused on bishops as successors to the apostles in their teaching office; from Tertullian we learn that the bishops of his day saw themselves as successors to St. Peter in the "power of the keys" that gave them the authority to absolve grave sins. Irenaeus the bishop probably exercised such power; Tertullian the layman tells us how the Catholic bishops justified their claim to do so.

9
ROME AND ALEXANDRIA IN THE EARLY THIRD CENTURY

R ome and Alexandria ranked first and second among the great cities of the Roman Empire, and the Council of Nicaea, in 325, recognized the bishops of those cities as having authority that extended over a considerable region beyond the limits of their own churches. Canon 6 of that council decreed:

> The ancient customs of Egypt, Libya and Pentapolis shall be maintained, according to which the bishop of Alexandria has authority over all these places, since a similar custom exists with reference to the bishop of Rome. Similarly in Antioch and the other provinces the prerogatives of the churches are to be preserved.[1]

Although the council did not specify the region over which the bishop of Rome had authority, it is generally understood to have included central and southern Italy. It is noteworthy that in 325 the regional authority of the bishops of Rome and Alexandria was recognized as sanctioned by "ancient custom." A custom going back less than a century would hardly qualify as ancient, so we can conclude that by the year 225 the bishops of Rome and Alexandria must have enjoyed a well-established authority in their own churches, for otherwise they could hardly have possessed it over the neighboring churches as well.

This chapter shall present some documentary evidence dating from the early third century that tends to confirm the conclusion I have drawn from the decree of Nicaea. For the church of Rome I shall consider a document known as *The Apostolic Tradition,* commonly attributed to a Roman writer named Hippolytus. For Alexandria I shall cite

171

some texts from the writings of the two great Alexandrian teachers, Clement and Origen.

HIPPOLYTUS OF ROME

The church historian Eusebius mentions a bishop named Hippolytus, who authored a number of books, including one entitled *Against All Heresies*.[2] The entire treatise consisted of ten books. Until modern times, scholars knew of only the first, which was usually referred to with the title *Philosophumena*. However, in 1842 books 4 through 10 were discovered at Mount Athos. Book 9 contains a scathing criticism of Callistus, a man whom the author judged unworthy to have leadership in the church because, among other reasons, of his practice of granting absolution for sins of adultery. So, whether or not the author of the "edict" that Tertullian criticized was Callistus, we know that this was his policy and that it had fierce opponents in Rome as well as in North Africa.

It has commonly been believed that Eusebius's reference to Hippolytus as a bishop (without naming his see) is a hidden reference to the fact that he broke off communion with Callistus and had himself elected as "antipope." No doubt this title is anachronistic, and recently Allen Brent has argued that Hippolytus was not even a bishop in the full sense of the term, but simply a leading member of a Christian community in Rome that opposed Callistus as an innovator.[3] In any case, after Callistus died Hippolytus was reconciled with a successor of his named Pontian (230–35). During the persecution of the emperor Maximinus, he, along with Pontian, was condemned to labor in the mines of Sardinia. They both died there of ill treatment and are venerated together as martyrs of the church of Rome.

In 1851 excavations in a place associated with the veneration of the martyr Hippolytus uncovered the statue of a person seated on a chair, which was inscribed with the titles of thirteen books. Ancient sources indicated that Hippolytus had written some of these books, and the person represented by the statue was identified with Hippolytus. He was then credited as the author of the works listed on the chair, one of which bore the title *Apostolic Tradition*.

Such a work was previously unknown, but two eminent patristic scholars, E. Schwartz and R. H. Connolly, working independently, concluded that it was the original source of a work known as *The Egyptian Church Order*.[4] This was one of a number of such "church orders," which laid down regulations for such matters as the celebration of the liturgy, the roles of clergy and laity, and various church practices.

Subsequently, Gregory Dix and Bernard Botte reconstructed what they believed to be the original text of the work of Hippolytus, piecing it together on the basis of an early Latin translation of part of it and its use in the composition of *The Egyptian Church Order* and other similar documents.[5]

In recent years much doubt has been cast on the identification of the person represented by the statue as Hippolytus and on his authorship of *The Apostolic Tradition*. Allen Brent recently proposed that the statue represents an allegorical figure rather than a historic person, that it was erected by the Roman "school" to which Hippolytus belonged, that the titles inscribed on it were works written by members of that community or "school," and that *The Apostolic Tradition* is better understood as the product of that community than as the work of Hippolytus alone.[6]

THE APOSTOLIC TRADITION

Whatever the historical role of Hippolytus in its composition, the important fact is that most scholars do accept, at least in its main lines, the reconstruction of *The Apostolic Tradition* by Dix and Botte and recognize it as a work of the early third century. This gives us a fairly reliable picture of the way the Roman church did things not only at that time but for several decades before that, that is, toward the end of the second century. In the following passage of the *Prologue,* the author declares his intention to describe "the tradition that has continued until now," which he insists should be maintained by "those who are at the head of the Church."

> *Prologue:* And now...having come to our most important topic, we turn to <the subject> of the Tradition which is proper for the Churches, in order that those who have been rightly instructed may hold fast to that tradition which has continued until now, and fully understanding it from our exposition may stand the more firmly <therein>. <This is now the more necessary> because of that apostasy or error which was recently invented out of ignorance and <because of certain> ignorant men. The Holy Ghost bestows the fullness of grace on those who believe rightly that they may know how those who are at the head of the Church should teach the tradition and maintain it in all things.[7]

Comment

Concerning the reliability of the author's claim to present "the tradition which has continued until now," I quote the comment Dom Gregory Dix makes in his *General Introduction:*

> Besides what I will venture to call the probability that when the book was written Hippolytus was still formally a presbyter of the Roman Church—albeit an exceedingly loosely attached one—we must bear in mind the circumstances of the book's publication. He is openly attacking what he considers the innovating tendencies of those with whom he is at loggerheads on other grounds by making a public appeal to the past. In the circumstances it is of the very essence of his case that he should, for the most part at least, be really doing what he says he is doing, setting down the genuine old Roman customs and rules of which the memory of Roman Christians then "went not back to the contrary."[8]

The work, as Dix and Botte have reconstructed it, consists of three parts: The first deals with the clergy, the second with the laity, and the third with various church observances. In keeping with the purpose and limitations of this book, I shall focus almost exclusively on the first part, especially on what it tells us about the ordination and ministry of bishops, presbyters, deacons and other members of the clergy. It begins with a description of the ordination of a bishop.

ii. Of Bishops

1. Let the bishop be ordained being in all things without fault chosen by all the people. 2. And when he has been proposed and found acceptable to all, the people shall assemble on the Lord's day together with the presbytery and such bishops as may attend. 3. With the agreement of all let the bishops lay hands on him and the presbytery stand by in silence. 4. And all shall keep silence praying in their hearts for the descent of the Spirit. 5. After this one of the bishops present at the request of all, laying his hand on him who is ordained bishop, shall pray thus, saying....

Comment

This paragraph highlights the different roles assigned to the people, the presbytery and the bishops. All the people take part in the choice of the man to be ordained bishop, and all pray in silence for the descent of the Spirit. We can presume that the presbyters have taken part in the choice of the bishop and also stand by and pray in silence for the descent of the Spirit, but only the bishops present lay hands on him. There is no mention here of a minimum number of bishops required; the Council of Nicaea would require no less than three.[9]

Evidently the bishops present for the ordination of the new bishop have come from other neighboring churches. The presence of a number of bishops, all of whom lay hands on the candidate, suggests a recognition of the collegial nature of the episcopate. Only those already belonging to this body were qualified to introduce others into it; the laying-on of their hands would signify their acceptance of this man into their college.

This account of how a bishop was chosen and ordained answers some questions left open in the letters of Ignatius of Antioch. Likewise, this document of the early third century gives clear evidence of the presence in Rome of the threefold structure, consisting of bishop, presbyters and deacons, that was already established in Antioch and in churches of Asia Minor by the early second century.

iii. Prayer for the Consecration of a Bishop

1. O God and Father of our Lord Jesus Christ, Father of mercies and God of all comfort, Who dwellest on high yet hast respect unto the lowly, who knowest all things before they come to pass; 2. Who didst give ordinances unto Thy church by the Word of thy grace; Who didst foreordain from the beginning the race of the righteous from Abraham, instituting princes and priests and leaving not Thy sanctuary without ministers; Who from the foundation of the world hast been pleased to be glorified in them whom Thou hast chosen; 3. And now pour forth that Power which is from Thee, of the princely Spirit which Thou didst deliver to Thy Beloved Child Jesus Christ, which He bestowed on Thy holy Apostles who established the Church which hallows Thee in every place to the endless glory and praise of Thy Name. 4. Father who knowest the hearts [of all] grant upon this Thy servant whom Thou hast chosen for the episcopate to feed Thy holy flock and serve as Thine high priest, that he may minister blamelessly by night and day, that he may unceasingly [behold and] propitiate Thy countenance and offer to Thee the gifts of Thy holy Church, 5. And that by the high priestly Spirit he may have authority to forgive sins according to Thy command, to assign lots according to Thy bidding, to loose every bond according to the authority Thou gavest to the Apostles, and

that he may please Thee in meekness and a pure heart, offering
to Thee a sweet-smelling savour, 6. through Thy Child Jesus
Christ Our Lord, through Whom to Thee be glory, might and
praise, to the Father and to the Son with the Holy Spirit now
[and ever] and world without end. Amen.

Comment

This prayer was most likely not a fixed formula from which the ordaining bishop could not deviate. However, we may assume that it provides a
good example of the kind of prayer used in ordaining a bishop in Rome at
the end of the second century. It sheds precious light on what the Church
of that period thought about the nature and source of episcopal ministry. It
begins by attributing to God the institution of priests for the ministry of
the sanctuary and the choice of those to fulfill this ministry. Later (no.4)
the prayer expresses the confidence that the Father who knows the hearts
of all has chosen this man for the episcopate. This indicates an assurance
that the choice made by all the people will identify the one chosen by God.

The main body of the prayer is an *epiclesis,* that is, a prayer invoking the
gift of the Spirit upon the one being ordained, to equip him with the
power and gifts for episcopal ministry. The prayer (which in this part is
preserved in the original Greek) uses two adjectives of the Spirit: *hegemonikou,* which Dix renders "princely," and *archieratiko,* "high-priestly."
A comparison with the prayers for the ordination of a presbyter and of a
deacon shows that in each case the words that qualify the Spirit to be
given are appropriate to the kind of ministry the man will have. Thus, for
the presbyter, the bishop prays that the Father would impart "the Spirit of
grace and counsel," while for the deacon he asks "the Spirit of grace and
earnestness and diligence."

The two adjectives used in the prayer for the bishop, then, likewise correspond to the kind of ministry he will have. The first adjective, *hegemonikou,* is translated in the lexicon of Arndt and Gingrich as "guiding"
or "leading." It would not seem incorrect, then, to translate the term
hegemonikou pneumatos as "the Spirit of leadership." Significantly, while
the Father is asked to pour out "the power which comes from Him" of
this Spirit, the prayers for the ordination of presbyters and deacons do not
speak of power in connection with the Spirit they are to receive.

The Spirit invoked upon the bishop is also described as "high-priestly,"
and his ministry is "to serve as high priest" *(archierateuein).* The prayer
spells out what this priestly ministry involves: to "feed the flock" (presumably with the Word of God), to pray on behalf of the people, to offer the
Eucharist, to forgive sins, to "assign lots" and to "loose every bond." The
expression "to assign lots" *(klerous)* would mean "to appoint people to

the various orders in the church," and "to loose every bond" would mean reconciling those who had been excommunicated.

The authority *(exousia)* with which the bishop will exercise these ministries is described as "the authority *[exousia]* Thou gavest to the Apostles," just as the "power *[dunamis]* of the princely Spirit" invoked upon the new bishop is that which Jesus bestowed upon the holy apostles. This clearly expresses the conviction that the mandate Jesus gave his apostles and the authority he gave them to carry it out is handed on through ordination to the episcopate.

It is true that the gift of the Spirit had to be invoked anew each time a man was ordained to share this ministry. Jesus, who received the Spirit from the Father, bestowed it on his apostles, but we find no suggestion that the ordaining bishop actually gave the Spirit to the ordinand. The Spirit, each time, was given in answer to prayer: first the prayer of the whole community, and then the prayer of the ordaining bishop. However, from the fact that only the bishops laid hands on the candidate and that only one of the bishops pronounced the solemn prayer, we can conclude that the Roman church at the end of the second century understood that only those who belonged to the episcopal order could aggregate others to it and so share their apostolic mandate with them. In this way the new bishop's authority would derive from the authority Jesus had given to his apostles.

Three Factors in the Ordination of a Bishop

In the ordination of a bishop as described in *The Apostolic Tradition* we can distinguish three factors: the ecclesiological, the christological and the pneumatological. By the ecclesiological I mean the part played by the church over which the man was to be the bishop. We have seen that he had to be "chosen by all the people" and "found acceptable by all." Further, the ordination took place in the presence of the whole community, and all took part in the prayer for the descent of the Holy Spirit. Finally, the ordination was celebrated with a view to this man's ministry as bishop to this particular church. Immediately after being ordained he was joined by the presbyters of his church in celebrating the Eucharist for the first time as its bishop.[10] Because his ordination would make him the bishop of *this* church his church had an indispensable part to play in his ordination.

The christological factor consists in the link ordination established between the new bishop and Christ: namely, that by his incorporation into the episcopal body, he began to share in the authority Christ gave to his apostles. The prayer of ordination called down upon him that "power of the princely Spirit" that Jesus received from the Father and in turn bestowed on his apostles. The laying-on of the hands of several bishops symbolized the sharing of the mandate that linked the new bishop to Christ as the original source of the authority he would now have to forgive sins and to "loose every bond" in the Lord's name.

The pneumatological factor consists in the gift of the Holy Spirit for which first the whole community and then one of the bishops prayed. This prayer is an *epiclesis;* the ordaining bishop did not confer the Spirit, he prayed that it be given from on high. The prayer clearly expresses the mind of the late second-century church that only a man upon whom the Spirit had come in power could fulfill the ministry of a bishop. At the same time, the attitude was one of serene confidence that the Spirit would be given in answer to the church's prayer. In the language of a later development of Christian theology, we can say that we find here a sense of what will be termed the sacramental efficacy of the prayer of ordination when this is pronounced over a suitable candidate by a bishop in the apostolic succession.

Following his ordination as a bishop, he celebrated the Eucharist assisted by deacons and presbyters.[11]

iv. < The Liturgy>
1. And when he has been made bishop let every one offer him the kiss of peace saluting him, for he has been made worthy *<of this>*. 2. To him then let the deacons bring the oblation and he with all the presbyters laying his hand on the oblation shall say giving thanks *[euchariston]*:

After the eucharistic prayer and other blessings reserved to the bishop, there follows the description of the ordination first of presbyters and then of deacons. Since several elements in the ordination of deacons shed light on the role of presbyters as well, I shall first give the texts for both ordinations, and then offer my comments.[12]

viii. Of Presbyters
1. And when a presbyter is ordained *[cheirotonein]* the bishop shall lay his hand upon his head, the presbyters also touching him. And he shall pray over him according to the aforementioned form which we gave over the bishop,[13] praying and saying: 2. O God and Father of our Lord Jesus Christ, look upon this Thy servant and impart to him the spirit of grace and counsel, "that he may share" in the presbyterate "and govern" Thy people in a pure heart. 3. As Thou didst look upon the people of Thy choice and didst command Moses to choose presbyters whom Thou didst fill with the spirit which Thou

hadst granted to Thy minister. 4. So now, O Lord, grant that there may be preserved among us unceasingly the Spirit of Thy grace, and make us worthy that in faith we may minister to Thee in singleness of heart praising Thee. 5. Through Thy Child Christ Jesus through Whom to Thee be glory, might *<and praise>* in the holy Church now and for ever and world without end. Amen.

ix. Of Deacons

1. And a deacon when he is appointed shall be chosen according to what has been said before, the bishop *[alone]* laying hands on him. Nevertheless we order that the bishop alone shall lay on hands at the ordination of a deacon for this reason: 2. That he is not ordained for a priesthood, but for the service of the bishop that he may do the things commanded by him. 3. For he is not *[appointed to be]* the fellow-counsellor of the clergy but to take charge *<of property>* and to report to the bishop whatever is necessary. 4. He does not receive the Spirit which is common to the presbyterate, in which the presbyters share, but that which is entrusted to him under the bishop's authority. 5. Wherefore the bishop alone shall ordain the deacon. 6. But upon the presbyter the *<other>* presbyters also lay their hands because of the similar Spirit *<which is>* common to *<all>* the clergy. 7. For the presbyter has authority *(exousia)* only for this one thing, to receive. But he has no authority to give holy orders *(kleros)*. 8. Wherefore he does not ordain a cleric *(klerikos)*, but at the ordination of a presbyter he blesses (*lit.* seals *sphragizein*) while the bishop ordains *(cheirotonein)*. 9. Over a deacon, then, let him say this: 10. O God who hast created all things and hast ordered them by the Word, Father of our Lord Jesus Christ whom Thou didst send to minister Thy will and reveal unto us Thy desire; 11. Grant the Holy Spirit of grace and earnestness and diligence upon this Thy servant whom Thou hast chosen to minister to Thy church and to bring up in holiness that which is offered to Thee by Thine ordained high priests to the glory of Thy Name; so that ministering blamelessly and in purity of heart he may by Thy goodwill be found worthy of this exalted office, praising Thee, 12. through Thy Child Jesus Christ through whom to Thee with Him be glory, might and praise with the Holy Spirit now and ever and world without end. Amen.

Comment

The author of *The Apostolic Tradition* seems particularly concerned to differentiate between presbyters and deacons. Although presbyters do not have the power to ordain, they take part in the ordination of a presbyter by touching (blessing) the candidate while the bishop lays his hand on him. This is explained by the fact that the presbyters share a common Spirit, which the deacons do not share; hence only the bishop lays hands on the man being ordained deacon. The different gifts of the Spirit for which the bishop prays suggests the difference between their ministries. For the presbyter the bishop prays for "spirit of grace and counsel," that he may "govern" the people of God in a pure heart; for the deacon it is the Spirit of grace and earnestness and diligence, so that he may minister to the church and to the bishop. This suggests that the presbyters assist the bishop by their counsel in the government of the local church. The text also suggests that they share in the priesthood, especially in the explanation that the bishop alone lays hands at the ordination of a deacon because a deacon is not ordained for a priesthood.

Because the author specifically notes this difference between deacons and presbyters, it would seem reasonable to conclude that presbyters were "ordained for a priesthood," even though the prayer for their ordination makes no mention of this. We have seen above that when the bishop celebrated the Eucharist, the presbyters laid their hands on the oblation along with him. Nothing is said about the possibility that the bishop might delegate one of them to celebrate the Eucharist in his absence. However, they are described later on (no. xxi) as the ministers of baptism.[14]

The description of the ordination of a deacon is followed by a brief section on "confessors," which raises a question about their ordination if they are chosen to be presbyters or deacons.

x. Of Confessors

1. If a confessor has been in chains in prison for the Name, hands are not laid on him for the diaconate or the presbyter's office. For he has the office *[time]* of the presbyterate by his confession. But if he be appointed bishop, hands shall be laid on him. 2. And if he be a confessor who was not brought before a public authority nor punished with chains nor condemned to any penalty but was only by chance derided for the Name, though he confessed, hands shall be laid on him for every order *[kleros]* of which he is worthy.

Comment

In the introduction to his edition of *The Apostolic Tradition,* Bernard Botte comments on this text. He finds it improbable that the author, who attributes such importance to the gift of the Spirit in ordinations, would have thought that being imprisoned for the faith would suffice to confer the Spirit along with the presbyteral order, making the laying on of hands and the bishop's prayer unnecessary. He remarks that there is no trace elsewhere of such a practice. He believes it more likely that that such worthy confessors would be given a place of honor in the church equal to that of the presbyters, but would not actually be members of the presbyterate.[15]

After confessors, the text mentions the widows, who receive an official appointment to this group.

xi. Of Widows

1. When a widow is appointed she is not ordained but she shall be chosen by name....4. Let the widow be instituted by word only and let her be reckoned among the <*enrolled*> widows. But she shall not be ordained, because she does not offer the oblation *(prosphora)* nor has she a <*liturgical*> ministry *(leitourgia).* 5. But ordination is for the clergy on account of their *leitourgia.* But the widow is appointed for prayer, and this is <*a function*> of all <*Christians*>.

Comment

Here we can clearly see that the term *leitourgia* in Christian usage had come to mean an official service associated with the community's worship for which persons were ordained. We know that the bishop "offered the oblation" and that presbyters and deacons had their roles in celebrating the Eucharist and in the administration of baptism. According to *The Apostolic Tradition,* the ordained clergy consisted only of these three. The reader was appointed by the bishop handing him the book, but he did not have hands laid on him, nor were hands laid on the subdeacon.[16] The teacher who instructed candidates for baptism could be either an ecclesiastic *(ekklesiastikos)* or a layman *(laikos).*[17] At the end of each instruction the catechumens would pray together, after which the teacher would lay hands on them and pray before dismissing them.

In the celebration of baptism, each of the ordained had a distinctive role. The bishop first pronounced a "prayer of thanksgiving" over the oils with which the candidates would be anointed. The presbyter, assisted by deacons, actually administered baptism. After being baptized, the neophytes were led into the assembly, where the bishop laid his hand on each one, invoking the gift of the Holy Spirit. Then he anointed each with holy oil, saying: "I anoint thee with holy oil in God the Father Almighty and Christ Jesus and the Holy Ghost." And sealing (signing) each one on the forehead, he gave him the kiss of peace, saying, "The Lord be with you."[18]

MINISTRY AT ROME AND CARTHAGE COMPARED

At this point it would seem useful to compare what *The Apostolic Tradition* tells us about ministry at Rome in the early third century with what we have learned from Tertullian about ministry in North Africa during the same period. We can begin with what they tell us about the ministers of baptism.

According to Tertullian, the "supreme right" to baptize belonged to the bishop, and after him to the presbyters and deacons, by commission from the bishop. At Rome the bishop blessed the oils that would be used to anoint candidates while a presbyter, assisted by deacons, did the anointing and baptizing. After being baptized the neophytes were presented to the bishop, who laid his hand on them, invoked the Spirit and anointed them. Thus it is clear that at both Carthage and Rome the bishop had a presiding role in the initiation of new members into the church. In this context, Tertullian refers to the bishop as "high priest"; similarly the prayer for the ordination of a bishop in *The Apostolic Tradition* asks the Father to grant that he "serve as Thine high priest," and by the "high-priestly spirit" have authority to forgive sins. According to Tertullian bishops had the authority to forgive lesser sins, but he denied that they had the power to grant absolution for grave sins. He makes it clear, however, that Catholic bishops claimed to have such power on the grounds that they had inherited the power of the keys and the authority to loose and bind that Jesus had given to Peter. So also in *The Apostolic Tradition* the ordaining bishop prayed that the new bishop be given authority "to loose every bond according to the authority Thou gavest to the Apostles."

Despite the many differences between the writings of Tertullian and *The Apostolic Tradition,* together they give a consistent picture of the structure of ministry in the churches of Rome and North Africa in the early decades of the third century. The monepiscopal structure, with one bishop assisted by a number of presbyters and deacons, is presented as so firmly established in both churches that it must have been well developed in these regions by the end of the second century. We know that it was already present in Antioch and in churches of the Roman Province of Asia early in that century. I shall now consider the evidence for the presence of such a structure at Alexandria at the same period.

THE BISHOPS OF ALEXANDRIA

The fourth-century church historian, Eusebius of Caesarea, gives the names of ten bishops of Alexandria who had succeeded one another prior to Demetrius, who was bishop of that church from 189 to 232. Demetrius appointed Origen as head of the famous catechetical school there. St. Jerome, writing about two hundred years after the time Demetrius was bishop, made a statement about the early bishops of Alexandria that has been the subject of intense discussion among scholars. This statement occurs in a letter Jerome wrote to a fellow presbyter named Evangelus, in which he bitterly criticized the Roman deacons who put themselves above presbyters.[19] In order to prove the vast superiority of presbyters to deacons, Jerome argued that presbyters were really the same as bishops. He cited texts from the New Testament, such as Acts 20:28 and Titus 1:5–7, where the same persons are called both *presbuteroi* and *episkopoi*. Having proved to his satisfaction that originally they were the same, he offered an explanation of how they came to be distinct from one another.

> The fact that afterwards one was chosen who was placed above the others was done as a remedy for schism, to avoid having each one draw a following for himself and break up Christ's Church. For at Alexandria from Mark the Evangelist up to the bishops Heraclas and Dionysius the presbyters always chose one of their number, placed him in the higher rank and named him bishop, in the way in which the army makes an emperor or the deacons choose one of their own number whose dedication they recognize and call him "archdeacon." For, with the exception of ordinations, what does a bishop do that a presbyter does not do?[20]

William Telfer has argued strongly in favor of the reliability of St. Jerome's statement concerning the role played by the presbyters in appointing the early bishops of Alexandria.[21] He understands Jerome to mean that the presbyters not only chose one of their number as bishop, but actually ordained him. He attributes this to the fact that there were no other bishops available to do it, for up to the time of Heraclas and Dionysius, the church of Alexandria was the only one in Egypt with a bishop. Telfer adduced arguments from several later sources in support of his interpretation.

While a number of scholars have accepted Telfer's case as proven, E. W. Kemp[22] and Joseph Lécuyer[23] have strongly criticized the arguments he used to support it. It would take us too far afield to go into detail on this issue, so it will suffice to focus on one point brought out by Lécuyer: namely, that the writings of Origen not only do not support St. Jerome's statement, they contradict it. First of all, Heraclas and Dionysius followed Demetrius as bishops of Alexandria; hence, if Jerome and Telfer were correct, Demetrius himself would have been ordained by presbyters, there being no other bishop in Egypt to ordain him. But there is early witness to the fact that Demetrius summoned two episcopal synods to pass judgment on Origen— clear proof that there were other bishops in Egypt during that period.[24]

The writings of Origen also provide abundant evidence that he was very conscious of the difference between bishops and presbyters and would by no means have shared Jerome's opinion about their equality. Lécuyer also cites a passage in which Origen criticized how bishops were sometimes chosen: either by the living bishop, who might designate someone as his successor, or by the whole Christian community. This contradicts Jerome's idea that the presbyters would choose one of their own number to be bishop. Lécuyer also mentions how Origen saw a model for the ordination of a bishop in the way Moses laid his hands on Joshua in the presence of all the gathered people. Obviously Origen could not have recognized this as a model for the ordination of a bishop if his own bishop, Demetrius, had been ordained by a group of presbyters. One certainly has to agree that Origen proves a far more reliable witness regarding the structure of ministry at Alexandria in the early third century than St. Jerome, who wrote two centuries later.

From the texts cited by Lécuyer, it seems certain that by the time of Origen the church of Alexandria was led by a bishop, who was also ordained by a bishop. Of course, this does not answer the question whether, or when, the structure of ministry at Alexandria developed from presbyteral to monepiscopal leadership. One can hardly settle this question by referring to the list of names given by Eusebius as those of the bishops who had succeeded one another at Alexandria from the time of the apostles.

In the conclusion of his article, Lécuyer says he does not reject the hypothesis that at an earlier period, local churches, including that of Alexandria, may have been led by a group of presbyters, who would choose one of their number as their leader and make him their bishop. Presumably this hypothesis would include a further development leading to the conviction that a bishop must be ordained by other bishops. What I believe

Lécuyer has shown is that when Demetrius became bishop of Alexandria in 189 (four years after Origen was born), he was ordained by other bishops and not by the college of presbyters. Clement, Origen's predecessor in the school of Alexandria, must have witnessed this ordination, but it is typical of the genre of his writings that he does not mention it.

CLEMENT OF ALEXANDRIA

Clement was born about 150, probably at Athens, of pagan parents. After becoming a Christian, he traveled extensively, to Italy, Syria and Palestine, seeking instruction from the most famous Christian teachers. He settled in Alexandria as a disciple of Pantaenus, whom he judged the best of those teachers and whom he succeeded as head of the school for catechumens Pantaenus had founded. Clement left Alexandria during the persecution of Septimius Severus, around 203, and spent the rest of his life in Palestine, where he died around 215.

Three of Clement's works have been preserved; the best known is entitled *Stromata*, a title suggestive of its patchwork character, made up of varied pieces with no overall design. The most important topic treated in this work concerns the relationship between Christian faith and Greek philosophy. Clement insisted that while one finds the true knowledge of God only through the Christian religion, Divine Providence gave philosophy to the Greeks, just as it gave the Law to the Hebrews, to prepare them for the Gospel. Philosophy now helps Christians attain that higher knowledge of their faith which Clement extolled as the true *gnosis*, in contrast to that claimed by the heretical Gnostics, to whose refutation Clement devoted a good part of his work.

In response to the question of what information Clement provides about the structure of ministry in the church of Alexandria at the end of the second century, the answer is: hardly any. On this I again quote the Protestant patristic scholar, Von Campenhausen. After explaining Clement's idea that a person who has attained genuine Christian *gnosis* will undertake the instruction and pastoral care of Christians less mature than himself, Von Campenhausen says:

> It is a perpetual astonishment to the reader how little is said in this context about the Church as a social reality and organisation, its official superstructure, its worship, and its public methods of discipline. That all these things were already present in Clement's environment cannot be doubted; and he himself has no thought of polemising against them. The gnostic is not to

avoid the normal forms of public worship, but for him himself they are dispensable; they are of no significance to him—at least of no essential and decisive significance. Moreover, just as Clement himself and his own teachers are outside the ranks of the professional clergy, and remain laymen, so too in his spiritual instruction he hardly ever finds occasion to speak of the "shepherds" belonging to his church....Although Clement knows Irenaeus, the latter's combination of the argument from tradition with the concept of episcopal succession is never mentioned by him.[25]

Without doubt, toward the end of the second century, when Clement wrote his *Stromata,* the church of Alexandria had the threefold structure of bishop, presbyters and deacons. However, it is typical of Clement's approach that, in a rare reference to this structure, he saw it as an imitation of the heavenly hierarchy. Here is the passage, as quoted by Quasten.[26]

According to my opinion the grades here in the Church of bishops, priests and deacons are imitations of the angelic glory and of that economy which, the Scriptures say, awaits those who following the footsteps of the apostles, have lived in perfection of righteousness according to the Gospel.

We shall have to be content with the little Clement tells us about the official ministry in the church of his day and turn now to his successor in the school of Alexandria.

ORIGEN

Origen was born around 185, probably at Alexandria, of Christian parents. His father Leonidas suffered martyrdom in the persecution of Septimius Severus in 202. At only eighteen years of age, Origen was put in charge of the catechetical school of Alexandria by Bishop Demetrius. Not long after this he castrated himself, most likely for ascetical reasons. He became enormously successful and famous as a teacher, and on the occasion of a visit to Palestine, around 216, the bishops of Caesarea and Jerusalem invited him to preach and explain the Scriptures to their communities. That Origen, a layman, had been authorized to preach in the presence of bishops greatly displeased Bishop Demetrius, who ordered Origen to return to Alexandria at once. He did return and continued to teach and write there, but fifteen years later, when he again visited Palestine, the bishops there ordained him to the presbyterate. This displeased Demetrius even more, objecting that his castration excluded Origen from such ordination and, in any case he should not have been ordained without the approval of his own bishop. Demetrius summoned two synods of bishops to deal with the case; the first excommunicated Origen and the second deposed him from the priesthood. When Heraclas, who succeeded Demetrius in 232, also excommunicated him, Origen left Alexandria and spent the rest of his life teaching and writing at Caesarea in Palestine, where he continued to be recognized as a priest. He suffered torture during the persecution of Decius (250–51) and died in 253.

Controversy arose during the third century about some of Origen's opinions, and this became more heated during the following centuries. Under the emperor Justinian I, a synod of Constantinople in 543 condemned nine propositions attributed to him, notably concerning the preexistence of human souls and the final restoration of all the damned. As a result, most of his works in the original Greek were destroyed, but many have been preserved in translation.

While the Church later rejected some of his opinions, there can be no doubt about Origen's intention to remain faithful to the apostolic tradition. He expressed this intention very clearly in the preface to his great work *On First Principles*.[27]

> 1. Preface. Many of those who profess to believe in Christ are not in agreement, not only on points of small or minimal significance, but even on questions of great or very great importance, i.e., concerning God or the Lord Jesus Christ himself or the Holy Spirit and not only on these questions, but also on the subject of his creatures such as the Dominations or the holy Powers. For all these reasons, it seems necessary to start by laying down a definite line on each of these things and a clear rule and then to proceed from there to ask questions about other matters. Many Greeks and barbarians have promised the truth but, starting from the moment when we came to believe that Christ is the Son of God, we recognized that their ideas were only false opinions. Similarly there are many who think they are Christian believers, yet many of these same people in fact believe differently from those who went before them. The Church's preaching has been handed down through an orderly succession from the Apostles and remains in the Church until the present. That alone is to be believed as

the truth which in no way departs from ecclesiastical and apostolic tradition.

Origen's writings give evidence of his familiarity with the work of Irenaeus
against the Gnostics. The above passage from the preface of Origen's work
On First Principles shows that he shared Irenaeus's view of the role the
"orderly succession from the Apostles" had played in handing on the apostolic tradition and that he also shared Irenaeus's intention to remain faithful to that tradition.

Origen on the Clergy of His Day

While Clement of Alexandria had hardly ever mentioned the clergy in his
writings, Origen did so frequently, especially in his homilies. But, as Von
Campenhausen points out, more than half of the relevant passages strike a
note of bitter criticism and concern.[28] He explains this as due to the fact that
Origen proposed the "gnostic" ideal of a deeper knowledge of the faith, and
a spiritual way of life consonant with such knowledge, as the norm all those
in positions of leadership in the Church should follow. In Origen's view, the
essential task of bishops and priests consisted of serving as spiritual guides to
the faithful, setting them an example of spiritual perfection and mediating
the higher gifts to them. In his view, therefore, the cleric was called to practice an ascetical way of life. He had to be free of earthly concerns and devote
himself wholly to the study of God's word, so as to be able to share his
higher knowledge with others. This resulted in Origen setting a standard of
perfection for the members of the clergy, which evidently many of them
failed to meet. And this explains why so many of his references to the clergy
in his homilies cited their faults and failings.

Von Campenhausen describes Origen as "the first penitential preacher
of the clerical profession." He intended his criticism to educate the members of the clergy to a more spiritual conception of their authority and calling and to awaken in them a personal spiritual life and a deeper sense of
responsibility. He did not direct his critique at the hierarchical structure as
such; Von Campenhausen observes that this was by now something so
long established that Origen would never dream of questioning it.[29]

For our purpose here, it will suffice to cite some passages of Origen's
homilies that throw light on the hierarchical structure of the churches of
Alexandria and Palestine where he taught and preached. Many of these
homilies explained sections of the Old Testament, where Origen saw the
role of the priest and levite as models for the Christian clergy. The following passage of a homily on Leviticus is typical in this regard.[30]

Let us see, therefore, by what sort of rite the high priest is installed. We read: "Moses called together the assembly and said to them: 'This is the word which the Lord has commanded.'"[Lev 8:5]. Although the Lord gave precepts for establishing the high priest, and the Lord chose him, nevertheless the assembly is also called together. For at the ordination of a priest the presence of the people is also necessary, so that all might know and be sure, because that man is chosen for the priesthood who is more outstanding among the whole people, more learned, holier, more eminent in every virtue. And this is done in the presence of the people lest anyone later have second thoughts, or anyone should remain doubtful. This is what the Apostle commanded for the ordination of a priest when he says: "He should also have a good attestation from those who are outside" [1 Tim 3:7].

In this passage, where Origen saw the installation of the high priest by Moses as the model for the ordination of the Christian priest, he clearly used the term "priest" to refer to the bishop. In a passage from a homily on the Book of Numbers, Origen spoke of abuses in the way bishops were being chosen, contrasting the way Moses left the choice of his successor up to God with how a Christian bishop might try to designate a member of his own family to succeed him.[31]

Let us admire the greatness of Moses. As he was about to depart from this life, he prayed God to choose a leader for his people....Would that the princes of the Church, instead of designating in their wills those linked to them by ties of blood or family relationships and instead of trying to set up dynasties in the Church, might learn to rely on God's judgment and far from choosing as human feelings urge, would leave the designations of their successors entirely in God's hands....If a great man like Moses did not take upon himself the choice of a leader from the people, the election of his successor, who then will dare, among this people which gives its vote under the influence of emotion, or perhaps of money; who will dare then, even in the ranks of the priests, judge himself capable of pronouncing on this, unless by means of a revelation obtained through prayers and supplications addressed to the Lord?

In the previous chapter, we saw evidence in Tertullian's writings that in the church of North Africa a member of the clergy whose wife had died was forbidden to remarry. Origen witnesses to the fact that the churches of Egypt and Palestine also observed this rule. In a homily on Luke, he remarked: "Not only fornication, but also second marriages exclude a person from ecclesiastical dignities; for neither the bishop nor the presbyter nor the deacon nor the widow can be twice married." Albano Vilela, who quotes this text, observes that the widows associated with the clergy were officially enrolled and served the community by their works of charity.[32] Here we also have one of the many instances where Origen refers to the threefold hierarchy of bishop, presbyter and deacon.

The following passage shows that Origen attributed priesthood to the bishop and presbyter, but not to the deacon.

> Do you think that those who exercise the priesthood and glory in their priestly order, conduct themselves in a way that accords with their order, and do everything in a way that befits their order? Likewise, do you think that deacons conduct themselves in keeping with their order of ministry? How does it happen, then, that we often hear people blaspheming and saying: Look what kind of a bishop, what kind of presbyter, what kind of deacon that is? Are not such things said when a priest or a minister of God is observed acting in a way that is unbecoming his order, and doing what is contrary to the priestly or levitical order?[33]

Clearly the bishop and presbyter belong to the priestly order, while the deacon belongs to the levitical order. Other texts, such as the following, show that even in Origen's day clergy had ambitions for promotion from a lower order to a higher. Origen compared them to the Pharisees whom Jesus criticized for seeking the first places at banquets.

> Even in the Church of Christ one finds men who organize banquets, and who love to have the first places, who scheme first of all to become deacons, and then are ambitious to obtain the chair of the priests, and, not content with that, scheme to be called bishops by men.[34]

Origen saw bishops as those holding the highest rank among the clergy. He described them as leaders *(hegoumenoi);* princes of the churches *(ecclesiarum principes);* high priests *(sacerdotes magni).*[35] At the same time, we find passages where he associated presbyters with the bishops in the leadership of the church, even as sharing with them the reproach the Lord spoke through the prophet Jeremiah: "Fools my people are,/they know me not..." (Jer 4:22).[36] One must recall that Origen delivered most of these homilies as a presbyter of the church of Caesarea and would have had other presbyters listening to him. Von Campenhausen says that in those later years of his life Origen "entered wholeheartedly into clerical life, preached to the congregation, attended synods, disputed with heretics, and generally proved himself the churchman that he wished to be."[37]

The final test of his loyalty to the church came during the persecution of the emperor Decius, when he suffered the imprisonment and torture that left his health so shattered that he died a year later. This persecution, which ended Origen's life, marked the first year of the episcopate of Cyprian, bishop of Carthage, the subject of our next chapter.

10
CYPRIAN, BISHOP OF CARTHAGE

Caecilius Cyprianus Thascius was born between 200 and 210 in North Africa, probably at Carthage, the son of a wealthy and cultivated pagan family. As a young man he gained great fame as a rhetorician and master of eloquence in Carthage. He converted to the Christian faith about the year 245 and became a member of the clergy. Within four years Cyprian was chosen bishop of Carthage with the enthusiastic approval of the laity, but against the opposition of some elderly presbyters.

He had not been bishop of Carthage for more than a year when the persecution of the emperor Decius broke out, which obliged all the subjects of the Empire to offer sacrifice to the gods under penalty of imprisonment, torture or death. Cyprian fled to a safe place in the country; from there he kept in touch with his flock by frequent letters. The persecution of Decius lasted only one year, but a great many Christians, including members of the clergy, succumbed to the pressure inflicted upon them either by offering sacrifice to the gods or by bribing an official to grant them a certificate falsely attesting to their having done so.

When the persecution ended, a great many of these "lapsed" Christians sought reconciliation with the church, and some of the presbyters who remained in Carthage during Cyprian's exile began to offer such reconciliation without requiring the fulfillment of a period of public penance. Cyprian insisted that reconciliation of the lapsed should be delayed until the bishops of North Africa formulated a common policy about this in council. However, five of his presbyters, those who had opposed his election as bishop, formed a schismatic group and subsequently got one of their number ordained as a rival bishop of Carthage. This schism, as well as the schism caused by Novatian, a presbyter of the church of Rome who got himself ordained as a rival to Cornelius, the rightful bishop there, provides the background against which Cyprian wrote his treatise *On the Unity of the Catholic Church.*[1]

Cyprian was absent from his church for a little more than a year while the persecution of Decius lasted. During that period he wrote a number of letters to the clergy and lay faithful of his church, and he kept up a frequent correspondence with other bishops during the seven years that followed, up to the time of his martyrdom in the persecution of Valerian in 258. These letters, some of which are more like treatises, provide precious information not only about Cyprian's life and thought, but about the Christian church at the middle of its third century.[2]

Eighty-two letters have come down to us, a few of which were written to Cyprian rather than by him. The most famous of these is a letter by Firmilian, bishop of Caesarea in Cappadocia. In it Firmilian strongly attacks Stephen, the bishop of Rome, for insisting that churches in Asia Minor, as well as those of North Africa, follow the Roman tradition with regard to reconciling people who had been baptized in a heretical or schismatic sect to the Catholic Church. The Roman tradition held that such people should not be rebaptized, whereas Cyprian and Firmilian held that they must be baptized in the Catholic Church, as baptism conferred outside it was always invalid. Despite Cyprian's refusal to conform to the Roman custom in this matter and the sharp words he addressed to Stephen in rejecting his demand for conformity, there is no indication that this resulted in a break of communion between them. Stephen died in 257, and Cyprian suffered martyrdom the following year.

Most of the passages cited in this chapter are taken from his letters. Rather than following the chronological order of the letters, it seems better to use a systematic ordering of the material, citing passages that illustrate various themes Cyprian treated. In keeping with the purpose of this book, only passages that throw light on his theory and practice of the ministry, especially that of the bishop, are included.

The Church and the Episcopate Are Founded by Christ on Peter

Let. 33.1.1 Our Lord, whose precepts it is our duty to fear and to follow, regulates the dignity of His bishops and the structure of His Church, when He speaks as follows in the gospels, addressing Peter: *I say to you that you are Peter, and on this rock I will build my church, and the gates of hell will not prevail*

against it. And to you I will give the keys of the kingdom of
heaven and whatsoever you have bound on earth will be bound
also in heaven, and whatsoever you have loosed on earth will be
loosed in heaven.

From this source flows the appointment of bishops and the
organization of the Church, with bishop succeeding bishop
down through the course of time, so that the Church is
founded upon the bishops and every act of the Church is gov-
erned through these same appointed leaders.

1.2 This establishment has been founded, then, in this way by
the law of God. I am, therefore, astounded that certain people
have had the outrageous audacity to take upon themselves to
write to me a letter "in the name of the church," whereas, in
fact, the church has been established upon the bishop, the
clergy and all those who remain faithful.[3]

Comment

Those who have written a letter to Cyprian "in the name of the church"
are a group of people who "lapsed" during the persecution. They now
arrogantly demand reconciliation with the church on their own terms and
not on those to be established by the bishops when they meet in council.
Cyprian begins his reply by showing that in thus flouting the authority of
the bishops, they in effect deny the divine origin of the episcopate, which
Christ founded when he gave to Peter the keys of the kingdom and the
authority to "bind and loose." Cyprian consistently interpreted the
"Petrine text" of Matthew 16:18–19 as he does here, not in the sense of
powers given exclusively to Peter, but as the divine founding of the church
and its episcopal structure. It is therefore "the law of God" that bishop
should succeed bishop down through the course of time.

Note that when Cyprian says that the church was founded "upon the
bishops," he is identifying the apostles as "bishops." One finds another
example of this identification in Letter 3.3.1, where he says:

For their part, deacons should bear in mind that it was the
Lord who chose Apostles, that is to say, bishops and appointed
leaders *[episcopos et praepositos]*, whereas it was the Apostles
who, after the ascension of Our Lord into heaven, established
deacons to assist the Church and themselves, in their office of
bishop *[apostoli sibi constituerunt episcopatus sui et ecclesiae
ministros]*.[4]

The Treatise De Unitate Ecclesiae Catholicae

Soon after returning to Carthage at the end of the persecution of Decius, Cyprian delivered his treatise *On the Unity of the Catholic Church* to the clergy and people. As mentioned, the context of this work was the schism threatening the churches of both Carthage and Rome. Here again he insisted that Christ founded the church and its unity upon Peter.

> *De Unitate* 3. All this has come about, dearest brethren, because men do not go back to the origin of [the Christian] realities, because they do not look for their source, nor keep to the teaching of their heavenly Master.
>
> 4. But if anyone considers those things carefully, he will need no long discourse or arguments. The proof is simple and convincing, being summed up in a matter of fact. The Lord says to Peter: [he then quotes Matt 16:18–19]. And he says to him again after the resurrection: "Feed my sheep." It is on him that He builds the Church, and to him that He entrusts the sheep to feed. And although He assigns a like power to all the Apostles, yet He founded a single Chair, thus establishing by His own authority the source and hallmark of the [Church's] oneness. No doubt the others were all that Peter was, but a primacy is given to Peter, and it is [thus] made clear that there is but one Church and one Chair. So too, even if they are all shepherds, we are shown but one flock which is to be fed by all the Apostles in common accord. If a man does not hold fast to this oneness of Peter, does he imagine that he still holds the faith? If he deserts the Chair of Peter upon whom the Church was built, has he still confidence that he is in the Church?
>
> 5. The authority of the bishops forms a unity, of which each holds his part in its totality *(Episcopatus unus est cuius a singulis in solidum pars tenetur)*. And the Church forms a unity, however far she spreads and multiplies by the progeny of her fecundity; just as the sun's rays are many, yet the light is one, and a tree's branches are many, yet the strength deriving from its sturdy root is one.[5]

Comment

By a careful study of the manuscript evidence, Maurice Bévenot has proven that this is what Cyprian wrote in the original version of his *De*

Unitate and that several years later, during his dispute with Pope Stephen, he revised this part of his text, omitting the reference to "the primacy given to Peter" and the question: "If he deserts the Chair of Peter upon whom the Church was built, has he still confidence that he is in the Church?" While Catholic scholars held this version to be genuine, seeing in it a clear witness to the papal primacy, many Protestant scholars claimed that these phrases had been subsequently interpolated into his text. Bévenot has shown not only that this version was genuine, but also that when Cyprian said "a primacy is given to Peter," he meant something quite different from what "papal primacy" came to mean in the following centuries.

Cyprian used the term in its original sense of "priority." In the fact that Christ had *first* given to Peter the power he later gave to all the Twelve, Cyprian saw a clear expression of the Lord's intention to found a church that would be built on the unity of the apostles and of the bishops who would be their successors. In this context, the "one Chair," which is also "the Chair of Peter," is the "one episcopate" by whose unity the oneness of the Church is maintained. Bévenot explains: "In Cyprian's mind, the legitimate bishop of *every* see occupied a place in the 'one chair' which Christ inaugurated with Peter."[6]

In another context Cyprian also recognized that the episcopal see of Rome had a special claim to be called the "chair of Peter," and we shall see the consequences that had, in his view, for the kind of authority he recognized the bishop of Rome to possess. However, there can be no doubt that the primary meaning the "chair which Christ founded upon Peter" had for Cyprian was the unity of the episcopate which it signified and established. Another, among many expressions of this idea, is the following.

> Let. 43.5.2 God is one and Christ is one: there is one Church and one chair founded, by the Lord's authority, upon Peter. It is not possible that another altar can be set up, or that a new priesthood can be appointed, over and above this one altar and this one priesthood. Whoever gathers elsewhere, scatters. Whatever is so established by man in his madness that it violates what has been appointed by God is an obscene outrage, it is sacrilege.[7]

Comment

For Cyprian, "priesthood" and "episcopacy" were synonymous terms; bishops were both *episcopi* and *sacerdotes*. In his usage, the first of these terms pointed to the bishops' role of government, and the second, as here, stressed their liturgical functions. Hence, to "set up another altar" was to introduce a rival bishop into a local church. Again, it is clear that

Cyprian believed the unity of each church under one bishop to be of divine institution, manifested by the fact that Christ originally conferred this authority on one man, Peter.

In *De Unitate,* and also in his letters, Cyprian develops the theme that just as the unity of each local church depends on the leadership of one duly appointed bishop, so the unity of the Catholic Church is maintained by the communion of all these legitimate bishops with one another. The following passage is one of many that expresses this idea.

> Let. 55.24.2 Moreover, there is but one Church founded by Christ but it is divided into many members throughout the world; likewise, there is but one episcopate but it is spread amongst the harmonious host of all the numerous bishops. And yet, despite this arrangement established by God, despite this unity in the catholic Church which is universally linked and locked together, he [Novatian] is now attempting to set up a man-made church and he is sending out to numerous cities upstart apostles of his own in order to lay down brand-new foundations for an establishment of his own devising.[8]

Comment

Because the bishops Novatian is "sending out to numerous cities" are, as Cyprian sees it, really founding a new church, he sarcastically calls them "apostles." This reflects his sense that Christ's apostles were also the first bishops, of whom the legitimate bishops are the divinely appointed successors.

Bishops Are the Successors to the Apostles

> Let. 45.3.2 Above all other goals, my brother, we strive, and ought to strive, to achieve this, to maintain to the limits of our ability that unity which was laid down by the Lord and handed on through the apostles to us their successors.

> Let. 66.4.2 And these things I say not by way of boasting; I mention them only in sorrow, for you are now appointing yourself judge over God and Christ, and He did say to his apostles, and thereby to all the leaders who are successors to the apostles, appointed to replace them: *He who hears you hears*

me, and he who hears me hears Him who sent me. And he who despises you despises me and Him who sent me.[9]

Comment

The first of these passages comes from a letter of Cyprian to his brother-bishop, Cornelius, bishop of Rome. The second, of very different tone, is from the reply Cyprian addressed to a man named Puppianus, who had accused Cyprian of grave dereliction of his duty as bishop. The Latin of the phrase "leaders who are successors to the apostles, appointed to replace them" is *praepositos qui apostolis vicaria ordinatione succedunt.* The expression *vicaria ordinatione succedunt* highlights the fact that, in Cyprian's usage, *ordinatio* often meant "appointment to office" rather than the liturgical rite of ordination and that just as the bishop of Rome was called "vicar of Peter" (long before he was called "vicar of Christ"), so all bishops could be seen as "vicars of apostles." These passages, along with other similar ones in his writings, make it obvious that in Cyprian's day, it was generally understood that duly appointed bishops were the lawful successors to the apostles.

Unity of the Church Maintained through the Unity of the Bishops

In the same letter to his critic Puppianus, Cyprian reminds him that the church is one through the unity of its bishops.

> Let. 66.8.3 You ought to realize that the bishop is in the Church and the Church is in the bishop, and whoever is not with the bishop is not in the Church. You must understand that it is to no avail that people may beguile themselves with the illusion that whilst they are not at peace with the bishops of God they may still worm their way in and surreptitiously hold communion with certain people. Whereas in truth, the Church forms one single whole; it is neither rent nor broken apart but is everywhere linked and bonded tightly together by the glue of the bishops firmly sticking to each other.[10]

Writing to Stephen, the bishop of Rome, and urging him to intervene so as to restore peace to the church of Arles in Gaul, Cyprian reminds him of a duty that follows from this close bond of unity among bishops.

Let. 68.3.2 Now, dearly beloved brother, there is good reason why our body of bishops is at once so generously large and yet so tightly bound together by the glue of mutual concord and by the bond of unity: it is so that should anyone from our sacred college attempt to form a heretical sect and thus to savage and devastate the flock of Christ, there should be others to come to the rescue, and being practical and kindhearted shepherds, they should gather the Lord's sheep back in to the fold.[11]

Unity Among Bishops Maintained by Councils and by Correspondence

While the persecution of Decius was still in effect and Cyprian was still absent from his church, he insisted on postponing any decision about terms for reconciling those who had lapsed. He explains his reason for this in a letter to a bishop named Antonianus.

Let. 55.4.3 My idea was that when peace and tranquility had been restored and God in His goodness allowed the bishops to gather together, then that was the time for everyone to contribute and exchange their views together and to deliberate upon them, and it was after that that we should determine what ought to be done....

6.1 And, in accordance with what had been planned beforehand, when the persecution died down and opportunity offered for us to convene together, there gathered in Council a generous number of bishops who had been preserved safe and unharmed thanks to their own staunch faith and the protection of the Lord. Scriptural passages were produced, in a lengthy debate, on both sides of the issue and eventually we arrived at a balanced and moderate decision, striking a healthy mean....

6.2 And in case anyone might regard the number of bishops who met in Africa to have been too few, you should know that we wrote to Rome also on this matter, to our colleague Cornelius. And he, meeting in Council with a large number of his fellow bishops, has agreed upon the same verdict as ours, after debating with equal seriousness and striking the same healthy balance.[12]

Comment

The statement "We wrote to Rome also on this matter" points to the custom of communicating to other churches the decisions taken at regional councils as well as to the frequent correspondence between the churches of Carthage and Rome. In a letter to Cornelius, bishop of Rome, Cyprian takes pains to explain why he had not written to him about two schismatic bishops recently introduced into North Africa.

> Let. 59.9.1 And I can explain, dearly beloved brother, why I did not write to you at once about that pseudo bishop Fortunatus who has been set up by a mere handful of chronic heretics. The simple answer is that this was not a matter which needed to be brought to your attention at once and in great haste as being of the most formidable and gravest importance.... 9.2 As a matter of fact, the faction of Novatian is also said to have now appointed here as their pseudo bishop the presbyter Maximus, who was lately sent over to us by Novatian as his representative and who was rejected from our communion. 9.3 And yet I did not write to you on this subject either, for we are contemptuous of all such matters, and, besides, I did send to you very recently the names of the bishops here in Africa who govern the brethren within the catholic Church with integrity and soundness of faith. Indeed, it was a unanimous resolution of our Council to write this list to you for the express purpose that it would be a quick way for removing error and perceiving the truth clearly, and that, therefore, you and our colleagues would know to whom it is proper for you to write and from whom, in turn, it is proper for you to accept letters.[13]

Comment

This passage shows how important it was for maintaining communion among the Catholic bishops that they know who, in other regions of the church, were the bishops with whom they should correspond. The first qualification of such bishops was that they had been chosen and appointed according to the rightful procedure. In several letters, Cyprian explains what this required.

The Election and Ordination of Bishops

Fabian, the bishop of Rome, suffered martyrdom in January, 250, the earliest known victim of the persecution of Decius. Because the persecution lasted through that year, the election of Fabian's successor, Cornelius, was delayed until March, 251. Novatian, one of the leading Roman presbyters, strongly contested his election and subsequently had himself ordained as a rival bishop. In a letter Cyprian wrote to a bishop who seemed to give credence to Novatian's charges against the legitimacy of Cornelius's election, he explained the reasons why he and the other African bishops recognized Cornelius as the rightful bishop of Rome.

> Let. 55.8.4 He was made bishop by a large number of our colleagues who were present at the time in the city of Rome and who have sent to us on the subject of his appointment testimonials which acclaim his honour and esteem and cover him with glory by their praises. Moreover, Cornelius was made bishop by the choice of God and of His Christ, by the favorable witness of almost all of the clergy, by the votes of the laity then present, and by the assembly of bishops, men of maturity and integrity. And he was made bishop when no one else had been made bishop before him, when the position of Fabian, that is to say, the position of Peter and the office of the bishop's chair, was vacant. But that position once having been filled by the will of God and that appointment having been ratified by the consent of us all, if anyone wants to be made bishop after that, it has to be done outside the Church; if a man does not uphold the Church's unity, it is not possible for him to have the Church's ordination.... 9.1 So, then, Cornelius took on this office of bishop, obtained neither through any corruption nor any extortion, but through the will of God, who is the one who makes bishops.[14]

Comment

Three times in this passage Cyprian asserts that Cornelius was made bishop "by the choice of God" or "by the will of God." He firmly believed that the approval of a candidate by laity, clergy and bishops gave a certain indication of the will of God and that ultimately "it is God who makes bishops." In this case, he had to say "by almost all of the clergy" because of Novatian's known opposition. In Cyprian's assertion that the appointment of Cornelius had been "ratified by the consent of us all," the "us all" includes at least the bishops of North Africa and may also include bishops of other regions. The election of a bishop, especially of Rome, would be communicated to the other principal churches.

In letter 67, in which he defended the legitimacy of the election of a bishop named Sabinus, Cyprian argued that the lawful procedure being followed in the choice of bishops was based on "divine teaching and apostolic observance." He found the divine teaching in the instruction the Lord gave to Moses to make Aaron's son Eleazar a priest *in the presence of all the assembled people* (Num 20:25 f.), and the "apostolic observance" in the fact that "when Peter addresses the people on the subject of appointing a bishop to replace Judas, we read: *Peter stood up in the midst of the disciples, for a large number was gathered together."* (Note that this is another instance of the fact that Cyprian thought of the apostles as "bishops.") Cyprian's letter continues:

> Let. 67.5.1 Hence we should show sedulous care in preserving a practice which is based on divine teaching and apostolic observance, a practice which is indeed faithfully followed among us and in practically every province. And it is this: when an episcopal appointment is to be duly solemnized, all the neighboring bishops in the same province convene for the purpose along with the people for whom the leader is to be appointed; the bishop is then selected in the presence of those people, for they are the ones who are acquainted most intimately with the way each man has lived his life and they have had the opportunity thoroughly to observe his conduct and behaviour. 5.2 And we note that this procedure was indeed observed in your own case when our colleague Sabinus was being appointed: the office of bishop was conferred upon him and hands were laid upon him in replacement of Basilides, following the verdict of the whole congregation and in conformity with the judgment of the bishops who had there convened with the congregation as well as of those who had written to you about him.[15]

Comment

This passage puts an even greater emphasis than the previous one on the role of the people in approving a candidate for the office of bishop. It is worth noting that Cyprian attributed his own election to the "voice of the people." He encountered strong opposition from five of the presbyters and evidently the enthusiasm of the congregation moved the bishops to ordain him, even though he had been a Christian for only about four years.

The passage about the election of Sabinus also mentions that a bishop was ordained by having "hands laid upon him." In Cyprian's usage, the Latin word *ordinatio* refers more often to "appointment to office" than to the liturgical rite.

The Ministry of Bishops

The words Cyprian most commonly used for a bishop were *episcopus* and *sacerdos*. As equivalent to *episcopus* he also used *praepositus* and *rector;* and for *sacerdos* he sometimes substituted *antistes*. The first of these words points to the leadership role of the bishop; the second to his liturgical and spiritual ministry. It should be noted that while we are accustomed to speaking of presbyters as "priests," Bévenot concludes his study of Cyprian's use of *sacerdos* by saying: "We are justified, then, in saying that when Cyprian speaks of Christian 'sacerdotes' he always means the bishops *(episcopi).*"[16]

Cyprian describes his episcopal ministry in his reply to an extremely offensive letter he had received from a man named Puppianus, who had judged Cyprian so unworthy of the episcopacy that he deemed his whole ministry invalid. Cyprian, who had been an accomplished rhetorician, employed his gift for sarcasm to the full in replying to this man who had appointed himself judge over his bishop.

> Let. 66.5.1 What an insolent sense of swollen self-importance, the high and mighty presumption of it all! Fancy anyone issuing a summons to bishops, the appointed leaders, *[praepositos et sacerdotes]* to attend his court of inquiry. And unless we are cleared before your bench and are acquitted by your verdict, the brethren will have had no overseer *[episcopum]* these last six years, the people no leader *[praepositum]*, the flock no shepherd *[pastorem]*, the Church no helmsman *[gubernatorem]*, Christ no priest *[antistitem]*, and God no bishop *[sacerdotem]*! 5.2 But only let Puppianus fly to the rescue! Let him issue his sentence and declare ratified the judgment God and Christ have already passed! Otherwise it could be thought that the great number of the faithful who have been called away to their rest during our time may have departed without the hope of peace and salvation; it could be considered that a whole new flock of converts may have received through us no grace of baptism and the Holy Spirit; it could be judged that the reconciliation and restoration to communion which we have conferred, after examination,

upon so many of the penitent lapsed may be rendered null and void by the authority of your verdict.[17]

Comment

The list of titles Cyprian attributes to himself in 5.1 gives a very good idea of how he understood his role as bishop. In 5.2 we see that his ministry included pastoral care of the dying, the reception of converts with baptism and the gift of the Holy Spirit, and the reconciliation of penitent sinners. In another letter, addressed to a fellow bishop, he speaks of their role as priests, offering the eucharistic sacrifice.

> Let. 63.17.1 And because at every sacrifice we offer we mention the passion of our Lord (indeed, the passion of our Lord is the sacrifice we offer), then we should follow exactly what the Lord did. And Scripture confirms that as often as we offer the cup in remembrance of the Lord and His passion, we are doing what all are agreed the Lord did before us.[18]

In another letter, Cyprian also speaks of the bishop's special role in Christian initiation, seeing it as patterned on what Peter and John did when they laid hands on the Samaritans whom Philip had baptized:

> Let. 73.9.2 And this same practice we observe today ourselves: those who are baptized in the Church are presented to the appointed leaders of the Church, and by our prayer and the imposition of our hands they receive the Holy Spirit and are made perfect with the Lord's seal.[19]

The bishop had another important role—choosing and ordaining clergy for his own church. While Cyprian was absent from Carthage during the persecution of Decius, he wrote a letter addressed to the presbyters and deacons and to all the laity of his church. It began as follows:

> Let. 38.1.1 Dearest brethren, it is our custom when we make appointments to clerical office to consult you beforehand, and in council together with you to weigh the character and qualities of each candidate. But there is no need to wait for evidence from men when already God has cast his vote. 1.2 Our brother Aurelius is a young man with a splendid record; he has already received the Lord's approbation and is dear to God. Tender in years he may be, but he is far advanced in glory for his faith and courage; though junior in terms of natural age, he is senior in honour. He has striven in a double contest: twice he has made

confession and twice he has covered himself with the glory of victorious confession.... 2.1 Such a man deserved higher grades of clerical appointment and greater advancement, judged as he should be not on his years but on his deserts. But it has been decided, for the time being, that he begin with the duties of reader.... 2.2 You should therefore know, dearly beloved brothers, that I and my colleagues who were present have appointed this man to office. I know that you warmly welcome this action just as you are anxious that as many men as possible of this calibre should receive appointments in our church.[20]

Comment

The young man Aurelius had "made confession" twice during the persecution; the first time he was exiled, and the second time he suffered torture, but evidently was released despite his refusal to offer sacrifice to the gods. The reader may recall that, according to *The Apostolic Tradition,* a "confessor" could be placed among the presbyters without having hands laid on him.[21] Cyprian does not say that hands were laid on Aurelius, but his mention of the participation of other bishops ("my colleagues") suggests a liturgical rite of ordination. It is worth noting that Cyprian would normally consult his clergy and laity even about the appointment of readers, who ranked lowest among the clergy.

Another letter Cyprian wrote to his clergy during his absence from Carthage shows that his episcopal ministry included solicitude for the widows, the sick, the poor and strangers.

Let. 7.2 I urge that you be scrupulous in your care for the widows, the sick, and all the poor, and further, that you meet the financial needs of any strangers who are in want out of my own personal funds which I have left in the care of our fellow presbyter Rogatianus. In case these funds have already been completely expended, I am sending to Rogatianus by the acolyte Naricus a further sum, to ensure that the work of charity amongst those in difficulties may be carried out the more generously and readily.[22]

The Ministry of Presbyters

The passages we have just seen show that the bishop consulted presbyters about appointments to the clergy and that presbyters shared in his care for the poor. Other letters Cyprian wrote to them during the year he spent in hiding show that, at least in his absence, presbyters celebrated the Eucharist and reconciled penitent sinners. One letter speaks of their offering the Eucharist in prison on behalf of the confessors there.

> Let. 5.2.1 And so take counsel and care that moderation makes visiting safer; in particular the presbyters who celebrate the offering there before the confessors should take it in turns to go individually, accompanied each by a different deacon, because the risk of resentment is diminished if the people who visit and meet together change and vary.[23]

Likewise, in his absence presbyters were authorized to reconcile penitents in danger of death.

> Let. 18.1.2 In the case of those who have received certificates from the martyrs and can, consequently, be helped by those martyrs' privileged position before God, should they be seized by some sickness or dangerous illness, they need not wait for our presence, but they may make confession of their sin before any presbyter in person, or if a presbyter cannot be found and their end is coming fast, even before a deacon. In this way, after hands have been laid on them in forgiveness, they may come to the Lord with that peace which, in their letter to us, the martyrs requested should be granted to them.[24]

Comment

While presbyters certainly celebrated the Eucharist in Cyprian's absence, his letters do not make it clear whether they did so while he was in Carthage. As seen above, he used the term *sacerdos* only of bishops. However, there is a passage (Let. 61.3.1) in which he speaks of the presbyters of Rome as "united with that bishop [Cornelius] in the dignity of the priesthood [*sacerdotali honore coniuncti*]." In another letter he insists on the observance of the rule laid down by a council that excluded any member of the clergy from being named in a will as a guardian or trustee. He explains the reason for this rule as follows.

> Let. 1.1.1 The reason being that everyone honoured with the sacred priesthood and appointed to clerical office ought to dedicate himself exclusively to altar and sacrifices, and devote himself entirely to prayer and supplication. For it is written: *No soldier fighting in God's service entangles himself in the anxieties of this world, thereby enabling himself to be free to please Him who enlisted him.*[25]

Comment

Because the appointment of a presbyter as trustee of a will occasioned this letter, it is obvious that Cyprian included presbyters among those who "ought to dedicate themselves exclusively to altar and sacrifices." One can conclude that even though Cyprian reserved the term "priest" to bishops, he associated presbyters with them in priestly functions and in the dignity of the priesthood.

Some of the presbyters also undertook the ministry of teaching the catechumens. In a letter informing his clergy that he had appointed a confessor named Optatus as reader, Cyprian explained how he had first tested him: "As for Optatus, when we were recently putting under careful examination readers for the teacher-presbyters, we appointed him one of the readers for the teachers of catechumens."[26]

Cyprian and the Roman Presbyters

More than a year elapsed between the death of Pope Fabian and the election of his successor Cornelius. The correspondence between Cyprian and the church of Rome during that interval shows how the Roman presbyters felt called upon, while the episcopal chair was vacant, to exercise collegially the kind of authority the bishops of Rome had customarily exercised. In the collection of Cyprian's letters, the first letter from the Roman presbyters is addressed to the clergy of Carthage, giving them instructions on dealing with those who lapsed during the persecution. In his commentary on this letter, Clarke says: "The mood in which the Roman clergy address the Carthaginian is notably imperative, authoritative, indeed, episcopal."[27] They applied to themselves the term *praepositi*, which Cyprian regularly used for bishops.

> Let. 8.1.1 Now we are clearly the leaders *[praepositi]* and it is accordingly our duty to keep watch over the flock, acting in the place of our shepherds....[28]

While not addressed to Cyprian, the letter evidently came to his attention, and he wrote a letter to the Roman clergy that shows his respect for the authority they were exercising during the fourteen months while Rome had no bishop. He had the impression that they were critical of his absence from his church during the persecution, and he felt it necessary to give them an account of his conduct.

> Let. 20.1.1 I have discovered, beloved brethren, that the reports being made to you on our actions both past and present

are not completely candid and accurate. I have therefore considered it necessary to write to you this letter in order that I might
render to you an account of our conduct, our maintenance of
Church discipline, and our zeal.[29]

Cyprian goes on to explain his motives for going into hiding and insists
that he had continued to exercise pastoral care of his flock through the
many letters he had sent to his clergy and faithful; in fact, he sends copies
of thirteen of them to the Roman presbyters. Toward the end of his letter
he says:

> 3.2 And furthermore I have read your message which you
> recently sent to our clergy by the hands of the subdeacon
> Crementius. You counselled that comfort should be given to
> those who fell ill after their lapse and being penitent, were anx-
> ious to be admitted to communion. I have, therefore, decided
> that I too should take my stand alongside your opinion,
> thereby avoiding that our actions, which ought to be united
> and in harmony on every issue, might differ in any respect.[30]

From the tone and contents of this letter, it is clear that Cyprian respected
the authority of the presbyters of Rome while the episcopal chair was
vacant. He gives no indication that he thought they were overstepping
their authority when they gave instructions to the clergy of Carthage
about the reconciliation of those who had lapsed; in fact, he brought his
own policy into line with theirs. This correspondence sheds a good deal of
light on the collegial leadership Cyprian recognized presbyters to have, at
least *sede vacante*, as well as on Cyprian's respect for the authority of the
church of Rome. We shall return to this last point after saying something
about the ministry of deacons.

The Ministry of Deacons

Cyprian was one of many Fathers who saw the institution of the diaconate in the appointment of the "Seven" by the apostles in Acts 6:1–6. We
have quoted the passage in which he says that the apostles appointed these
men "as ministers of their office as bishops" *(episcopatus sui ministros)*.[31]
From this we can see that Cyprian saw deacons as primarily in the service of
the bishop. This included assistance to the bishop in the celebration of the
Eucharist, at which the deacons administered the chalice to the laity (on this
see *De Lapsis* 25). As noted earlier, the presbyters who celebrated the

Eucharist in prison for the confessors were accompanied by a deacon. In the immediate danger of death, and when no presbyter was available, Cyprian authorized his deacons to reconcile penitents.[32] Deacons were also involved in the care of widows, orphans, and others in need of financial assistance. That deacons would have charge of funds for this purpose is clear from what Cyprian writes about one named Nicostratus.

> Let. 52.1.2 As for Nicostratus, he has been stripped of the administration of his holy office of deacon, having sacrilegiously embezzled moneys belonging to the church and having refused to return deposits lodged by widows and orphans.[33]

CYPRIAN AND THE BISHOPS OF ROME

The Bishops of Rome and the Chair of Peter

As we have seen above, Cyprian did not interpret the "Petrine text" of Matthew 16:18–19 in the sense of powers given exclusively to Peter, but rather as the founding of the episcopacy in which all the apostles shared. In giving the keys and the power to bind and loose first to Peter, Cyprian understood the Lord to have expressed his will that there be only one episcopate, of which each bishop should have his part. Because the symbol of the bishop's role was his *cathedra,* Cyprian could say that in giving episcopal authority first to Peter, Christ had "founded a single chair." Hence he could also use the term "the chair of Peter" to refer to the episcopate as inaugurated in Peter, and, for that reason, as necessarily one.

At the same time, however, Cyprian also recognized that the Roman episcopate had a special claim to the title "chair of Peter." He accepted the tradition that the bishops of Rome were the successors of Peter; indeed, given his description of the apostles as bishops, it is likely that he thought of Peter as having been the first bishop of Rome.[34] It is not surprising, then, that in the letter in which he defended the legitimacy of the election of Cornelius, he described the bishop's chair at Rome as *locus Petri.*[35] Subsequently, in a letter to Cornelius, Cyprian expressed his indignation that the rebels in his own church had tried to get their schismatic bishop approved at Rome.

> Let. 59.14.1 They have had heretics set up for them a pseudo bishop, and on top of that they now have the audacity to sail off carrying letters from schismatics and outcasts from religion even to the chair of Peter, to the primordial church, the very

source of episcopal unity; and they do not stop to consider that they are carrying them to those same Romans whose faith was so praised and proclaimed by the Apostle, into whose company men without faith can, therefore, find no entry.[36]

Comment

The terms used by Cyprian here—*ad Petri cathedram atque ad ecclesiam principalem unde unitas sacerdotalis exorta est*—have often been cited by Catholics as proof that Cyprian recognized papal primacy in the sense it later came to have. However, while on the one hand the term "chair of Peter" clearly means the Roman episcopate in this instance, it must also be understood here as referring to the one episcopate inaugurated by Christ when he founded his church upon Peter. For this reason Rome, as Peter's church, is the "primordial" or "original" church from which "the unity of the episcopacy took its origin." Bévenot stresses the past tense of *exorta est;* Cyprian is looking back to the moment when Christ founded the church upon Peter.[37]

Cyprian Called upon the Bishop of Rome to Use His Authority in an Affair of the Church of Gaul

After the deaths of Cornelius and his successor Lucius, who were both venerated as martyrs, Stephen became the next bishop of Rome. In 257 he also died as a martyr, preceding Cyprian by a little more than a year. Relations between Cyprian and Stephen were initially cordial, but later became strained over the question of baptism administered outside the Catholic Church. Before that question arose, Cyprian wrote to Stephen urging him to intervene in a dispute involving Marcianus, the bishop of Arles, one of the major sees of Gaul. Marcianus was allied with the schismatic bishop Novatian and, like him, refused to grant absolution to penitents who had lapsed during the persecution of Decius. The following communicates the substance of what Cyprian wrote to Stephen:

> Let. 68.1.1 Marcianus has departed from the truth of the catholic Church and from the harmony of our corporate body of bishops by espousing the perverse and pitiless tenets of that presumptuous heresy....
>
> 1.2 It is incumbent upon us, beloved brother, to help remedy and rectify such a situation as this....

2.1 It is, therefore, your duty to write in the most explicit terms to our fellow bishops in Gaul: they should not suffer Marcianus, that obstinate and arrogant enemy of the mercy of God and the salvation of his brothers, to continue any further to scoff at our college of bishops, taunting us on the grounds that he does not appear so far to have been excommunicated by us....

3.1 I exhort you, therefore, to direct letters to that province and to the faithful who dwell at Arles, urging that after Marcianus has been excommunicated, a successor be appointed in his place....

5.1 It is our duty to preserve the honour of those glorious predecessors of ours, the blessed martyrs Cornelius and Lucius. But much as we, for our part, honour their memory, you, dearly beloved brother, far more than anyone else, are in duty bound to bring honour upon that memory, and to uphold it, by exerting the full weight of your personal authority; after all, you are the one who had been appointed to replace and succeed them. And they, being filled with the spirit of the Lord and the glory of martyrdom, declared that reconciliation was to be granted to the fallen, and they indicated in their letters that when penance had been done, its reward of reconciliation and restoration to communion was not to be denied.

5.2 And throughout the world without exception we all made the same declaration on the matter....Let us know who precisely it is who is appointed to replace Marcianus at Arles, so that we may be informed as to whom we are to direct our brethren and to whom we are to write ourselves.[38]

Comment

Cyprian urges Stephen to "exert the full weight of his personal authority" (*gravitate et auctoritate tua*) in this affair of the church of Arles. It is important, then, to note what exactly he expects Stephen to do. Clearly this is not a question of simply deposing Marcianus and appointing his successor, as a modern pope might do. On the other hand, Stephen has a "duty" to write to the bishops of that province and the faithful of the church of Arles so that Marcianus will be excommunicated and a successor appointed in his place. Clearly they are expected to accomplish this. Cyprian feels confident that they will do it, as he asks Stephen to let the bishops of North Africa know who has been appointed to replace Marcianus.

This shows a very nuanced appreciation of the authority the bishop of Rome could exercise beyond the limits of his own province. Cyprian insisted that it was Stephen's duty to intervene in the affairs of the church in Gaul, but he expected him to use his authority to persuade rather than to command. Evidently Cyprian also expected Stephen's intervention to be effective in moving the bishops of the province and the faithful of Arles to depose Marcianus and appoint his successor. This would indicate that the bishop of Rome had a certain role in overseeing the churches of Gaul as well as those in Italy. The next question would test the limits of the authority Cyprian would recognize the bishop of Rome to have.

CONTROVERSY OVER THE RECEPTION OF THOSE BAPTIZED BY HERETICS

Different answers were given to the question of whether those baptized in heretical or schismatic sects should be baptized if later they were received into the Catholic Church. A North African council had decided that they should be baptized, and Cyprian believed this to be the only theologically sound decision. He felt convinced that only in the true church would the Holy Spirit be given and that baptism that did not give the Holy Spirit did nothing at all. However, the Roman tradition recognized the validity of baptism, if administered correctly, outside the Catholic Church and hence insisted that it should not be repeated; all that was needed when a baptized person was received was the imposition of the bishop's hands for the gift of the Holy Spirit.

The only letter Cyprian addressed to Stephen on this question simply communicated to him the decisions taken at the North African council of 256, namely, that those baptized outside the Catholic Church should be baptized when received into it and that those ordained outside should be received only as laymen. Cyprian presents the theological grounds for these decisions, but not in an argumentative way, even though he may well have known that the Roman tradition was different. In concluding this letter he writes:

> Let. 72.3.1 We bring these points to your notice, dearly beloved brother, in a spirit of mutual respect and sincere affection. We believe that matters which conform to piety and truth will recommend themselves to you also, knowing as we do your true piety and faith. However, we are aware that there are some who refuse to lay aside notions acquired in the past

and do not readily change their viewpoint; they keep as their own certain practices adopted amongst them in the past but without, however, rupturing the bonds of peace and harmony with their colleagues. 3.2 We are not forcing anyone in this matter; we are laying down no law. For every appointed leader has in his government of the Church the freedom to exercise his own will and judgment, while having one day to render an account of his conduct to the Lord. We wish that you, dearly beloved brother, may ever fare well.[39]

Comment

Cyprian probably aims the reference to "some who refuse to lay aside notions acquired in the past" at some African bishops who opposed the decision taken at the council, for it was only on them whom the council could have "laid down the law." The idea that "every appointed leader has in his government of the Church the freedom to exercise his own will and judgment" and that he is "responsible to God alone" was a basic element of Cyprian's concept of episcopal authority.[40] In his view, the unity of the church was maintained by preserving harmony among bishops, even though they might differ from one another on matters of discipline.

Cyprian returned to this theme at the end of the following letter, addressed to a bishop named Iubianus, in which he argued strongly against recognizing the validity of baptism given outside the Catholic Church. He even describes those who held that position as "perverters of the truth," "betrayers of church unity" (Let. 73.11.2) and as "partners in the blasphemies of heretics" (18.3). However, at the end of the letter he could still say:

> 73.26.1 For our part, we do our very best to refrain from quarreling over this question of heretics with our colleagues and fellow bishops; we keep with them the harmony God has ordained and the peace the Lord has given us....[41]

Cyprian in Controversy with Pope Stephen

The letter addressed to Iubianus, with its highly uncomplimentary remarks about those who held the Roman position on this matter, came to the knowledge of Pope Stephen, who then wrote a letter to Cyprian. Unfortunately this has not been preserved. However, Cyprian quotes a key passage from it in a letter he wrote to a bishop named Pompeius.

Let 74.1.2 There is much that is arrogant, irrelevant, self-contradictory, ill-considered, and inept in what he has written; but he has even gone so far as to add this remark: "And so, in the case of those who may come to you from any heresy whatsoever, let there be no innovation beyond what has been handed down: hands are to be laid on them in penitence, since amongst heretics themselves they do not use their own rite of baptism on other heretics when they come to them, but they simply admit them to communion." 2.1 He has forbidden that anyone who comes from any heresy whatsoever should be baptized in the Church.[42]

Comment

It seems clear that Stephen had forbidden this not only in his own church, but in the whole Catholic Church. A later passage of Cyprian's letter indicates that Stephen threatened to excommunicate any bishop who continued to baptize those already baptized outside the Church.

74.8.2 Does he give honour to God who, far from upholding the unity and truth prescribed by God, champions the cause of heretics against the Church? Does he give honour to God who, being a friend of heretics and the foe of Christians, considers that those priests of God who seek to protect the truth of Christ and the unity of the Church deserve to be excommunicated?[43]

Comment

In his commentary on this passage, Clarke invokes the testimony of St. Augustine, who, while "well aware of Stephen's threat of excommunication, insisted that Cyprian displayed model forbearance in refusing to cause a schism."[44] Clarke concludes that while there was "a scandalous breakdown in fraternal relations, there was no formal excommunication in the modern canonical sense."[45] However, this threat of excommunication reemerges in the letter Cyprian received from Firmilian of Caesarea.

The Letter of Firmilian of Caesarea

This letter tells us that Stephen attempted to impose the Roman tradition not only on the churches of North Africa but on those of Asia Minor as well. It also gives important information about the grounds on which Stephen based his authority to do this.

Let. 75.5.2 Firstly, there is the claim made by Stephen that the apostles not only forbade that those who come from heresy should be baptized but that they have handed down this teaching to be observed by posterity.... 6.1 And anyone can see that those who are in Rome do not observe in all particulars those things which were handed down from the beginning; it is pointless, therefore, for them to parade the authority of the apostles. For we can appreciate the fact that in the celebration of the season of Easter and in many other points of religious observance we notice that there are certain differences to be found among them; their practices are not all exactly the same as those in Jerusalem. This is as we find in very many other provinces: there is a great deal of diversity, just as the places and peoples themselves vary. And yet it does not follow from this that there has been any departure at all from the peace and unity of the catholic Church.

6.2 But Stephen has now had the hide to make just such a departure. He breaks off peace with you, a peace which his predecessors always preserved with you in a spirit of mutual love and respect. And besides that, he traduces the blessed apostles Peter and Paul, claiming that it was they who handed down this tradition, whereas, in fact, in their epistles they execrated heretics and warned us to shun their company.[46]

Comment

Firmilian's remarks about the celebration of the Easter season remind us of Victor's effort to impose the Roman tradition on the churches of the province of Asia and of the remonstrance made by Irenaeus when Victor threatened to break off communion with the churches that continued to observe Easter on the 14th of Nisan. Here we learn also that Stephen had appealed to Peter and Paul as the authors of the Roman tradition concerning baptism given outside the church. Further along in Firmilian's letter we learn more about how Stephen justified his position.

Let. 75.17.1 At this point I become filled with righteous indignation at Stephen's crass and obvious stupidity. He is a man who finds the location of his bishopric such a source of pride, who keeps insisting that he occupies the succession of Peter, upon whom the foundations of the Church were laid; and yet, by using his authority to defend heretical baptism, he is introducing many other rocks and he is laying the foundations of and building up many new churches....

17.2 Whereas Stephen, who vaunts that he has succeeded to the occupancy of the chair of Peter, is stirred by no such zeal against heresy; instead, he concedes to heretics not some modest but the very greatest power to confer grace, going so far as to claim and assert that they wash away the filth of the old man by their holy rite of baptism, that they pardon the ancient and deadly sins, that they generate sons of God through the heavenly rebirth, and that by the sanctification of the divine waters they revivify them for eternal life.[47]

Comment

This provides the first clear proof, in Christian literature, that bishops of Rome based their authority over other churches on their being the successors to Peter in occupying the episcopal chair of the church of Rome. We should note that Firmilian's "righteous indignation" was not stirred so much by Stephen's making such a claim (although he accused him of pride in so insisting on it), as on the fact that he used his authority to "defend heretical baptism." No doubt if Firmilian could have refuted Stephen's claim to the authority associated with his occupancy of the chair of Peter, he would have done so. The absence of such an argument by a writer so intent on demolishing the position of his opponent strongly suggests that by the middle of the third century it was generally recognized, throughout the Christian Church, that the bishops of Rome were the successors to St. Peter and that this gave them a special kind of authority. However, the reaction of Cyprian and Firmilian to Stephen's attempt to impose the Roman tradition on them shows that there could be a considerable difference between the authority a bishop of Rome might claim and the authority other bishops conceded to him. In fact, I think one could broadly describe the history of papal primacy as the interplay between the claims made by the bishops of Rome and the varying responses given to them by the rest of the episcopate.

As we have seen, St. Augustine assures us that the conflict between Cyprian and Stephen did not lead to formal excommunication or schism. A new persecution broke out in 257, ordered by the emperor Valerian. In August of that year Stephen died as a martyr, and Cyprian was put on trial and exiled to a distant place in North Africa named Curubis. He spent a year there before being recalled to Carthage, where he suffered martyrdom by being beheaded on September 14, 258.

11
SUCCESSORS BY DIVINE
INSTITUTION?

In the first chapter we saw that the question of whether bishops are the successors to the apostles by divine institution divides the churches, with Catholic, Orthodox and Anglican churches on one side of the issue and the Protestant churches on the other. This issue also involves such divisive questions as whether episcopal ordination in the apostolic succession is necessary for valid orders and ministry and whether it confers on bishops an authoritative teaching role. The answer to these questions depends on whether one views the episcopate as the result of a purely human, historical development or of divine institution. In the first case, it would constitute a possibly useful, but not obligatory way to organize ministry; in the second it would prove an indispensable element of the structure of the Church.

As was also noted in the first chapter, most Christian scholars from both sides of this divide agree that the threefold structure of ministry, with one bishop along with a number of presbyters and deacons in each local church, does not appear in the New Testament. There is a broad consensus among scholars that the historical episcopate developed in the post–New Testament period, from the local leadership of a college of presbyters, who were sometimes also called *episkopoi*, to the leadership of a single bishop. Scholars also agree that this development took place sooner in the churches of Antioch and of western Asia Minor than in those of Philippi, Corinth and Rome. Scholars differ on details, such as how soon the church of Rome was led by a "monarchical" bishop, but hardly any doubt that the church of Rome was led by a group of presbyters for at least part of the second century.[1]

The question dividing the churches is not whether or how rapidly the development from the leadership of a college of presbyters to that of a single bishop took place, but whether the result of that development is rightly judged an element of the divinely ordered structure of the Church. This is a question of the theological significance of a post–New Testament development, and history alone cannot give the answer. On the other hand, accurate knowledge of the history proves essential in arriving at the answer, for the question concerns whether the historical development took place in such a way that the resulting episcopate could rightly be accepted by the Church as essential to the structure God willed for it.

An accurate knowledge of the history is also necessary if one wishes to avoid making assertions that cannot stand the test of historical investigation or critical exegesis. The first chapter mentioned one such assertion, made in the Vatican Response to the Final Report of ARCIC I.[2] In this final chapter, then, I shall first recall some of the key points of that history and then discuss the theological grounds that I believe justify the assertion of Vatican II that "bishops have by divine institution taken the place of the apostles as pastors of the Church" (*LG* 20).

REVIEW OF THE HISTORY

I am in substantial agreement with the consensus of modern scholars that the historical episcopate was not already present in the New Testament church, but a development that took place in the course of the second century, from the earlier collegial to the later monepiscopal leadership of the local churches. Recently, David Albert Jones, O.P., challenged this consensus in his article "Was there a Bishop of Rome in the First Century?"[3] In reviewing some of the main points of the history sketched out in the preceding chapters, I shall take into account the alternative view presented by Father Jones.

Ministry of the Apostles

The first point concerns the ministry of the apostles. Known primarily from Acts and the Letters of St. Paul, this ministry included both their work of founding new churches and the ongoing pastoral care of the churches they had founded. While Paul was actually present in one of those churches, he no doubt presided over it. But there is no indication, nor is it at all likely, that he ever took up permanent residence in any one church. Nor do the

Pastoral Letters present Timothy and Titus as presiding in a permanent way over the churches of Ephesus or Crete. They were to rejoin Paul when they had completed the commission he had given them. If we recognize James the "brother of the Lord" as an apostle, as Paul seems to have done, then he would be the only apostle described in the New Testament as presiding permanently over a local church. Luke gives this impression when he notes how, on his final visit to Jerusalem, "Paul accompanied us on a visit to James, and all the presbyters were present" (Acts 21:18).

In the light of these facts, I have to differ with Jones when he says: "The supposition that there was no central figure in the local church in the days of the apostles is demonstrably false, for we know that, at least in some cases, the apostles themselves presided over particular local churches."[4] One certainly has to qualify this statement. Paul exercised pastoral care over the churches he founded, by letters and by sending them his coworkers, but he can hardly be said to have "presided" over them except when present, and there is no likelihood that he ever intended to stay permanently in any one of them.

Mono-episcopacy in the New Testament?

Jones sees evidence for "mono-episcopacy" in the New Testament in the fact that *episkopos* occurs there in the singular. He finds it striking that "of the five New Testament occurrences of *episkopos* in the sense of an officeholder, three are in the singular...." After noting that, by contrast, *presbuteros* is almost always used in the plural, he argues:

> Thus the attempt to exclude any connotation of mono-episcopacy from the three references to *episkopos* in the pastoral letters, *all* in the singular, is unconvincing. For one would have to combine the coincidence that bishop occurs there always in the singular with the coincidence that when a single chief presbyter does clearly become the norm, it is under the same title of *episkopos*.[5]

First, I am puzzled by Jones's statement that the word *episkopos* occurs five times in the New Testament in the sense of an officeholder and that three of these instances are found in the Pastoral Letters. He does not give the references to these places, and I can find only two: 1 Timothy 3:2 and Titus 1:7. Actually, the third time the word occurs in the singular it refers not to an officeholder, but to Christ (1 Pet 2:25). Secondly, both times the word occurs in the Pastorals, the phrase is *dei ton episkopon,* where the singular is best taken as generic. Thirdly, *episkopon* as used in Titus 1:7 clearly refers to the same officeholders that verse 5 calls presbyters. Therefore most scholars have good reasons for not thinking that the use of *episkopos* in the singular in the Pastorals indicates the presence of the monepiscopate in the churches of Ephesus and Crete during the New Testament period.

In my opinion, there are also good reasons why most scholars agree that one does not find in the New Testament the structure of leadership whereby one member of a local church stands out as presiding over the presbyters and the rest of the community. Jones agrees that we have little evidence for the existence of such chief presbyters contemporary with the apostles, but still believes that there must have been such a chief presbyter or head bishop in each church. He attributes the lack of evidence to the fact that during the time of the apostles, such local leaders would not have stood out. In his opinion, "the very existence of a *purely* collegiate *presbyterion* is itself a speculative fiction."[6]

In response to this assertion, I point out three passages from the later books of the New Testament that speak of the role of presbyters in a local church. The first is the farewell discourse of St. Paul to the presbyters of the church of Ephesus (Acts 20:17–35). There Luke presents Paul as addressing the whole group when he says: "Keep watch over yourselves and over the whole flock of which the holy Spirit has appointed you overseers." If it were true, as Jones claims, that one of them stood out as the "overseer," it would seem very strange that Paul's discourse gives no hint of the special responsibility such a "chief presbyter" or "bishop" would have after his departure.

A second text is 1 Peter 5:1–5, where the author, who describes himself as a "fellow presbyter," addresses an exhortation to presbyters. Here also the whole group have the pastoral role of "tending the flock of God" and are urged not to "lord it" over those assigned to them. I would think that if one of them had stood out as the "chief presbyter" or "bishop," the warning not to "lord it" over the others would more appropriately have been addressed to him than to the whole group.

Finally, there is the text in 1 Timothy, which indicates that some within the group of presbyters "presided well" and some "toil in preaching and teaching" (1 Tim 5:17). In each case, the reference is to several presbyters; there is no indication that any one of them was seen as the "chief presbyter" who would preside over the community in Timothy's absence.

Jones objects that to conclude that there was no one "bishop" in these churches is to argue from silence. I would respond that, in each case, we have good reason to think that had there been such a "bishop" in charge of the local church, the context was such that we would rightly expect him to be mentioned. Hence I stand with the majority of scholars who agree that one does not find evidence in the New Testament to support the theory that the apostles or their coworkers left one person as "bishop" in charge of each local church. The only person described in the New Testament as having such a role is James, the "brother of the Lord," and he would better be termed a "resident apostle" than a "bishop."

One Bishop the Rule Everywhere in Early Second Century?

When we come to the post–New Testament period, Jones says that "we find from the beginning of the second century a threefold pattern of a single figurehead with a college of presbyters and assisting deacons has become the rule everywhere." It is true that by the second decade of that century we find such a pattern in the churches of Antioch and those in the vicinity of Ephesus. It is also true that Ignatius of Antioch speaks of bishops "appointed throughout the world" (Eph. 3:2) and says that nothing lacking a bishop, presbyters and deacons can be called a church (Trl. 3:1). However, as we have seen above,[7] it remains uncertain whether these statements corresponded to the reality of the Church throughout the world of his day. The very urgency with which he exhorted the Christian communities to unity with their bishops can be seen as an indication that the episcopal structure was not yet so firmly established so he wanted it to be.

Furthermore, in the letter that Polycarp, the bishop of Smyrna, wrote to the church of Philippi shortly after Ignatius had stopped there on his way to Rome, he speaks of presbyters and deacons in that church, but makes no mention of a bishop. Although an argument from silence, it is persuasive, as the purpose of Polycarp's letter is such that it would have called for mention of the bishop had there been one in Philippi. (One cannot build such an argument from the failure of Ignatius to mention a bishop in his letter to the Romans, for there he says nothing about presbyters or deacons either; that letter was very different from his others.)

A Bishop of Rome in the First Century?

Jones then comes to the question that formed the title of his article "Was there a Bishop of Rome in the First Century?" As the reader will recall, I have expressed agreement with the consensus of scholars that the available evidence indicates that the church of Rome was led by a college of presbyters, rather than by a single bishop, for at least several decades of the second century. Jones, on the contrary, finds the argument for a "loose presbyteral government" of the church in Rome in the late first century "terribly weak."[8] In his opinion, "there seems little reason to doubt the presence of a bishop in Rome already in the first century." It seems worthwhile, therefore, to recall why scholars generally doubt such a presence.

The first reason is the probability that in the 90s, when *I Clement* was written, the structure of leadership at Rome did not differ much from that at Corinth—and that letter gives us good reasons to conclude that there was no bishop in charge of the church of Corinth at that time. The terms used in that letter to describe the leaders of the Corinthian church, *hegoumenoi, episkopoi, presbuteroi, archontes,* are all in the plural. The term most frequently used is *presbuteroi;* Clement calls upon those guilty of the schism to "submit to the presbyters," and to allow the "flock of Christ to be at peace with its duly appointed presbyters."[9]

It seems inconceivable that, if there had been a bishop in charge of the church of Corinth at that time, Clement would not have said something about the obligation of the guilty parties to submit to their bishop or about his role in restoring good order to his church. However, Jones finds a hint of the existence of a bishop in Corinth in the analogy Clement gives for good order: namely, that in the liturgy of the Old Law the high priest, priests, Levites and laity each had their proper tasks. As noted above, this is one of several examples Clement offers of good order, and nothing in the letter supports the conclusion that the Corinthian church must also have had its "high priest."

The other reason for the common opinion that a college of presbyters led the church of Rome well into the second century is based on *The Shepherd of Hermas,* a work generally agreed to have been written in Rome during the first half of that century. As in *I Clement,* the terms used here to refer to people in leadership roles are all in the plural: "leaders" *(prohegoumenois);* "presbyters who preside over the church" *(tôn presbuterôn tôn proistamenôn tês ekklesias);* "leaders of the church and occupants of the seats of honor" *(prohegoumenois tês ekklesias kai tois prôtokathedritais). The Shepherd* makes no reference to any one person having a role of leadership in the church. However, the argument is not based merely on silence about a bishop; in my view the stronger evidence in both *I Clement* and *The Shepherd* is the consistent use of the plural in referring to those in positions of leadership. Hence I cannot agree with Jones's judgment that there seems little reason to doubt the presence of a bishop in Rome already in the first century.

SUCCESSORS OF APOSTLES BY DIVINE INSTITUTION?

No doubt proving that bishops were the successors of the apostles by divine institution would be easier if the New Testament clearly stated that before they died the apostles had appointed a single bishop to lead each of the churches they had founded. Likewise, it would have been very helpful had Clement, in writing to the Corinthians, said that the apostles had put one bishop in charge of each church and had arranged for a regular succession in that office. We would also be grateful to Ignatius of Antioch if he had spoken of himself not only as a bishop, but as a successor to the apostles, and had explained how he understood that succession. Unfortunately, the documents available to us do not provide such help. They do indicate that in the course of the second century, in the churches of Corinth, Philippi and Rome, there was a transition from the leadership of a college of presbyters to the leadership of a single bishop, but they do not throw any light on how that transition took place. To that question one can only offer what seems the most probable answer.

The answer I find most probable is based on the New Testament evidence that the apostles shared their mandate with both their missionary coworkers and with the leaders in the local churches and that when the apostles died both of these groups carried on their ministry. The Pastoral Letters witness to how the coworkers continued to exercise oversight over various churches, and Luke's account of Paul's farewell address to the presbyters of Ephesus shows that presbyters continued to exercise leadership in local churches after Paul's departure. There were therefore two lines of apostolic succession in the postapostolic church, each perpetuating the mandate given to the apostles by Christ.

I think it most likely that a development along both lines of apostolic succession gave rise to the monepiscopate during the second century. This could have happened in two ways. A man who had exercised oversight over the churches of a region could have taken up residence in the major church of that region and become its bishop. In another church one of the presbyters might have shown himself so superior to the others in leadership qualities and in ability to teach that the community would recognize him as its chief pastor. In either case, a local church that accepted such an individual as its bishop would have had good reason to recognize him as standing in the line of apostolic succession. They could establish his link with the apostles either through earlier coworkers or through a succession of presbyters in their church.

I realize that someone might raise an objection to this explanation on the grounds that it would mean that the specifically episcopal powers of ordaining and teaching with authority would have been handed on not only by the apostles' coworkers but also by presbyters in the local churches prior to the emergence of the episcopate. One might object to the idea that a group of presbyters not only would have possessed and transmitted such episcopal powers, but would have conferred them on the person whom they chose as the first bishop of their church.

To this objection I would reply that the evidence both from the New Testament and from such writings as *I Clement,* the Letter of Polycarp to the Philippians and *The Shepherd of Hermas* favors the view that initially the presbyters in each church, as a college, possessed all the powers needed for effective ministry. This would mean that the apostles handed on what was transmissible of their mandate as an undifferentiated whole, in which the powers that would eventually be seen as episcopal were not yet distinguished from the rest. Hence, the development of the episcopate would have meant the differentiation of ministerial powers that had previously existed in an undifferentiated state and the consequent reservation to the bishop of certain of the powers previously held collegially by the presbyters.

I propose this as a reasonable explanation of the transition from the collegial to the monepiscopal structure. We simply do not have documentary evidence on which to base a historically certain account of how it took place. Does this eliminate the possibility of sustaining the claim that the monepiscopate is an element of the divinely willed structure of the church and that bishops are the successors of the apostles by divine institution? Historical evidence is important, but this alone cannot sustain this claim; for that we must also invoke theological reflection.

THE FACTOR OF
THEOLOGICAL REFLECTION

The Catholic belief that bishops are the successors of the apostles by divine institution is based on a combination of historical evidence and theological reflection. Since theology, by definition, is "faith seeking understanding," theological reflection will necessarily presuppose faith. The reflection I propose is based on belief that Christ founded the Church, that he continues to guide it through the abiding gift of the Holy Spirit and that the Holy Spirit maintains the Church in the true faith. I propose a theological reflection in three steps:

1. The post–New Testament development is consistent with the development that took place during the New Testament period.

2. The episcopate provided the instrument that the post–New Testament Church needed to maintain its unity and orthodoxy in the face of the dangers of schism and heresy threatening it.

3. The Christian faithful recognized the bishops as the successors to the apostles in teaching authority. The reception of the bishops' teaching as normative for faith is analogous to the reception of certain writings as normative for faith. The Holy Spirit guided the Church in determining both norms, for error about the norms would have led to untold errors in faith.

1. The Post–New Testament Development Is Consistent with the Development That Took Place During the New Testament Period.

As a first step here we recall the development of ministry that took place during the period of the New Testament. The Gospels tell us that Jesus gathered disciples around himself and gave a structure to their community by his choice of the Twelve, with Peter as their spokesman and leader. Jesus shared his ministry of preaching and healing with these Twelve during his lifetime, and after his resurrection he sent them out as his apostles with the mandate to make disciples and teach them to observe all he had commanded them.

However, when they set out on their task, they faced a great number of questions that Jesus had not answered. For instance: Were they supposed to preach the Gospel to Gentiles? If so, should they oblige Gentile Christians to keep the Mosaic Law? How should they structure the communities they would form by their preaching? Would their own supervision over those communities be sufficient, or should they appoint local pastors? Some sayings of Jesus had suggested his return to judge the world within their own lifetime. Did that mean that they need not make provision for a structure of leadership that would last beyond the present generation? Raymond Brown has summed up the questions facing the apostles by saying that Jesus had not given them a blueprint to follow in building the church.[10]

As we read the letters of Paul and the Acts, we see that the apostles met each of these problems as they arose and relied on the Holy Spirit for help in solving them. Let us recall a few examples. In their pastoral care of the Jerusalem community the Twelve saw the need to share their ministry with others, as Jesus had shared his with them, and they appointed the Seven as leaders of the group of Hellenists. Similarly, Paul enlisted coworkers to help him found new churches and provide pastoral care for those he had founded. His letters also make it evident that he did not leave those churches without local leaders. The part he himself played in their choice and appointment remains unclear, but in any case he put his own authority behind theirs, as when he tells the Thessalonians to "respect those...who are over you in the Lord and admonish you" (1 Thess 5:12) and the Corinthians to "be subordinate" to the household of Stephanas (1 Cor 16:16). While Paul relied on the Holy Spirit to provide ministry for his churches by the distribution of charisms, he also saw to their pastoral care by letters, by sending them his coworkers and by supporting the authority of the local leaders. When he died, in the mid-60s, there were two groups of people with whom he had shared his ministry and who could carry it on: his coworkers and the local leaders in his churches.

In looking to the parts of the New Testament written during the sub-apostolic period, especially 1 Peter, Acts and the Pastorals, we see that as the church began to think in terms of future generations, it also developed a form of local leadership to provide for continuity in doctrine and practice. 1 Peter 5, Acts 20 and the Pastorals all witness to the fact that by the 80s, each local church, including those of the Pauline tradition, had a group of leaders that they called either elders or overseers. 1 Peter and the Pastorals also witness to the continuation of the pastoral care exercised over a number of churches by coworkers of an apostle (as in the Pastorals) or by one who writes in the name of the apostle himself (as in 1 Peter). Furthermore, Acts 20:17–35 and 2 Timothy 4:1–8 witness to the conviction of Christians of the subapostolic period that Paul himself, when foreseeing his own death, entrusted the ongoing care of the church of Ephesus to its presbyters and bequeathed his own ministry of evangelization to Timothy.

The Pastorals also witness to the concern of the subapostolic church for the safeguarding and faithful transmission of the "deposit," which the careful selection of leaders would ensure. These would be "able to teach" (1 Tim 3:2) and would "hold[ing] fast to the true message as taught so that [they] will be able both to exhort with sound doctrine and to refute opponents" (Titus 1:9). These letters also make clear that an important task of the apostolic coworkers consisted of selecting the right persons for ministry in the local churches and ordaining them by the laying on of hands.

The development of ministry as just described took place in the churches of the Pauline and Petrine traditions. 2 and 3 John give a different picture, but provide such fragmentary evidence that we cannot be sure how the ministry developed in the Johannine churches. In any case, we stand on solid ground when we understand 1 Peter, Acts and the Pastorals as witnessing to a development of ministry that took place in mainline Christian churches during the subapostolic period. This development came about as the communities realized that provision had to be made for the continued life of the Church and that this required a stable structure of ministry. Such structure would guarantee the faithful handing on of all the Church had received from the apostles. While this did not mean the end of charismatic ministry (cf. 1 Peter 4:10–11), it did call for the choice and ordination of responsible pastors and teachers: "faithful people who will have the ability to teach others as well" (2 Tim 2:2). The choice and ordination of such people remained in the hands of individuals like Timothy and Titus, but the local leadership was entrusted to a group of presbyters, among whom some "preside well" and some "toil in preaching and teaching" (1 Tim 5:17).

With the exception of James, the "brother of the Lord," the New Testament does not describe any one person as having been left in charge of a local church. We can only surmise why. Perhaps because at this time most Christians were recent converts, it was thought that giving such authority to any single one would be too risky and thus group leadership would be safer. Likewise, up to the end of the subapostolic period, there were still coworkers of the apostles to provide a remedy should a group of local presbyters become divided into factions and threaten the unity and stability of a local church.

Our second step involves showing how the postapostolic development of ministry was consistent with what took place during the period of the New Testament. Just as during the subapostolic period the need for a structure that would provide stable and continuing leadership in the churches was recognized and met by the development of the presbyterate, so also in the postapostolic period the growing threats to unity, and the need for leadership that could more effectively maintain unity in the face of those threats, led to the development and general acceptance of the episcopate.

2. The Episcopate Provided the Instrument That the Post–New Testament Church Needed to Maintain Its Unity and Orthodoxy in the Face of the Dangers of Schism and Heresy Threatening It.

Let us recall some of the growing threats to unity that the church faced during the postapostolic period. First of all, the apostles and their immediate coworkers were no longer on the scene. Peter and Paul were martyred in the mid-60s, and men like Timothy and Titus probably did not live into the second century. While they may have been succeeded by others who would exercise oversight over a number of churches, the strong leadership provided by the apostles and their original coworkers was no longer available.

Secondly, the number of Christians in each city continued to grow, which resulted in a corresponding increase in the number of "house-churches" where they gathered to celebrate the Eucharist. It was quite impossible for members of a forbidden religion to construct large churches where the whole Christian community could meet together. The necessity of meeting in a number of small congregations could have led to a diminished sense of being one church and to the emergence of factions. *I Clement* and the letters of Ignatius of Antioch witness to this danger.

The greatest threat to the unity of the church in the second century came from the spread of Gnosticism. This danger was particularly evident in the church of Rome. Various exponents of this heresy established themselves there and formed communities of followers, claiming to possess a secret apostolic tradition that surpassed the teaching in the ordinary Christian communities.

During the second century, the church met the growing threat to its unity by developing and accepting the stronger leadership that having a single bishop over the church in each city provided. There is little need to prove this assertion, as even scholars who see the development of the episcopate as a merely natural response to a sociological need for stronger leadership in the church recognize it as true. Catholic scholars now generally agree that developing the episcopacy was the church's way of responding to the threats to its unity that it faced during the second century. However, they also believe that they are as justified in seeing the guidance of the Spirit in this development as they are in seeing it in the development of the presbyterate that took place during the subapostolic period of the New Testament.

Raymond Brown has well expressed the belief that the Spirit has guided development of the episcopate when he said:

> I am not so naive to think that every development within the Church is the work of the Spirit, but I would not know what guidance of the Church by the Spirit could mean if it did not include the fundamental shaping of the special ministry which is so intimately concerned with Christian communal and sacramental life.[11]

3. The Christian Faithful Recognized the Bishops as the Successors to the Apostles in Teaching Authority. The Reception of the Bishops' Teaching as Normative for Faith Is Analogous to the Reception of Certain Christian Writings as Canonical and Normative for Faith. The Holy Spirit Guided the Church in Determining Both Norms, for Error about the Norms Would Have Led to Untold Errors in Faith.

In my opinion, this provides the strongest reason for seeing the Spirit's guidance in the development of the episcopate. Here we must distinguish between historical facts and theological reflection on those facts. That, by the end of the second century, bishops were recognized as the rightful successors of the apostles and that what they taught in common was recognized as normative for Christian faith are facts to which the writings of Irenaeus, Tertullian and Origen bear witness. The move from these facts to the conclusion that the Spirit guided the development of the episcopate calls for reflection on the theological significance of the church's reception of the norms for its faith.

We can begin by reflecting on the significance of the church's reception of certain writings (and not others) as normative for its faith. There is no doubt that the consensus of Christian churches during the second and third centuries concerning the reception of four Gospels, the letters of St. Paul, the Acts of the Apostles and some other writings established the canon of the New Testament. By virtue of this consensus the Church recognized that collection of writings as normative for Christian faith. An erroneous decision about the norm of its faith would obviously have led the Church into incalculable errors on particular matters of faith. If one believes, as most Christians do, that the Holy Spirit maintains the Church in the true faith, one must also believe that the Holy Spirit guided the Church in its discernment of the books that would constitute a written norm for its faith.

Because the Gnostics also appealed to these writings during the second century, the church needed another norm to use in judging which interpretation of the New Testament corresponded to the authentic apostolic faith. The Gnostics claimed to base their interpretation on a secret tradition originating from one of the apostles and handed down by a succession of their teachers. Christian writers, such as Hegesippus, Irenaeus, Tertullian and Origen, responded by appealing to the tradition handed down from the apostles by the succession of bishops in the churches. The fact that in all those churches one found the same "rule of faith," in contrast to the great diversity of Gnostic teachings, proved that the churches led by bishops had maintained the genuine apostolic doctrine. These writers, from different regions of the church, witness to the fact that the bishops were recognized as the authoritative bearers of the apostolic tradition and their teaching was received as normative for Christian faith.

A wrong decision about the living norm of faith used in countering the threat of Gnosticism would have been just as disastrous for the church as a wrong decision about the reception of the New Testament as its written norm. We have just as good reason for believing that the Spirit guided the church in recognizing its bishops as successors of the apostles and authoritative teachers of the faith as we have for believing that the Spirit guided it in discerning the books that comprise the New Testament.

From this it follows that we also have good reason to believe that the Spirit guided the development of the episcopate itself, for it was to play such a primary role in maintaining the Church in the true faith. Without the leadership of its bishops, the early Church could hardly have achieved a consensus on the canon of Scripture, recognizing the Old Testament as also Word of God for Christians and settling on the writings of the New Testament. Neither could it have overcome the very real threat Gnosticism posed to its unity and orthodoxy.

While most Catholic scholars agree that the episcopate is the fruit of a post–New Testament development, they maintain that this development was so evidently guided by the Holy Spirit that it must be recognized as corresponding to God's plan for the structure of his Church. This structure was in development during the New Testament era, but even at the close of that period the Church did not yet have a structure adequate to meet the challenges it would face during the second century. Catholics see no reason to think that the Holy Spirit, who guided the Church during the period of the New Testament, would have ceased to guide it during the development of the basic structure necessary for its long-term survival. I conclude by quoting Raymond Brown again: "Although development of church structure reflects sociological necessity, in the Christian self-understanding the Holy Spirit given by the risen Christ guides the church in such a way that allows basic structural development to be seen as embodying Jesus Christ's will for his church."[12]

AFTERWORD

During the summer of 2000, while this book was at Paulist Press being edited for publication, the Congregation for the Doctrine of the Faith (CDF) issued two documents that confirmed in a rather dramatic way what I had said in the first chapter about episcopal ordination in the apostolic succession being a church-dividing issue. The first of these documents, "Note on the Expression 'Sister Churches,'" was approved by Pope John Paul II on June 9, 2000, and communicated to all the Catholic episcopal conferences along with a letter signed by Cardinal Ratzinger on June 30th.[1] The second document is the Declaration *Dominus Iesus*, "On the Unicity and Salvific Universality of Jesus Christ and the Church," which was approved by Pope John Paul II on June 16, 2000, and released to the public on September 5th.[2] The critical comments expressed by a number of Anglicans and Protestants about these documents have focused on statements made in them to the effect that Christian communities lacking valid episcopal orders are not churches in the proper sense. (Neither document specifies which communities are meant, but it is well known that Pope Leo XIII declared Anglican orders invalid and that few Protestant churches claim to have preserved the episcopate in the historic succession.) As seen in the first chapter, Vatican II spoke of the Christian bodies that lacked valid orders as "ecclesial communities" rather than "churches," and the subsequent discipline of the Catholic Church with regard to the sharing of the Eucharist with other Christians has been based on the same distinction.

Since Vatican II, official Catholic documents have commonly distinguished between "churches" and "ecclesial communities," with judgment based on their possession or lack of valid orders. In light of this, one might wonder what caused the strongly negative reaction to the documents issued in the summer of 2000. I suggest that it stems from the hope raised during more than thirty years of productive dialogues between the

231

Catholic Church and the Anglican and Protestant churches, and the sense that the recent documents had thrown a dash of cold water on it. The hope was that the Catholic Church might be moving toward a more favorable evaluation of the ecclesial status of the communities with which it has been in dialogue. The dialogues had shown broad agreement not only between Catholics and Anglicans but also between Catholics and Lutherans on Eucharist and ministry as well as on the doctrine of justification. Many on both sides thought that the recognition of common faith on such important matters would justify a more positive evaluation of the churches involved.

In what way has the CDF in its recent documents disappointed this hope? First of all, it makes no mention of the agreements Catholics have reached in dialogues with Anglicans and Protestants during the past three decades, and thus gives no encouragement to the idea that those agreements could justify a more positive evaluation of their churches than was expressed at Vatican II. Secondly, rather than speaking more positively than Vatican II did about those communities, the CDF has ignored a positive statement made about them at the council, which Pope John Paul II repeated in his encyclical *Ut Unum Sint*. And finally, the CDF has spoken in a more negative fashion than Pope Paul VI had when it said that communities lacking episcopal orders may not be called "sister churches," and in a more negative fashion than Vatican II when in *Dominus Iesus* it said that such communities "are not churches in the proper sense." Let us consider these three points in a bit more detail.

Perhaps one might justify the silence of these recent documents regarding agreements reached in ecumenical dialogues with Anglicans and Protestants on the grounds that the document on "sister churches" dealt mainly with the Orthodox churches and *Dominus Iesus* principally concerned the other religions. However, the disappointing fact remains that negative remarks were made about Christian communities with which the Catholic Church has been in prolonged and productive dialogue. Furthermore, there was no hint that judgments being made at Rome concerning those communities might reflect the progress made in recognizing the extent to which we share common faith.

Secondly, I pointed out that the CDF has ignored a positive statement made about the "ecclesial communities" at Vatican II. *Dominus Iesus* says only of the Orthodox Churches and others having valid episcopal orders that "the Church of Christ is present and operative in them." However, that this can be said, although with some qualifications, of the other Christian communities was affirmed at Vatican II by its Doctrinal Commission. The commission explained and justified the council's use of the expression "ecclesial communities" in the following way:

It must not be overlooked that the communities that have their origin in the separation that took place in the West are not merely a sum or collection of individual Christians, but they are constituted by social ecclesiastical elements which they have preserved from our common patrimony, and which confer on them a truly ecclesial character. In these communities the one sole Church of Christ is present, albeit imperfectly, in a way that is somewhat like its presence in particular churches, and by means of their ecclesiastical elements the Church of Christ is in some way operative in them.[3]

Pope John Paul II recently confirmed this positive assessment of the "ecclesial communities" expressed at Vatican II in his Encyclical *Ut Unum Sint*, when he said: "Indeed, the elements of sanctification and truth present in the other Christian communities...constitute the objective basis of the communion, albeit imperfect, which exists between them and the Catholic Church. To the extent that these elements are found in other Christian communities, the one church of Christ is effectively present in them...."[4]

Despite what both Vatican II and Pope John Paul II have said, the recent document of the CDF gives the impression that the Church of Christ is present and operative only in those it calls "true particular Churches."

Finally, we come to the statements that have elicited the strongest reactions from critics of these documents: namely, that communities lacking episcopal orders are not to be called "sister churches"[5] and are not "churches in the proper sense."[6] In the letter Cardinal Ratzinger sent to the presidents of the Conferences of Bishops along with the "Note on the Expression 'Sister Churches,'" he specifically mentioned the Anglican Communion as one to which the expression "sister Church" had been improperly applied. The "Note" goes on to explain that this expression is properly used only in referring to particular churches that have preserved a valid episcopate and Eucharist. And yet, one would think that some members of the CDF must have been present at the canonization of the forty martyrs of England and Wales on October 25, 1970, when Pope Paul VI spoke as follows:

There will be no seeking to lessen the legitimate prestige and the worthy patrimony of piety and usage proper to the Anglican Church when the Roman Catholic Church—the humble "Servant of the Servants of God"—is able to embrace her ever beloved Sister in the one authentic communion of the family of Christ: a communion of origin and of faith, a communion of

priesthood and of rule, a communion of the Saints in the freedom and love of the Spirit of Jesus.[7]

It is true that the "embrace in the one authentic communion" was still an
object of hope, but Pope Paul VI did not hesitate to use the term
"Anglican Church" when referring to the contemporary Anglican
Communion. Likewise, his use of the phrase "ever beloved Sister" is hardly
consonant with the idea that only if the Catholic Church were to recognize
Anglican orders as valid could she be acknowledged as a "sister Church."

However, this is obviously what the CDF means to say in its "Note on
the Expression 'Sister Churches.'" It evidently bases its decision that this
expression should not be used of the communities judged as lacking valid
episcopal orders on the statement it makes about them in *Dominus Iesus*,
namely, that they "are not churches in the proper sense." While the
Second Vatican Council distinguished between "churches" and "ecclesial
communities," it never flatly declared, as the CDF has now done, that the
ecclesial communities "are not churches in the proper sense." I believe
that critics of *Dominus Iesus* have had reason to see in this hardening of
language a counter-indication to the hope that the progress made during
more than thirty years of ecumenical dialogue with those communities
could justify a more positive evaluation of their ecclesial character.

Perhaps at this point a reader might pose the following question to me.
In the light of the thesis defended in this book, that the episcopate in
apostolic succession is an indispensable element of the divinely willed
structure of the Church, is there really any way the Catholic Church could
arrive at a more positive evaluation of the ecclesial character of the
Anglican and Protestant communities?

I would reply that we might find a way forward on this issue by following a suggestion made in the official Catholic response to the "Lima
Report": "Baptism, Eucharist and Ministry" (BEM). In chapter 1 I spoke
of this groundbreaking ecumenical document as indicating the progress
toward convergence that had been made among Christian communities
on the question of apostolic succession.[8] Among the many unique features
of this report was the urgent request the Faith and Order Commission
directed to officials of all the churches involved that they study the report
and respond to it. They received so many responses that their publication
required six volumes.[9] The Secretariat for Promoting Christian Unity in
collaboration with the Congregation for the Doctrine of the Faith prepared the response of the Roman Catholic Church.[10] The section that
deals with what BEM proposed for the "mutual recognition of ordained
ministries" includes the following paragraph:

It must be clear that the recognition of ordained ministry cannot be isolated from its ecclesiological context. The recognition of the ordained ministry and of the ecclesial character of a Christian community are indissolubly and mutually related. To the extent that it can be recognized that a communion now exists between churches and ecclesial communities, however imperfect that communion may be, there is implied some recognition of the ecclesial reality of the other. The question that follows is what does this communion imply for the way in which we perceive the ministry of the other? This perhaps is one question that should be taken up when attention is given to the fundamental ecclesiological dimension of the problem of the recognition of the ordained ministry.

I find particularly significant the idea that recognition of the ordained ministry and of the ecclesial character of a Christian community are not only indissolubly related, but also mutually related. This clearly means that one can not only begin with a judgment about the ministry in a community and draw conclusions about its ecclesial character; one can also begin with a judgment about its ecclesial character and draw conclusions about its ministry. As is obvious, the approach taken by the CDF in its recent documents moves in only one direction: from a negative assessment of the ordained ministry in the ecclesial communities to a negative conclusion about their ecclesial character. Because they lack the episcopate in the apostolic succession, they are "not churches in the proper sense."

However, the official Catholic response to BEM authorizes another approach, which many Catholic ecumenists favor: one can begin with reasons for a positive assessment of the ecclesial character of Christian communities and draw conclusions about the authenticity of their ministry. If one asks where they find the reasons for a positive assessment of the ecclesial character of the Anglican and Lutheran communities, I have no doubt they would reply that such reasons are based on the growing recognition of the degree of communion that exists between them and the Catholic Church. At the very beginning of the Catholic Church's involvement in the ecumenical movement, Vatican II already recognized that all baptized Christians are joined in a real, even though imperfect, communion. It further affirmed that communities not in full communion with the Catholic Church carry out liturgical actions that can truly engender a life of grace and that the Holy Spirit uses such communities as means of salvation for their members.[11] Many Catholic ecumenists say that thirty-five years of dialogue have shown that a much higher degree of communion in faith and liturgical practice exists between the Catholic Church and such communities as the Anglican and

Lutheran than was known to the bishops at Vatican II. Through these dialogues, it has become evident that when Anglican and Lutheran communities gather to celebrate the Eucharist their belief about what they are doing and what they are receiving is substantially what Catholics believe. It is also evident that they believe Christ instituted the ministry of word and sacrament and that only those duly ordained are qualified to preside at the Eucharist. The most striking fruit of years of patient dialogue is the fact that the Catholic Church and the churches of the Lutheran World Federation could affirm together that there is no longer any serious disagreement between them on the crucial doctrine of justification.[12]

Perhaps even more important than recognizing the degree of communion in faith achieved through ecumenical dialogue is recognizing the level of communion that exists in the practice of the Christian life according to that faith. This recognition is the fruit not only of ecumenical dialogue, but of the many fraternal contacts between Christians of different communities by which they have come to know and appreciate one another as brothers and sisters in Christ. One can hardly recognize the authentic Christian life of another community without forming a positive judgment about the ordained ministry that nurtured and fostered that life.

The official Catholic response to BEM affirmed that the recognition of the ordained ministry of a community and of its ecclesial character are mutually related. We need not limit ourselves to arguing, as the CDF has done, from a negative judgment about the ministry in other communities to the conclusion that they are not churches in the proper sense. We may also argue from the reasons for recognizing the truly ecclesial character of those communities to the fruitfulness and genuineness of their ministry.

I believe we have sound reasons to hold that Christian ministry, in order to be fully valid, must be related to Christ and his apostles through the historic succession maintained in the college of bishops. At the same time, I believe that we have tended to pay too exclusive attention to the conditions for the validity of ministry and have not sufficiently explored the implications of the fruitfulness of a ministry that may not meet all the conditions we believe are required for validity. One implication, which certainly needs deeper exploration, concerns the ecclesial character of communities that have not retained the episcopate, but which for centuries have led numberless Christians to grace and salvation through the effective preaching of the Word of God and a fruitful pastoral ministry. I do not believe we have done full justice to such communities when we simply declare that they are not churches in the proper sense.

NOTES

APOSTOLIC SUCCESSION IN THE EPISCOPATE:
A CHURCH-DIVIDING ISSUE

1. *The Tablet,* 3 October 1998, p. 1271.

2. *One Bread One Body,* no. 117.

3. *UR* 22. This translation is by Walter Abbott, S.J., *The Documents of Vatican II* (New York: America Press, 1966). Cited text appears on p. 364.

4. *Origins* 28/8 (16 July 1998): 119. See Francis A. Sullivan, S.J., "A New Obstacle to Anglican–Roman Catholic Dialogue," *America* 179/3, August 1–8, 1998: 6–7.

5. *One Bread One Body,* no. 41.

6. *Together in Mission and Ministry. The Porvoo Common Statement with Essays on Church and Ministry in Northern Europe* (London: Church House Publishing, 1993).

7. W. A. Norgren, and Wm. G. Rusch, eds., *"Toward Full Agreement" and "Concordat of Agreement"* (Augsburg: Fortress Press, 1991).

8. "A Word in Due Season," *The Tablet,* 8 July 1998, pp. 935–36.

9. "In Line with the Apostles," *The Tablet* 248, 9 July 1994, p. 879.

10. Ibid.

11. See Francis A. Sullivan, S.J., *The Church We Believe In: One, Holy Catholic and Apostolic* (New York/Mahwah, N.J.: Paulist Press, 1988), pp. 185–209.

12. *Baptism, Eucharist and Ministry,* Faith and Order Paper No. 111 (Geneva: World Council of Churches, 1982), p. ix.

13. *LG* 20,b. Translation is by Austin Flannery, O.P., *Vatican Council II: Constitutions, Decrees, Declarations,* Revised edition (Northport, N.Y.: Costello Publishing Company, 1996), p. 27.

14. *LG* 20,c. Translation by Flannery, p. 28.

15. *LG* 21,b. Translation by Flannery, p. 29.

16. *LG* 25,b. Translation by Flannery, p. 35.

17. *DV* 7–8. Translation by Flannery, p. 101.

18. *DV* 10, b. Translation by Flannery, p. 103.

19. *CA* 28, 21; Theodore G. Tappert, ed. *The Book of Concord* (Philadelphia: Fortress Press, 1959), p. 84.

20. *LG* 20,c. Translation by Flannery, p. 28.

21. *LG* 20,c. Translation by Flannery, p. 27.

22. *LG* 21,b. Translation by Flannery, p. 29.

23. *Origins* 21/28 (19 Dec. 1991): 441–47. See also F. A. Sullivan, "The Vatican Response to ARCIC I," *Gregorianum* 73 (1992): 489–98, and *One in Christ* 28 (1992): 223–31.

24. *Origins* 21/28 (19 Dec. 1991): 446.

The Apostles

1. *Jesus and Community: The Social Dimensions of Christian Faith,* tr. John P. Galvin (Philadelphia: Fortress; New York: Paulist Press, 1984), p. 10.

2. Ibid., p. 22.

3. Ibid., p. 11.

4. See Anton Vögtle, "Ekklesiologische Auftragswörte des Auferstandenen," in *Sacra Pagina,* ed. J. Coppens, A. Decamps, E. Masseux (Paris: Gembloux, 1959), II, pp. 280–94, at pp. 291–94.

5. In his book, *Priest and Bishop: Biblical Reflections* (Mahwah, N.J.: Paulist Press, 1970), Raymond Brown seems to conclude from the fact that the Twelve did not go on the Gentile mission that they were not personally involved in missionary activities (see pp. 51–52). However, he also says: "Luke tells us relatively little about the Twelve, and they may have been much more active than the NT shows us"(p. 51).

6. The "they" could be taken to mean that Paul included James the brother of the Lord among the apostles to the circumcised. He names him among those to whom the risen Lord appeared; like the appearance to Kephas, it was to James alone (1 Cor 15:7). Paul says that when he went up to Jerusalem "to confer with Cephas," he "did not see any other of the apostles, only James the brother of the Lord" (Gal 1:18–19).

7. See James D. G. Dunn, *Unity and Diversity in the New Testament,* 2nd ed. (London: SCM Press, 1990), pp. 253–54.

8. "Apostel vor and neben Paulus," in *Schriften zum Neuen Testament* (München: Kösel Verlag, 1971), pp. 338–57.

9. Raymond E. Brown, Karl P. Donfried and John Reumann, eds., *Peter in the New Testament* (Minneapolis: Augsburg; New York: Paulist Press, 1973).

10. Dunn, *Unity and Diversity in the New Testament,* p. 385. This appreciation of Peter's role is particularly significant, coming as it does from a scholar who can hardly be accused of bias in favor of a Roman Catholic point of view.

SHARERS IN THE APOSTLES' MINISTRY

1. The "Hellenists" were Jewish Christians whose language and culture were Greek; the "Hebrews" were those whose language and culture were Aramaic. It seems likely that by this time, the Hebrews had developed some form of community organization among themselves, while the Hellenists had not done so.

2. Raymond E. Brown, *Introduction to the New Testament,* Anchor Bible Reference Library (New York: Doubleday, 1997), p. 293.

3. Joseph A. Fitzmyer, *The Acts of the Apostles,* The Anchor Bible, vol. 31 (New York: Doubleday, 1998), p. 351.

4. Brown, *Introduction to the New Testament,* p. 295.

5. Fitzmyer, *The Acts,* p. 345.

6. See above, ch. 2, note 5.

7. Luke attributes their separation to a "sharp disagreement" as to whether they should take John Mark along with them a second time, after he had left them during their first journey (Acts 15:37–39). However, a more serious reason for their separation may have been the fact that Barnabas had sided with Peter, rather than with Paul, in the dispute at Antioch (Gal 2:13).

8. See above, ch. 2, p. 28–29.

9. In Romans 12:8 Paul speaks of a spiritually gifted member of the community as *ho proistamenos;* the word is translated in the NRSV as "the leader."

10. Joseph A. Fitzmyer, *Romans: A New Translation with Introduction and Commentary,* The Anchor Bible, vol. 33 (New York: Doubleday, 1993), p. 731.

11. Pierre Grelot, "La structure ministérielle de l'église d'après S. Paul: à propos de l'Église de H. Küng," *Istina* 15 (1970): 389–424; "Sur l'origine des ministères dans les églises paulininnes," *Istina* 16 (1971): 453–69; *Église et Ministères. Pour un dialogue critique avec Edward Schillebeeckx* (Paris: Cerf, 1983).

12. On "spontaneous leaders" see Edward Schillebeeckx, *Ministry: Leadership in the Community of Jesus Christ* (London: SCM Press, 1981), p. 8, and *The Church with a Human Face: A New and Expanded Theology of Ministry* (London: SCM Press, 1985), pp. 77–78.

MINISTRY IN THE SUBAPOSTOLIC PERIOD

1. (New York/Ramsey, N.J.: Paulist Press, 1984, pp. 13–16.
2. Brown, *Introduction to the New Testament,* p. 695.
3. Ibid., p. 633.
4. (Collegeville, Minn.: Liturgical Press, 1992).
5. Collins had presented the fruit of his detailed study of the use of *diakonia* in the ancient sources in his previous book: *Diakonia: Reinterpreting the Ancient Sources* (New York/Oxford: Oxford University Press, 1990).
6. Fitzmyer, *The Acts,* p. 483.
7. *Antiquities* 20.9.200.
8. *HE* 2.23. All translations of this text, both here and following, are from Roy J. Deferrari, *Eusebius Pamphili, Ecclesiastical History,* Books 1–5 (New York: Fathers of the Church, Inc., 1953). Cited text appears on p. 125.
9. Fitzmyer, *The Acts,* p. 497.
10. Ibid., p. 535.
11. Thus, E. Nellesen, "Die Einsetzung von Presbytern durch Barnabas und Saulus," *Begegnung mit dem Wort,* J. Zmijewski et al., ed., Bonner biblische Beiträge 53 (Bonn, 1979): 175–93, at 185–86, 189.
12. Anton Vögtle, "Exegetische Reflexionen zur Apostolizität des Amtes und zur Amtssukzession," in R. Schnackenburg et al., ed., *Die Kirche des Anfangs* (Leipzig: St. Benno-Verlag, 1977), pp. 529– 82.
13. Brown, *Introduction to the New Testament,* pp. 718–22.
14. Ibid., p. 728.
15. Ibid., p. 737.
16. This view has been argued especially by Jerome Murphy-O'Connor, "2 Timothy Contrasted with 1 Timothy and Titus," *Revue Biblique* 98 (1991): 403–18.
17. The difference between the two versions is more easily explained if, as Murphy-O'Connor believes, these letters were written by different authors. It is also possible that Paul was joined by a group of presbyters in the laying on of hands. One must also note the difference between the authentic letters of Paul and the Pastorals regarding the source of charisms:

In the former they are directly distributed by the Spirit, while Timothy received his through human agency.

18. He notes that in 1 Timothy 3:2 one of the qualifications of the man to be chosen as *episkopos* is that he be "able to teach." See his article: "*Presbyteros* in the Pastoral Epistles," *Catholic Biblical Quarterly* 35 (1973): 323–45; reprinted in *The Mission of Christ and His Church* (Wilmington: M. Glazier, 1990), pp. 222–51.

19. Meier, "*Presbyteros* in the Pastoral Epistles," pp. 231–33.

20. It is worth noting that the word translated "people" is *anthropois;* the choice of this word could mean that for the author of 2 Timothy, women were not excluded from teaching, as they were for the author of 1 Timothy.

21. Brown, *Introduction to the New Testament,* pp. 398–99.

22. *Adversus Haereses* 4.27.1.

23. Raymond E. Brown, *The Epistles of John,* The Anchor Bible, vol. 30 (Garden City, N.Y.: Doubleday, 1982), p. 744.

24. See above, pp. 29–31.

25. See above, pp. 64–66.

26. See p. 13.

THE *DIDACHE* AND *I CLEMENT*

1. *HE* 3.25.

2. "Festal Letter" 39, in E. Preuschen, *Analecta.* Kurzere Texte zur Geschichte der alten Kirche und des Kanone. II Zur Kanongeschichte. 2nd ed. (Tubingen, 1910), p. 45.

3. J. P. Audet, *La Didaché: Instructions des Apôtres,* Études Bibliques (Paris: J. Gabalda, 1958), p. 199.

4. Kurt Niederwimmer, *The Didache: A Commentary,* Hermeneia, tr. Linda M. Maloney (Minneapolis: Fortress Press, 1998), p. 53.

5. Ibid., p. 212.

6. The translation of the texts that I shall cite from the *Didache, I Clement,* the letters of Ignatius, the Letter of Polycarp and *The Martyrdom of Polycarp,* and *The Shepherd of Hermas* will be taken from J. B. Lightfoot, J. R. Harmer and M. W. Holmes, eds., *The Apostolic Fathers,* 2nd ed. (Grand Rapids: Baker Book House, 1992).

7. The Lightfoot translation has: "after you have had enough."

8. See *HE* 3.37.

9. André de Halleux, "Les Ministères dans la *Didaché,*" *Irénikon* 53 (1980): 18.

10. The Lightfoot translation has "appoint," but, as it is the action of the whole community, the word is better translated "choose."

11. Willy Rordorf and André Tuilier, *La Doctrine des Douze Apôtres (Didaché)*, Sources Chrétiennes 248 (Paris: Cerf, 1978), pp. 49, 64, 72–73.

12. De Halleux, "Les Ministères," pp. 20–29.

13. *HE* 4.23. Translation by Deferrari, p. 259.

14. Raymond E. Brown and John P. Meier, *Antioch and Rome: New Testament Cradles of Catholic Christianity* (New York/Ramsey, N.J.: Paulist Press, 1983), p. 175.

15. As we have seen above (p. 51), Grelot argues strongly that he must have done so, but there is no textual proof that he did.

16. See above, pp. 65–66.

17. John Fuellenbach has given a full and detailed account of this dispute in his work: *Ecclesiastical Office and the Primacy of Rome: An Evaluation of Recent Theological Discussion of First Clement* (Washington, D.C.: The Catholic University of America Press, 1980).

IGNATIUS OF ANTIOCH

1. Brown and Meier, *Antioch and Rome,* p. 70.

2. Brown, *The Churches the Apostles Left Behind,* p. 139, n. 189.

3. Eusebius (*HE* 3.22) says that the first bishop of Antioch was Evodius. Ignatius does not mention his predecessor.

4. Theodore Zahn, *Ignatius von Antiochien* (Gotha: Perthes, 1873), and J. B. Lightfoot, *The Apostolic Fathers,* vol. 2 (London: Macmillan, 1885).

5. Robert Joly, *Le dossier d'Ignace d'Antioche* (Brussels: Editions de l'Université de Bruxelles, 1979); J. Ruis-Camps, *The Four Authentic Letters of Ignatius the Martyr* (Rome: Pontificium Institutum Orientalium Studiorum, 1979).

6. William R. Schoedel, *Ignatius of Antioch: A Commentary on the Letters of Ignatius of Antioch,* edited by Helmut Koster (Philadelphia: Fortress Press, 1985). On the question of authenticity, see pp. 4–7 and his article: "Are the Letters of Ignatius of Antioch Authentic?" *Religious Studies Review* 6 (1980): 196–201.

7. *Polycarp's Two Epistles to the Philippians* (Cambridge: University Press, 1936), pp. 79–106.

8. Schoedel, *Ignatius of Antioch: A Commentary,* p. 13.

9. Ibid., p. 46.

10. Ibid., p. 49.

11. "The Silence of the Bishop in Ignatius," *Harvard Theological Review* 43 (1950): 169–72.

12. The Lightfoot translation has "those who lead," but I have substituted "those who preside," since the same verb *(prokathemai)* is used here as of the bishop in 6:1.

13. Writing a few decades later, Justin Martyr says that the deacons "give to each one present a portion of the consecrated bread and wine and water, and they take it to the absent" *(First Apology,* 65).

14. Klaus Schatz, S.J., *Papal Primacy from Its Origins to the Present,* translated from the German by John A. Otto and Linda M. Maloney (Collegeville, Minn.: Liturgical Press, 1996), pp. 4–6.

15. Schoedel, *Ignatius of Antioch: A Commentary,* p. 160.

16. Docetism (from the Greek word *dokein,* "to seem") was an early form of Gnosticism that denied the reality of Christ's body. This was an error against which Ignatius argues strongly in several of his letters; cf. Trl. 9–10; Smr. 5–6.

17. "Bishops, Presbyters and Priests in Ignatius of Antioch," *TS* 28 (1967): 828–34.

18. H.-M. Legrand, "The Presidency of the Eucharist According to the Ancient Tradition," *Worship* 53 (1979): 413–38, at 427.

POLYCARP, HERMAS, JUSTIN AND HEGESIPPUS

1. *Adversus Haereses* III, 3.4; also in *HE* 4.14.

2. See note 7 to ch. 6.

3. See W. R. Schoedel, *The Apostolic Fathers: Vol. 5, Polycarp, Martyrdom of Polycarp, Fragments of Papias* (Camden, N.J.: Nelson, 1967), p. 40. A similar view is expressed by another recent commentator on this letter, Henning Paulsen, *Die Briefe des Ignatius von Antiochia und der Brief des Polykarp von Smyrna,* Handbuch zum Neuen Testament, 18 (Tübingen: J.C.B. Mohr [Paul Siebeck], 1985), p. 112.

4. 1 Cor 6:2.

5. He refers to the fact that the church of Smyrna was founded later than the churches founded by St. Paul.

6. In my remarks about the message of the work, its authorship and dating I am following the lead of Carolyn Osiek in the introduction to her work: *Shepherd of Hermas: A Commentary (Hermeneia)* (Minneapolis: Fortress Press, 1999).

7. See Osiek, *Shepherd,* pp. 18–19.

8. The translation is by Edward Rochie Hardy, in *Early Christian Fathers*, ed. by Cyril C. Richardson (Philadelphia: Westminster Press, 1953), pp. 285–88.

9. Eusebius has preserved this passage of the letter of Irenaeus to Victor: *HE* 5.24. For the text, see below, p. 152.

10. *HE* 4.22. Translation by Deferrari, pp. 253–54.

11. *Ecclesiastical Authority and Spiritual Power in the Church of the First Three Centuries*, tr. by J. A. Baker (Stanford: Stanford University Press, 1969), pp. 164–65.

12. The Deferrari translation has "list" instead of " succession" here; I have substituted "succession," following von Campenhausen.

IRENAEUS AND TERTULLIAN

1. *Adversus Haereses*. III.4.2–3.

2. The Latin text, along with fragments in other languages, was edited by W. W. Harvey (Cambridge: University Press, 1857); a more recent edition, with French translation, was published by A. Rousseau and L. Doutreleau, Sources Chrétiennes 211 (Paris: Éditions du Cerf, 1974). Unfortunately, these editions use different systems of numbering the chapters and paragraphs of the text.

3. By this the Gnostics meant their own secret tradition.

4. The English translation of this section is by Edward R. Hardy, in *Early Christian Fathers*, vol. 1, edited by Cyril C. Richardson (Philadelphia: Westminster Press, 1953), pp. 370–71.

5. See, for instance, his reference to such a presbyter in *Adversus Haereses* IV.42.2 (Harvey): "As I heard from a certain presbyter, who heard it from those who had seen the apostles and had been taught by them...." Likewise: "presbyters, disciples of the apostles, say..." (*Adversus Haereses* V.5.1).

6. The English translation of the following passages is by Robert B. Eno, in *Teaching Authority in the Early Church*, Message of the Fathers of the Church, 14 (Wilmington: Michael Glazier, 1984), pp. 45–50. He follows the numbering of chapters as given in Sources Chrétiennes.

7. Livre III, Tome 2, p. 33.

8. *HE* 5.6.1–2. The Greek is also given in Harvey, II, 10–15.

9. See above, pp. 141–43.

10. *De Praescriptione Haereticorum*, 32.2.

11. In the Harvey edition, this passage is found in IV.40.2.

12. See Y. Congar, "Pour une histoire sémantique du terme 'magisterium,'" *RSPT* 60 (1976): 85. Jerome D. Quinn studied the use of

charisma by the Latin translator of *Adversus Haereses* and came to the conclusion that in this text he took it to mean that bishops were endowed with a prophetic gift that assured the truth of their teaching. However, Quinn notes that this does not settle the question as to what Irenaeus had in mind. *"Charisma veritatis certum:* Irenaeus, *Adversus Haereses* 4.26.2," *TS* 39 (1978): 520–25.

13. *HE* 5.23–24.

14. *HE* 5.24. Translation by Deferrari, pp. 337–39.

15. This expression is found in a passage of a letter of Irenaeus, cited in *HE* 5.20; the Greek is also given in Harvey, II, pp. 471–73.

16. "Are we laymen not also priests?" (*Nonne et laici sacerdotes sumus? De exhortatione castitatis* 7.3). Jerome's statement is in his work *De viris illustribus,* 53.

17. The translation of this passage is by Eno, *Teaching Authority in the Early Church,* p. 57 ff. The Latin text is in *CCL* I, 199.

18. Translation by Peter Holmes, Ante-Nicene Fathers (Grand Rapids: Eerdmans, 1951), vol. 3, pp. 252–53. Latin text in *CCL* I, 202–3.

19. *I Clement* 42. See above, p. 94.

20. The translation of this and the following passages (nos. 36, 37, 41) is by Eno, *Teaching Authority,* pp. 6–64; Latin text in *CCL* I, 212–22.

21. The Latin reads: *"unde nobis quoque auctoritas praesto est"* (*CCL* I, 216). Eno translates: "which is also our closest apostolic see," but the Latin *unde* would point to Rome as the source of the apostolic authority of the church of Carthage.

22. Tertullian is the earliest witness to this story about the apostle John, which is now generally not taken to be historical.

23. Translation by Eno, *Teaching Authority,* pp. 65–66; Latin text in *CCL* I, 550–52.

24. Translation by Eno, *Teaching Authority,* pp. 63–64; Latin text in *CCL* I, 221–22.

25. Translation by Ernest Evans, *Tertullian's Homily on Baptism* (London: 1964), pp. 35–37. Latin text in *CCL* I, 291.

26. *I Clement* 40.5; above, p. 93.

27. M. Bévenot, S.J., "Tertullian's Thoughts about the Christian Priesthood," in *Corona Gratiarum,* Misc. E. Dekkers, vol. 1 (Bruges, 1975), pp. 125–37, at pp. 130–31.

28. To the Smyrnaeans 8.1; See above, p. 119.

29. No doubt he refers to 1 Timothy 3:1 and 12; and Titus 1:6, where a man to be chosen bishop, deacon or presbyter must be a "husband of one wife." It is to be noted that for Tertullian this meant being chosen into the "sacerdotal order."

30. Translation by Eno, *Teaching Authority,* pp. 54–55; Latin text in *CCL* II, 1024–25.

31. *De Exhort. Cast.* 11.2; *CCL* II, 1031: *"et offeres pro duabus et commendabis illas duas per sacerdotem de monogamia ordinatum...?"*

32. Translation by William P. LeSaint, *Tertullian: Treatises on Penance,* Ancient Christian Writers 28 (Westminster: The Newman Press, 1959), pp. 54, 118–22. Latin text in *CCL* II, 1281–82.

33. Cyprian, *Letter* 55.21.

34. The translation of the following passages from *De Pud.* 21 is by LeSaint, in *Treatises on Penance,* pp. 118–22. Latin text in *CCL* II, 1326–28.

35. Eph 5:11.

36. Mark 2:7.

37. He most likely refers to the story of David and the prophet Nathan: 2 Kings 12:1–14.

38. *De Pud.* 18:18; *CCL* II, 1319.

39. *pro consanguinitate doctrinae, De Praescr.* 32.6, *CCL* I, 213.

Rome and Alexandria in the Early Third Century

1. Norman P. Tanner, S.J., ed., *Decrees of the Ecumenical Councils,* vol. 1 (London: Sheed & Ward; Washington, D.C.: Georgetown University Press, 1990), pp. 8–9.

2. *HE* 6.20 and 22. In the prologue, Hippolytus describes himself as among the successors of those to whom the apostles had imparted the Holy Spirit and as sharing with them the same grace of high priesthood and teaching authority.

3. Allen Brent, *Hippolytus and the Roman Church in the Third Century: Communities in Tension Before the Emergence of the Monarch-Bishop* (Leiden/New York/Cologne: E. J. Brill, 1995), pp. 398–426.

4. E. Schwartz, *Über die pseudo-apostolischen Kirchenordnungen,* Schriften der wissenschaftlichen Gesellschaft in Strassburg, vi (1910); R. H. Connolly, *The So-called Egyptian Church Order and Derived Documents,* Cambridge Texts and Studies, viii, 4 (1916).

5. Gregory Dix, *The Treatise on The Apostolic Tradition of St. Hippolytus of Rome* (London, 1937); reissued with corrections, preface and bibliography by Henry Chadwick (London: Alban Press, 1992). Bernard Botte, *Hippolyte de Rome, La Tradition Apostolique d'après les anciens versions,* Sources Chrétiennes 11 bis, 2nd ed. (Paris: Cerf, 1984).

6. Brent, *Hippolytus and the Roman Church,* pp. 460–61.

7. English translation by Dom Gregory Dix, *The Treatise on The Apostolic Tradition*, pp. 1–2. Words and phrases enclosed within < > have no authority from any of the versions but have been introduced by him to assist the sense.

8. Dix, *The Treatise on The Apostolic Tradition*, p. xxxviii.

9. Canon 4; Tanner, *Decrees of the Ecumenical Councils*, vol. 1, p. 7.

10. This eucharistic liturgy is described in *The Apostolic Tradition*, no. iv; Dix, *The Treatise on The Apostolic Tradition*, pp. 6–9.

11. Dix, *The Treatise on The Apostolic Tradition*, p. 6

12. The texts are given in Dix, *The Treatise on The Apostolic Tradition*, pp. 13–18.

13. Dix interprets the phrase "according to the aforementioned form which we gave over the bishop" to mean that the prayer for the ordination of the presbyter would begin with the first three paragraphs of the prayer for the ordination of a bishop. Botte differs, describing this as "peu probable," because the typology developed there concerns only the bishop, and the prayer for the presbyter has its own typology: the seventy elders chosen by Moses who receive a share of his spirit. See Botte, *Hippolyte de Rome*, p. 57, n. 2.

14. Dix, *The Treatise on The Apostolic Tradition*, pp. 33–38.

15. Botte, *Hippolyte de Rome*, pp. 27–28.

16. Dix, *The Treatise on The Apostolic Tradition*, pp. 21, 22.

17. Ibid., p. 30.

18. Ibid., pp. 38–39.

19. This is Letter 146; text in *CSEL* 56: 308–12.

20. English translation by Joseph T. Lienhard, S.J., in *Ministry*, Message of the Fathers of the Church, 8 (Wilmington, Del.: Michael Glazier, Inc., 1984), pp. 161–62.

21. W. Telfer, "Episcopal Succession in Egypt," *JEH* 3 (1952): 1–13.

22. "Bishops and Presbyters at Alexandria," *JEH* 6 (1955): 125–42.

23. "La succession des évêques d'Alexandrie aux premiers siècles," *BLE* 70 (1969): 80–99.

24. Lécuyer, "La succession," p. 84. He refers to Photius, who quotes the Defense of Origen of which Eusebius speaks in *HE* 6.23.

25. Von Campenhausen, *Ecclesiastical Authority*, pp. 200–201.

26. *Patrology*, vol. 2, p. 27. He gives the English translation of *Stromata* 6, 13, 107 from *Ante-Nicene Fathers*.

27. Translation in Eno, *Teaching Authority*, p. 81.

28. Von Campenhausen, *Ecclesiastical Authority*, p. 248.

29. Ibid., p. 254.

30. Homily 6 on Leviticus 3. English translation in Lienhard, *Ministry*, p. 62.

31. Translation in Eno, *Teaching Authority,* p. 84.

32. Albano Vilela, *La Condition Collégiale des Prêtres au IIIe Siècle,* Théologie Historique, 14 (Paris: Beauchesne, 1971), p. 59.

33. Homily on Numbers 2, 1; *GCS* 30, 10; Latin text cited by Vilela, *La Condition,* p. 85; my translation.

34. *Comm. Mat.* Ser. 12 (*GCS* 38, 22), cited by Vilela, *La Condition,* p. 68, my translation.

35. References to the places where Origen described bishops with these terms are given by Vilela, *La Condition,* p 96.

36. Vilela cites a number of such passages, *La Condition,* p. 96 f.

37. Von Campenhausen, *Ecclesiastical Authority,* p. 249.

CYPRIAN, BISHOP OF CARTHAGE

1. Text and translation by Maurice Bévenot, *Cyprian: De Lapsis et de Ecclesiae Catholicae Unitate* (Oxford: Clarendon Press, 1971), pp. 56–99.

2. In quoting passages of these letters, I shall use the translation by G. W. Clarke, *The Letters of Cyprian of Carthage,* 4 vols., Ancient Christian Writers, vols. 43, 44, 46, 47 (New York: The Newman Press, 1984–89).

3. Clarke, *The Letters,* vol. 2, p. 40.

4. Ibid., vol. 1, p. 56.

5. Bévenot, *De Lapsis et de Unitate,* pp. 61–65.

6. Ibid., p. 63, n. 5.

7. Clarke, *The Letters,* vol. 2, p. 64.

8. Ibid., vol. 3, p. 48.

9. Ibid., vol. 3, p. 119.

10. Ibid., vol. 3, pp. 121–22.

11. Ibid., vol. 4, pp. 29–30.

12. Ibid., vol. 3, pp. 35–36.

13. Ibid., vol. 3, pp. 75–76.

14. Ibid., vol. 3, pp. 37–38.

15. Ibid., vol. 4, p. 24.

16. Maurice Bévenot, "'Sacerdos' as Understood by Cyprian," *JTS* 30 (1979): 413–29 at p. 423.

17. Clarke, *The Letters,* vol. 4, p. 119.

18. Ibid., vol. 3, p. 107.

19. Ibid., vol. 4, p. 59.

20. Ibid., vol. 2, pp. 52–53.

21. See above, p. 180

22. Clarke, *The Letters,* vol. 1, p. 67.

23. Ibid., vol. 1, p. 62.

24. Ibid., vol. 1, p. 98.

25. Ibid., vol. 1, p. 51.

26. Let. 29.1.2; Clarke, *The Letters,* vol. 2, p. 25.

27. Ibid., vol.1, p. 203.

28. Ibid., vol. 1, p. 68.

29. Ibid., vol. 1, p. 101.

30. Ibid., vol. 1, pp. 102–3.

31. Above, p. 194.

32. Clarke (*The Letters,* vol. 1, p. 298) notes that early in the next century the Council of Elvira, in Spain, also decided that in danger of death a deacon could absolve a penitent if the bishop so ordered.

33. Clarke, *The Letters,* vol. 2, p. 82.

34. Irenaeus had more correctly distinguished between apostles and bishops. He described Peter *and Paul* as the founders of the church of Rome, who had made Linus its first bishop. Hence, in his list, Hyginus was the eighth in succession. However, for Cyprian, Hyginus was the ninth, indicating that he saw Peter as the first in the list of Roman bishops. See Let. 74.2.4 and Clarke's note concerning Hyginus, *The Letters,* vol. 1, p. 249.

35. Let. 55.8.4, see above, p. 201.

36. Clarke, *The Letters,* vol. 3, p. 82.

37. Bévenot, *De Lapsis et de Unitate,* p. xiv.

38. Clarke, *The Letters,* vol. 4, pp. 28–32.

39. Ibid., vol. 4, pp. 53–54.

40. See Maurice Bévenot, "A Bishop Is Responsible to God Alone (St. Cyprian)," *RechSR* 39 (1951): 397–415.

41. Clarke, *The Letters,* vol. 4, p. 69.

42. Ibid., vol. 4, p. 70.

43. Ibid., vol. 4, pp. 74–75.

44. Clarke refers to Augustine's *De bapt.* 1.18.28, 2.4.5, 5.25.36 and 6.5.7.

45. Clarke, *The Letters,* vol. 1, p. 244.

46. Ibid., vol. 4, pp. 80–82.

47. Ibid., vol. 4, pp. 88–89.

SUCCESSORS BY DIVINE INSTITUTION?

1. David Albert Jones, O.P., has recently questioned this consensus among scholars in his article: "Was there a Bishop of Rome in the First Century"? *New Blackfriars* 80 (1999): 128–43. I shall discuss his position later on in this chapter.

2. See above, p. 13.

3. See n. 1 above.

4. Jones, "Was there a Bishop," p. 136.

5. Ibid., pp. 131–32.

6. Ibid., p. 137.

7. See above, p. 107.

8. Jones, "Was there a Bishop," p. 141.

9. See above, p. 98.

10. Raymond E. Brown, *Biblical Crises Facing the Church* (New York/Paramus, N.J.: Paulist Press, 1975), pp. 52–55.

11. Raymond E. Brown, *Priest and Bishop: Biblical Reflections* (New York/Paramus, N.J.: Paulist Press, 1970), p. 4.

12. Brown, *Introduction to the New Testament,* p. 295.

AFTERWORD

1. *Origins* 30/14 (Sept. 14, 2000): 223–24.

2. Ibid., 209–19.

3. *Acta Synodalia Concilii Vaticani Secundi* III/2, 335.

4. *Ut Unum Sint,* no. 11.

5. "Note on the Expression 'Sister Churches,'" no. 12; *Origins:* 224.

6. *Dominus Iesus,* no. 17, *Origins:* 216.

7. *Acta Apostolicae Sedis,* 62 (1970), p. 753.

8. See above, pp. 8–9.

9. They were edited by Max Thurian with the title *Churches Respond to BEM* (Geneva: World Council of Churches, 1986).

10. The Secretariat is now the Pontifical Council. The Response was published in *Origins* 17/23 (Nov. 9, 1987): 401–16 and also in vol. 6 of the edition of the responses by Max Thurian.

11. Decree on Ecumenism, no. 3.

12. On October 31, 1999, the Joint Declaration on the Doctrine of Justification was signed by Cardinal Cassidy on behalf of Pope John Paul II, and by Bishop Krause, president of the Lutheran World Federation.

INDEX